MULTIPLE-CHOICE & FREE-RESPONSE QUESTIONS IN PREPARATION FOR THE AP ECONOMICS EXAMINATION

(MICRO and MACRO)

(FOURTH EDITION)

James Chasey
Homewood-Flossmoor High School (retired)
Flossmoor, Illinois

School of Continuing Studies
Northwestern University
Chicago, Illinois

Shaun Waldron
Niles West High School
Skokie Illinois

D&S MARKETING SYSTEMS, INC.
1205 38th Street Brooklyn, NY 11218

w w w . d s m a r k e t i n g . c o m

Moniz Martindin

ISBN # 978-1-934780-27-5 / 1-934780-27-8

Printed in the U.S.A.

PREFACE

This book is designed to help students prepare for the Advanced Placement Examinations in Microeconomics and Macroeconomics. Each of the examinations created by The College Board is comprised of a 70-minute multiple-choice section containing 60 multiple choice questions and a 60-minute free-response section containing three questions. This book is organized in a similar manner, containing both multiple-choice and free-response questions. The unit exams in the book are designed to test the basic concepts of each unit of study, and include both multiple-choice and free-response questions. Each unit exam will help students identify areas of strength and weakness in their understanding of economics. The two sample exams at the end of the Microeconomics and Macroeconomics sections are designed to provide a realistic assessment of students' knowledge of economics at the Advanced Placement level.

New to the 4th edition is a review of the content material in each of the 5 Microeconomics and 5 Macroeconomics units. Additionally, the multiple-choice questions for the 5 Microeconomics and 5 Macroeconomics units have each been expanded by 5 questions.

Every year the exam is different, and there is no substitute for actual classroom instruction. This book is designed to allow students to efficiently allocate their scarce resources. By reviewing the concepts they miss on these exams, they will hopefully learn more economics and perform better on the actual AP Examination in May. It is only with thoughtful instruction that students will succeed on the Advanced Placement Examination.

We would like to thank our editors, Professor Francis McMann, Jr. of George Washington High School in Cedar Rapids, Iowa, Scott McAlister of Homewood-Flossmoor High School in Flossmoor, Illinois, and Lauren Chasey of Homewood-Flossmoor High School in Flossmoor, Illinois. Their careful and thoughtful critiques of our work helped make the finished product what it is. As with all such works, any errors that remain are those of the authors.

We would like to dedicate this book to all of our former, present, and future economics students. We would also like to dedicate this book to our children who are a constant reminder that wants are unlimited and resources are scarce. James would like to also acknowledge that his wife, Julie, is glad this revision is complete and their house is now free of piles of paperwork, for the time being. Shaun would similarly like to thank Scott for his patience in this entire process.

All communications concerning this book should be addressed to:
D&S Marketing Systems, Inc.
1205 38th Street
Brooklyn, NY 11218
www.dsmarketing.com

Biography

James Chasey received his BA from Purdue University, his MA from the University of Illinois, and studied at the Graduate School of Business at the University of Chicago as the Christa McAuliffe Fellow for the State of Illinois. He taught economics at the high school level from 1969-2002, and part-time at the college level since 1985. He has enjoyed the privilege of being a grader and a table leader in AP Economics since 1996. One of his favorite professional activities is presenting at one-day workshops and week-long summer institutes for AP Economics. He is married and has two children, one of whom is currently teaching AP Psychology, and the other is a nurse. Mr. Chasey has written numerous works specifically for use in the teaching of AP Economics.

Shaun Waldron has taught AP Economics for 19 years at Niles West High School in Skokie, Illinois. She had the privilege of working for the College Board as a grader, table leader and question leader in AP Economics for nine years. She earned a B.A. in Economics from the University of Illinois and an M.S. from Northwestern University.

TABLE OF CONTENTS

TABLE OF CONTENTS

MICROECONOMICS: UNIT I

SCARCITY AND OPPORTUNITY COST

Economics is everywhere. Most students do not realize that the fundamentals of economics pervade their lives on a daily basis. In order to understand this, it is necessary to become fluent in the language of economics. This first unit introduces the economic concepts upon which future units will build and helps students begin to think like an economist.

Many students come to the first class thinking that they "know" economics. Maybe they've read *Freakonomics*, or played around in the stock market. Perhaps they follow a particular political candidate and can recite budget numbers. They might love tracking the business news. These are all worthwhile activities, of course, but often these activities do not ensure <u>economic</u> knowledge. This book is meant to help correct that and, as with every subject, understanding the topic begins with learning the language.

Scarcity

When students are asked, "What is 'scarcity'?" they often respond with the definition of "shortage." A shortage is a temporary deficiency in a particular item. A **scarcity**, though, is a permanent deficiency – there will never be enough to satisfy the desires of an individual person, or of society as a whole. There may be a shortage of milk at the corner grocery store, but there is a scarcity of time (is there ever enough time to get everything done?), resources (for example, are there enough rare metals that can be mined to meet our demand for computers and smart phones?), money (are most people truly satisfied with the amount of money they have?), and so on. This idea of scarcity represents the **key concept** behind any study of economics: **there are limited resources available, but people tend to have unlimited wants**. The question is, how do we distribute these limited resources to meet our wants in a way that best serves society?

1

Economic Systems

In order to answer this question, it is helpful to understand the various types of economic systems. Throughout history, societies have set up economies in ways that were meant to help distribute limited resources. Although the result is the same for all – goods and services are exchanged – the methods of such exchange have varied over time.

A society's economy is determined by how that society answers the following three questions:

What is produced?	What does society want? Does it want baked goods, shoes, weapons, alarm clocks, PlayStations?
How is it produced?	What materials are used? What type of labor is needed? Is the product made at home or in a factory? Domestically or overseas?
For whom is the product produced?	Who gets the good or service? Is it determined by hereditary privilege (i.e., only the nobles can have it)? By government planning (i.e., the government decides who gets what and how much)? By wealth (i.e., if a person has the money, she may purchase it)?

For centuries, the most common type of economy was the **traditional economy** where the job a person performed was determined by his place in society, and often by the job his father did. Thus, if your dad were a blacksmith or a farmer, you likely would be one as well. The answer to the first and second questions – what was produced and how it was produced – was determined by tradition: you produced goods/services with the skills passed to you from your ancestors using the natural resources available in your immediate vicinity. The last question, for whom is the product produced, was determined by whomever was able to pay, trade or barter for it.

Another type of economy is the **command economy**, in which the government makes decisions about the economy. That is, the government "commands" that the production and exchange of goods be done in a certain way. Often, students associate the pharaohs of Egypt or absolute monarchies where kings make all the decisions with this type of economy. While it is true that these types of dictatorships often had political and economic control centered at the top, these are not traditionally considered "command" economies because the kings and pharaohs usually did not control what happened in the town square on market day. Instead, command economies are ones where the government decides exactly how many pairs of shoes, for example, are going to be produced, how the shoe factories will obtain the materials (and what materials will be used, for that matter), and then how many pairs of shoes each person will be allowed to have. Historically, the best examples of command economies are those under Joseph Stalin in the Soviet Union or Mao Zedong in China. Under these leaders, their respective governments set goals for production and determined how their countries' resources were allocated in order to reach those goals, all with the purpose of ensuring that the citizens' basic needs were met (whether this really happened under these two leaders is another discussion).

The opposite of a command economy is a **market economy**, where buyers and sellers in the marketplace, instead of the government, answer all three questions. Buyers decide what they would like to purchase. Sellers provide the good or service. If a seller is making a product that no one wants, he will realize he should change the product or risk starvation. The seller also knows that he needs to make the product in a cost-efficient manner, using resources for which buyers will be willing to pay. Using an historical example, if I were going to sell plows at the market, I'd better make my plows out of steel rather than wood (which rots and is not very sharp) or iron (which is heavy and can become brittle with rust). Few buyers would be silly enough to buy a plow that will not cut through sod or is of poor quality and will quickly fall apart. Today, buyers want fewer plasma TVs as the technology in an LED TV produces a better picture; the sellers of plasma TVs know they need to change their product or risk becoming obsolete. The last question, who gets the TV or plow, is determined in a market economy simply by who can afford it. If a person has the money, he/she can purchase a TV (ignore the availability of credit cards for now, as you are not truly purchasing the product when you use a credit card – you are borrowing money from the credit card company); if you do not have the money, you will have to save until you do.

A **mixed economy** is a blend of the command and market economies, and is the most common economy in the world today. In this case, buyers and sellers interact in the market place to determine which goods/services are desired by society, and government involvement exists in order to ensure the well-being of society. During the Roman Empire and through the Middle Ages in Europe, the wealthy ate using plates and utensils made from lead, and drank wine with lead added to it. As such, lead poisoning was rampant, and some historians attribute it as one of the causes of the fall of the Roman Empire. Today, in order to prevent lead poisoning, such additives are forbidden by law – the manufacture of plates, glasses, jewelry, toys, and paint, for example, are all affected by this regulation. During the Industrial Revolution, it was common for workers, especially women and children, to have their clothing or limbs caught in machinery. Now, government regulations in the United States prohibit children from working until age 16, and also require many safety measures that are meant to ensure people don't lose body parts while at work. There are similar regulations for education (in order to guarantee a minimum level of education for the future workforce, countries often set curriculum standards at the national level, or like the U.S., at the state level), air travel (there are rules about maintenance requirements, flight paths, take-off and landing procedures, how long airlines can leave passengers sitting on runways…), and so on. Most countries in the world today have some form of mixed economy – sometimes a country might have more government involvement while another country has less – but generally, mixed economies are the most common.

Opportunity Cost

Like scarcity, **opportunity cost** is another important term in economics. Literally, it means an opportunity was given up or lost when a particular choice was made. For example, if I choose to spend hours updating my Facebook page, I give up the opportunity to study, go to the movies with my friends, or baby-sit for my next-door neighbor. Opportunity cost does not reflect whether the choice was a good one or a bad one, but simply it is the recognition that there are always tradeoffs in life, and people make them all day long.

Tradeoff:	Opportunity Cost:
Should I take a shower now or later?	If I shower now, the opportunity cost might be that I miss the bus and am late to work. If I shower later, the cost might be that I smell all day long and people avoid me.
Should I turn down this hallway to go to my locker or the next?	If I turn down this hallway, I might avoid the crowded main staircase, but I also might miss seeing the person I want to ask to the dance.
Should I stop at the stop sign, or take a chance and roll through it?	If I stop, I risk looking like I drive like my grandma to my friends, but if I roll through it, I might get a ticket, or worse, be involved in an accident.
Should I start my own skateboard design business or use my artistic skills to design greeting cards for a large company?	Starting my own business means being my own boss, but also means a less dependable paycheck. Working for a large company might mean more stability, but also perhaps more rigid expectations regarding work hours and artistic freedom.

Rational Decision Making and Marginal Benefits vs. Marginal Costs

When making decisions, people subconsciously (or consciously, at times) weigh the pros and cons of the potential outcomes of each option.

For example:

Pros of stopping at the stop sign: no ticket, no accident, no increase in insurance rates, no grounding from the parents, plus acknowledgement that laws exist to calm the chaos of the universe.

Cons: might be late, goes against my vow to disregard all means of authority, stop signs are just a hassle...

In economics "marginal" means "extra" or "additional," so **marginal benefit** is the additional benefit of obtaining one more unit of a good or service. **Marginal cost** is the additional cost of obtaining one more unit of a good or service.

Let's assume you can quantify the benefits received from consuming a good. A table that shows these benefits would look like this:

Units of a Good	Total Benefit
0	0
1	10
2	19
3	27
4	32
5	35
6	35

If I wanted to know how much benefit I received from increasing my consumption of this good from 1 unit to 2 units, I would look at the difference between the Total Benefit of the first good and the Total Benefit of the second good. Since $19 - 10 = 9$, the marginal benefit of consuming the 2nd unit is 9.

This concept is easier to understand if you think about a specific good:

Units of Chocolate Chip Cookies	Total Benefit Received from Consuming Chocolate Chip Cookies	Marginal Benefit Derived from Consuming an Additional Cookie
0	0	0
1	10	10
2	19	9
3	27	8
4	32	5
5	35	3
6	35	0

In the case of chocolate chip cookies, I get 10 units of satisfaction (economists call these "**utils**") from consuming the first cookie. Eating the second cookie adds 9 utils, for a total level of satisfaction of 19. If I consumed 6 cookies, I would get no satisfaction from that last cookie – in fact, it might result in a stomachache. Using this measure, should I only eat 1 cookie, where my marginal satisfaction is the highest? Or, being a cookie lover, should I eat all my cookies and risk the stomachache?

Of course, economists have vocabulary for this weighing of pros and cons. They call it **marginal analysis**. This means at every decision point ("at the margin"), people weigh their pros and cons ("benefits" and "costs," respectively) and come up with the best possible decision from the point of view of the decision maker (the role of "rational choice"). In this case, if each cookie can be obtained at a constant marginal cost of $5 per unit (it is a really good cookie), then the utility maximizing quantity for a rational consumer to purchase (that is, the point at which I would receive the most satisfaction) would be 4. I would not stop after eating only 3 cookies because I get more satisfaction from the 3rd cookie than it costs me (8 utils vs. $5, respectively). However, I would not consume the 5th cookie because the cost is greater than the benefit: the 5th unit has a marginal benefit of 3 utils but a marginal cost of $5. Eating 4 cookies is where my marginal benefits and marginal costs are in equilibrium, at 5 utils and $5. Lovely.

Units of Chocolate Chip Cookies	Total Benefit Received from Consuming Chocolate Chip Cookies	Marginal Benefit Derived from Consuming an Additional Cookie	Marginal Cost of Obtaining each Additional Cookie
0	0	0	$5
1	10	10	5
2	19	9	5
3	27	8	5
4	32	5	5
5	35	3	5
6	35	0	5

Utility Maximizing Rule

What if I wanted to compare the satisfaction received from eating a cookie to the satisfaction received from drinking a milkshake? According to the utility maximizing rule, I should allocate my money so that the last dollar spent on each cookie and milkshake gives me the same satisfaction (that is, the same marginal utility) for each. I calculate this using the formula:

$$\frac{\text{Marginal utility of cookie}}{\text{Price of cookie}} = \frac{\text{Marginal utility of milkshake}}{\text{Price of milkshake}}$$

Dividing by price allows me to compare a dollar's worth of cookies to a dollar's worth of milkshakes. Which option gives me more satisfaction? Weighing my marginal benefits and costs this way tells me if I should drink more milkshakes or eat more cookies.

Factors of Production

In the preceding discussion, there were references to "resources." Economists prefer the phrase "factors of production," and these can be divided into four categories:

Factors of Production:	Land	Labor	Capital	Entrepreneurship
Examples:	Forests Water Iron Ore	Workers	Hammers Computers Train Cars Oxen Harnessed to a Plow	Combining some or all of the other three into one productive activity

Some prefer using the term **natural resources** instead of **land** because, in essence, this factor encompasses all natural resources, not just the land beneath our feet. **Labor** refers to the physical exertion of humans involved in the productive process. In everyday usage, "capital" is often used to denote "money."

In economics, however, money can help a person obtain capital, but money itself it is not capital. Instead, **capital** refers to the tools, machines, or other resources used to make the productive process more efficient. Economists also talk of "human capital," which refers to the acquisition of knowledge that makes us more efficient (obviously, the more educated we are, the more productive we can be). The **entrepreneur** is the "risk taker," the one who brings together the other three factors, plus some money, in order to create a good or service. Think of the person who starts his own business – this is an entrepreneur.

Imagine a local dairy that raises its own cows and produces its own ice cream. While I'm not sure such places exist anymore, hypothetically I can divide the business according to the four factors of production:

My Ice Cream Factory				
Factors of Production:	**Land**	**Labor**	**Capital**	**Entrepreneurship**
Examples:	Cows Pastureland Raw sugar Fresh fruit	Farm workers Ice cream mixers Truck drivers (these might be the same person)	Barn Milking machines Metal bowls and buckets Delivery trucks	The dairy farm owner who combines the other three into a productive activity

Production Possibilities Curve

An easy way to visualize how the concept of opportunity cost applies to an economy is to use what is called a **production possibilities curve** (a "PPC" for short). This is drawn with two axes representing two different goods/services ("outputs" or "final products") and a curve that shows the various combinations of resources ("factors of production" or "inputs") used to create these final products.

For example, assume an economy produces two goods: corn and computer chips. Our PPC would look like this:

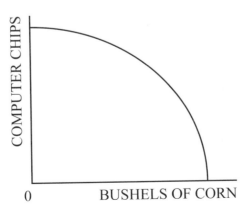

Graph A: Production Possibilities Curve

Remember that the curve, concave to the origin, represents this economy's many combinations of labor, capital, natural resources and entrepreneurship that go into the production of both corn and computer chips.

At any point along the curve, the economy is using its resources efficiently. The only difference between points A, B, and C are the relative amounts of computer chips and corn produced.

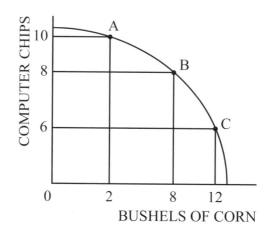

Graph B: Production Possibilities Curve

For example, if the people in this economy want more computer chips than corn, they would chose to produce at point A. If they would rather have more corn than computer chips, they would produce at point C. If they would like an equal amount of both, point B would be the best.

The most important concept of the PPC is that in order to move from one point to another, a choice needs to be made: do the people of this economy value computer chips more than corn, or corn more than computer chips? Any time a movement is made from one point to another, the people give up something.

Assume they prefer corn to computer chips; in this case, the ideal point of production would be point C. Here, using the resources available to produce the desired amount of corn, they end up with 12 bushels of corn and 6 computer chips. However, if they decide they now would like more computer chips, the only way they can build more chips with the resources they have is to shift some production from corn to computer chips – in this case, they give up four bushels of corn to gain 2 computer chips (moving from point C, where they had 12 bushels of corn and 6 computer chips, to point B, where they now have 8 bushels of corn but 8 computer chips). If they move all the way from point C to point A, they gain 4 computer chips but give up 10 bushels of corn.

Now, you may say, "Hey, they had to give up a lot of corn to get relatively few computer chips! Why would they do that?" The answer is that it is okay as long as society has decided that this movement away from corn to computer chips is the best use of the available resources. The idea of "giving up" something, in this case corn, represents the **opportunity cost** for this society. The society weighed its benefits and costs, and decided that producing a greater number of computer chips is more helpful – a better use of their scarce resources – than it is harmful.

As always, there are exceptions. What if this economy's use of resources resulted in a point of production that was not actually on the curve? Look at *Graph C* on page 9. What if the point was D? Or even E? What does that mean?

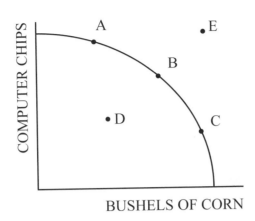

Graph C: Production Possibilities Curve

Remember that the curve represents efficient use of the resources available, whether production is located at points A, B, C or anywhere else on the curve. Once production moves off the curve, production is no longer efficient. Point D represents that situation where resources are not being used as efficiently as possible. Perhaps people are out of work, factories are sitting idle, banks are not making loans – in short, the resources exist, but they aren't being used. Point D, or any point inside or under the curve, usually occurs during a recession or worse, a depression. Only when the economy moves toward full employment will the PPC reflect the movement from point D to some point on the curve.

Point E represents the opposite problem: more resources are being used than are thought to exist, and thus production is expanded beyond what is possible with the current resources available. How can this be? This generally only happens in extreme circumstances. The best example is the U.S. economy during World War II. Remember that as U.S. involvement in the war picked up, the country needed to produce more weapons, ammunition, airplanes, food and military uniforms than it had before. How did the U.S. economy do this, especially since a huge part of the American workforce had become soldiers? Women (who generally were housewives at the time) replaced men in the workforce and factories began using double and triple shifts, working around the clock. Thus, the U.S. had access to more labor and more capital than previously, and production soared. This was a temporary situation, though; when the soldiers came home at the war's end, women left the factories in order to allow men to return to their jobs. Factories, which had changed from producing consumer goods (cars, typewriters) to war goods (airplanes, machine guns) now switched back again, and the economy moved from point E to somewhere along the curve once more.

Point E can become a permanent point of production if there is a fundamental change in the resources of the economy itself. There are six circumstances that may bring about this change:

A change in the quantity of resources	If the size of the labor force changes – there is a baby boom, the number of immigrants allowed into a country increases, the retirement age is extended, etc. – then there are more workers available, and thus the level of potential productivity increases.
A change in the quality of resources	If the existing workers become better educated, the level of potential productivity increases.
A change in technology	If more efficient means of production become available, then the level of potential productivity increases.
A change in the legal environment	If contracts and property rights are upheld by a strong judicial system, then individuals and companies will be willing to use their entrepreneurial skills and potential productivity will increase.
A change in access to trade	If countries are encouraged to specialize based on their comparative advantages (more on this later), then they can focus their production and potential productivity will increase.
A change between capital-intensive production and agricultural-intensive production	Countries that have a larger proportion of their workforce engaged in agriculture are less productive overall than countries where the population works mainly in industrial or service sectors.

Of course, the above changes can cause an economy's PPC to shift inward as well, meaning that Point D could end up being on the curve.

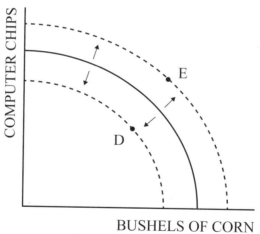

Graph D: Production Possibility Curve

This is usually the result of a recession or depression, but could be the result of a natural or man-made disaster; think of the U.S. recession of 2008 or Japan after the 2011 tsunami.

Productive, Allocative and Economic Efficiency

The terms "efficient" and "efficiency" have been used quite a bit thus far and, as one might suppose, they mean doing something – cleaning your room, making pancakes, running a business – with the least amount of waste possible. In the examples given, "waste" would mean wasting time, wasting flour, wasting energy, respectively. Economists have a more precise definition, depending on the type of efficiency. **Productive efficiency** means producing a good or service at the least cost. This type of efficiency is pretty intuitive: minimizing costs allows for greater profit. Allocative efficiency is a bit more complicated, and harder to measure: a society is reaching **allocative efficiency** if it is producing what society wants. A society that produces goods or offers services that no one wants is not using its resources in an allocatively efficient manner. Who wants laptops that weigh 10 pounds and are bulky to carry? Who wants MySpace when Facebook has more options and users? All the ingenuity, resources and time involved in the production of bulky laptops and obsolete social networking sites should be used to produce a different set of goods. This is true for all goods and services.

When a society has reached both productive and allocative efficiency, it is said to be economically efficient, or to have **economic efficiency**. To economists, this is the equivalent of economic heaven.

Microeconomics vs. Macroeconomics

What is the difference between these terms? One is small (micro) and one is large (macro), right? True, but how does this apply to economics? **Microeconomics** is the study of individual decisions – how one person, one company or one industry makes choices. **Macroeconomics** refers to the choices made by society as a whole – all the people, the companies, the industries in a particular country, or increasingly, in our global society. The basic principles of both Microeconomics and Macroeconomics are the same, but they have vocabulary, graphs and concepts that are unique to each.

Circular Flow

Just as the PPC is a visual representation of opportunity costs in an economy, economists have a diagram that shows how all of the components in an economy – buyers, sellers, resources and goods and services – fit together. This diagram is called a **circular flow diagram**, and it looks something like this:

```
          ┌─────────────────────────┐
          │   Resources or Inputs or │
          │   Factors of Production  │
          └─────────────────────────┘


 ┌──────────────┐                    ┌──────────────┐
 │   Sellers    │                    │    Buyers    │
 └──────────────┘                    └──────────────┘


          ┌─────────────────────────┐
          │  Goods / Services Output │
          │       or Products        │
          └─────────────────────────┘
```

Graph E

Of course, economists like to use economic vocabulary, so a preferred version shown in *Graph F* reflects this (but it means the same thing):

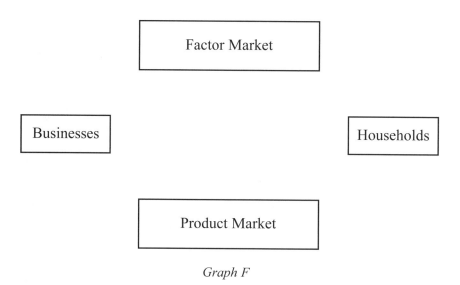

Graph F

In order for the diagram to make sense, there needs to be a relationship between the boxes. The arrows in *Graph G* reflect this.

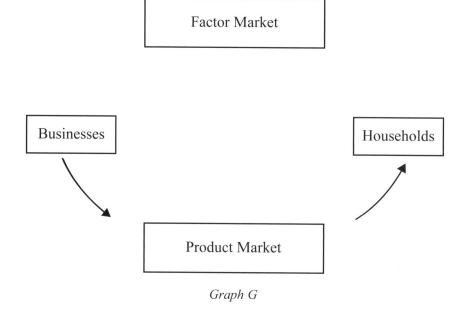

Graph G

Here, the arrows are showing that businesses create goods and services, which make up the product market. These goods and services (or, products) are then sold to households.

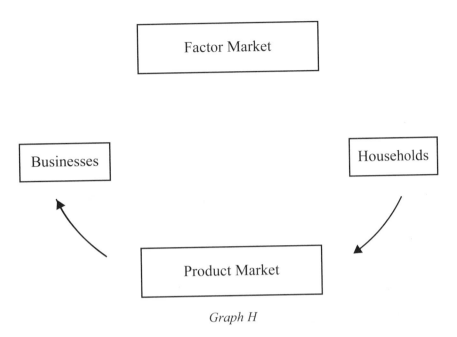

Graph H

The arrows in *Graph H* represent the flow of money (the "revenue") from Households to Businesses to pay for the goods and services.

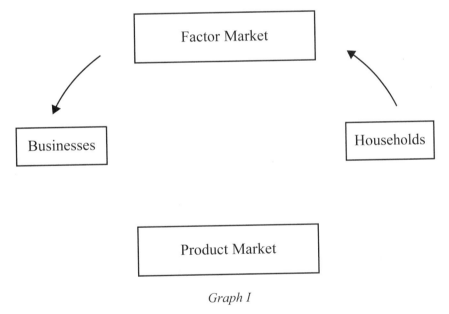

Graph I

The arrows in *Graph I* represent a trickier concept. Businesses have to hire resources to make their goods and services. They get these resources from Households, as this is where the labor, land, capital and entrepreneurship (the factors of production) are found. Without these, businesses cannot produce any goods or services.

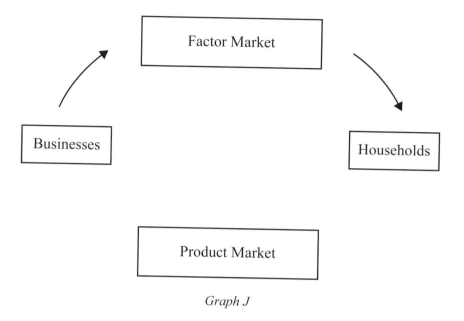

Graph J

The return arrows in *Graph J* represent the payments that Businesses make for the use of these factors of production. Of course, these payments have specific names in economics: labor is paid in **wages**, land is paid in **rent**, capital is paid in **interest**, and entrepreneurship is paid in **profit**.

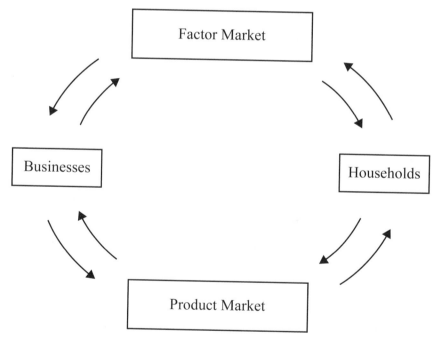

Graph K: The Circular Flow Diagram

In *Graph K*, all the arrows and boxes are put together. The inside arrows represent the flow of money, and the outside arrows represent the inputs and outputs that are used and created in this economy. Ideally, there should be a balance between all four boxes; when such a balance exists, the economy is operating at its most efficient level.

Short-run vs. Long-run

The ideas of "short-run" and "long-run" are meant to convey time periods. When most people use these terms, they mean "in the near future" and "some time in the distant future," respectively. In economics, both have very specific definitions. The **short-run** is a period where at least one factor of production is fixed, meaning it cannot be changed. The **long-run** denotes a period of time when all factors of production can be changed (economists say "all factors of production are variable").

Positive vs. Normative statements

These statements can be simplified as based on fact (**positive**) or based on opinion (**normative**). "It is hot today" is a normative statement – the person saying it might think so, but the person next to him might not agree. However, if the statement is, "It is 90 degrees today," that is a fact, one that is not in dispute. This latter example is known as a positive statement.

Both positive and normative statements often show up in the media and in everyday conversation, especially because people who think they know economics like to sound as if they understand economics. These same people often make statements that sound convincing but aren't necessarily based on fact. For example, the statement "Too many people are out of work" sounds like a fact. Few people like to be unemployed and we usually think of unemployment as a negative thing. From an economic point of view, though, there is more to this. "Too many people" could mean one person who would like a job cannot find one, or it could mean 10% of the civilian population who are willing and able to work do not have jobs. Thus, until one defines what "too many" means, this is a normative statement. A positive statement, on the other hand, would be something like, "The unemployment rate is currently 8.9%." This is a measurable, factual, and, therefore, positive statement.

Absolute and Comparative Advantage

When two people are trying to decide how to split up two jobs, they usually compare their marginal benefits and marginal costs – who is better at which job? Who can do the job faster? This is called weighing their advantages. Often, it is easy to divvy up a project. For example, if I am working on a lab report with my classmate, and I am quicker at writing but she is better at pouring chemicals into beakers, it is fairly obvious who should do which parts of the lab: she will do the actual experiment while I watch, offer suggestions and take notes.

Sometimes, however, a person has an **absolute advantage** – my lab partner might be better at both note-taking and beaker-pouring. How is the work divided then? Economists use **comparative advantage** to answer this question; how one divides up the work depends on whose opportunity cost is the least. Comparative advantage allows for specialization, and thus increases the overall production of goods and services.

Hopefully, you have noticed that the bottom line of all of these different concepts is that there are limited resources to meet our unlimited wants, and we must make choices about how to distribute the resources in the best (read: "most efficient") way possible. How I might distribute these resources is different from how you might do it. This dichotomy – analyzing all the varied ways humans attempt to solve the problem of scarcity, and understanding why some ways work better than others – is what makes economics so interesting.

Important Terms:

- Scarcity
- Command economy
- Market economy
- Traditional economy
- Mixed economy
- Opportunity cost
- Marginal benefits
- Marginal costs
- Marginal analysis
- Factors of production
- Natural resources/land
- Labor
- Capital
- Entrepreneur

- Production possibilities curve
- Productive efficiency
- Allocative efficiency
- Economic efficiency
- Microeconomics
- Macroeconomics
- Circular flow
- Short-run
- Long-run
- Positive statement
- Normative statement
- Absolute advantage
- Comparative advantage

MULTIPLE-CHOICE QUESTIONS

1. The study of economics is primarily concerned with

    (A) allocating scarce resources to eliminate scarcity.
    (B) allocating scarce resources to eliminate unlimited wants.
    (C) allocating scarce resources to achieve as many unlimited wants as possible.
    (D) prioritizing unlimited wants to maximize the use of scarce resources.
    (E) equating unlimited wants with scarce resources.

Questions 2-4 refer to the diagram below:

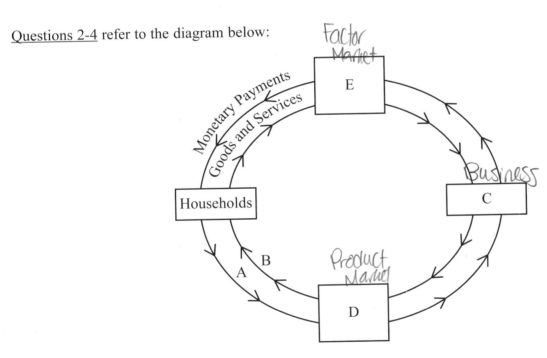

2. The circular flow diagram in the figure above is for a closed private economy. Letter "C" in the diagram represents

    (A) government.
    (B) business.
    (C) factor market.
    (D) goods market.
    (E) scarce resources.

3. The flow from households to box "D" represented by A in the diagram represents

(A) land, labor, capital, and entrepreneurship.
(B) wages, interest, rent, and profit.
(C) supply.
(D) demand.
(E) government.

4. Box "D" in the diagram represents

(A) business.
(B) government.
(C) goods market.
(D) resource market.
(E) equilibrium.

5. Which of the following economic systems provides for the most efficient allocation of resources?

(A) Market based economic systems
(B) Tradition based economic systems
(C) Government based economic systems
(D) Mixed based economic systems
(E) Command based economic systems

6. Production possibility curves are most often used to demonstrate

(A) opportunity costs.
(B) dollar costs.
(C) explicit costs only.
(D) fixed costs.
(E) production costs.

Questions 7-9 refer to the diagrams below:

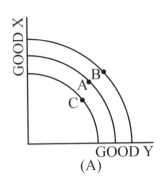
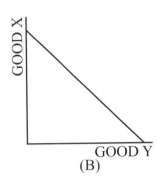
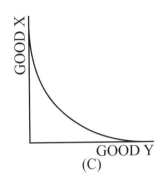

7. Select the order of the graphs to represent increasing opportunity cost, decreasing opportunity cost and constant opportunity cost respectively.

(A) A, B, C
(B) B, C, A
(C) C, B, A
(D) C, A, B
(E) A, C, B

8. Movement from point A to point B in graph A above could be achieved by

(A) employing all available resources.
(B) increasing consumer demand for the good in question.
(C) discovering additional resources.
(D) shifting production from Good X to Good Y.
(E) increasing the production cost of Goods X and Y.

9. Movement from point A to point C on the production possibility curve in graph A above could be caused by

(A) a movement toward more free unrestricted international trade.
(B) a decrease in consumer demand for Good X and Good Y.
(C) a technological breakthrough that reduces production costs for all goods.
(D) lower birth rates and increased governmental regulation.
(E) lower interest rates that result in an increase in the capital stock.

10. With which of the following would economists agree concerning positive and normative economics?

(A) Normative statements focus on facts while positive statements involve value judgments.
(B) Normative statements involve value judgments while positive statements focus on facts.
(C) Normative and positive statements both focus on facts and neither involve value judgments.
(D) Normative and positive statements both involve value judgments and neither focus on facts.
(E) Normative statements involve value judgments and focus on facts while positive statements only focus on facts.

11. If the land, labor, and capital used in the production of goods A and B are very different, but are still characterized by increasing opportunity costs, then the correct shape for the production possibility curve for these two goods is best represented by which of the graphs below?

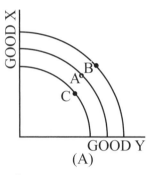
(A)

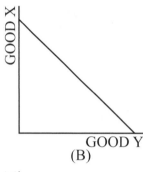
(B)

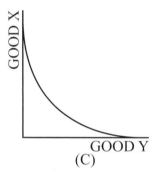
(C)

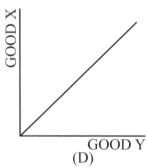
(D)

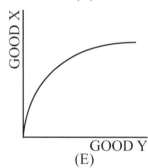
(E)

(A) A
(B) B
(C) C
(D) D
(E) E

Questions 12-13 refer to the diagram below:

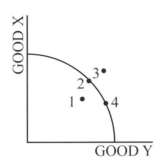

12. Points 1, 2, and 3 on the production possibility curve in the figure above best portray (in order)

   (A) an efficient level of production, an unattainable level of production, and an inefficient level of production.
   (B) an unattainable level of production, an efficient level of production, and an inefficient level of production.
   (C) an inefficient level of production, an efficient level of production, and an unattainable level of production.
   (D) an inefficient level of production, an unattainable level of production, and an efficient level of production.
   (E) an efficient level of production, an inefficient level of production, and an unattainable level of production.

13. Which of the following statements about the points in the figure above is correct?

   (A) The opportunity cost of moving from point 1 to point 2 is the amount of Good X sacrificed.
   (B) The opportunity cost of moving from point 2 to point 1 is the amount of Good X sacrificed.
   (C) The opportunity cost of moving from point 1 to point 4 is the amount of Good Y sacrificed.
   (D) The opportunity cost of moving from point 2 to point 4 is the amount of Good Y sacrificed.
   (E) The opportunity cost of moving from point 2 to point 4 is the amount of Good X sacrificed.

14. Which of the following would shift a production possibility curve inward (to the left)?

   (A) an increase in consumer demand
   (B) a decrease in consumer demand
   (C) continued depletion of non-renewable resources
   (D) a decrease in international trade restrictions
   (E) an increase in population

15. Based on the information in the figure below, the principle of rational choice would indicate that to maximize utility:

	Jim MU of Last One Consumed	Julie MU of Last One Consumed
$2.00 Juice	10 5	15 7.5
$1.00 Donuts	8	9

(A) Julie's next purchase would be juice.
(B) Jim's next purchase would be juice.
(C) Julie has a higher marginal utility per dollar spent on juice than donuts.
(D) Jim and Julie will both purchase juice next.
(E) Jim and Julie will both purchase donuts next.

16. The utility maximizing rule is

(A) MUA = MUB
(B) MUA × PA = MUB x PB
(C) MUA + PA = MUB + PB
(D) MUA – PA = MUB – PB
(E) MUA/PA = MUB / PB

17. Based on the information in the figure below, a rational consumer who is presently consuming 4 units of this good in order to maximize utility should

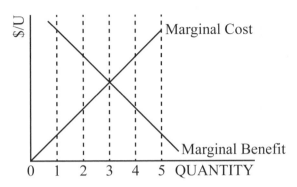

(A) continue to consume 4 units.
(B) increase consumption to 5 units.
(C) decrease consumption to 3 units.
(D) decrease consumption to 2 units.
(E) decrease consumption to 1 unit.

18. People tend to make bad decisions in their lives when

(A) costs are clear and benefits are clear.
(B) costs are unclear and benefits are clear.
(C) explicit costs equal explicit benefits.
(D) explicit costs are greater than explicit benefits.
(E) explicit benefits are greater than explicit costs.

Questions 19-20 refer to the following figure:

	Country A	Country B
Corn	10 $\frac{1}{2}$	5 $\frac{1}{3}$
Computers	20 2	15 3

19. Assume that countries A and B have identical technologies and equal amounts of resources. The figure above shows outputs produced per day if the countries were to make only one good or the other. On this basis

   (A) country A has an absolute advantage in the production of corn only.
   (B) country B has an absolute advantage in the production of corn only.
   (C) country A has an absolute advantage in the production of corn and computers.
   (D) country B has an absolute advantage in the production of corn and computers.
   (E) both countries are at an equal absolute advantage.

20. Based on the information in the figure above

   (A) country A has a comparative advantage in the production of corn.
   (B) country B has a comparative advantage in the production of corn.
   (C) country A has a comparative advantage in the production of both corn and computers.
   (D) country B has a comparative advantage in the production of both corn and computers.
   (E) country A has a comparative advantage in the production of computers.

FREE-RESPONSE QUESTIONS

1. The following is a production possibility table for the production of computers and corn.

	Combination				
Computers	0	2	4	6	8
Corn	30	27	21	12	0

(a) Demonstrate the various combinations of computers and corn by drawing a production possibilities curve.

(b) What is the significance of the points on the curve you drew in part (a), as opposed to points under (or inside) the curve?

(c) How would you demonstrate that this economy is experiencing unemployment on your graph?

(d) Assume that a technological improvement occurs in producing computers. Draw the new PPC that would result on your graph for part (a) and label it PPC-D.

(e) Now assume that a technological breakthrough occurs that positively impacts the production of all goods. Draw the new PPC that would result on your graph for part (a) and label it PPC-E.

(f) On your graph, demonstrate the effect of a change in tastes and preferences that results in society demanding more computers.

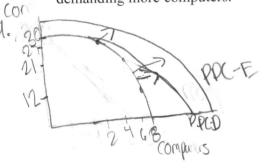

a.

b. The points on the curve occur when resources are being used efficiently, while the points on the inside occur when resources are used inefficiently

c. Putting a point inside of the curve.

25

2. Consumers behave in rational and predictable ways using cost and utility to guide their choices.

   (a) Define total utility.
   (b) Define marginal utility.
   (c) Based on the information below predict:
      i. what will typically happen to the marginal utility of the 11th ounce of candy as compared to the marginal utility of the 10th ounce of candy.
     ii. what a rational consumer would purchase next. Explain.

	Candy	Fruit
Price per ounce	$5.00	$7.00
Quantity Purchased	10 oz.	20 oz.
Marginal Utility of the Last Ounce Purchased	15	28

a) The total satisfaction received from consuming a given total quantity of a good or service.

b) The satisfaction gained from consuming an additional quantity of a good or service

c) i) decrease

ii) A consumer would purchase fruit next because the marginal utility per dollar is higher

3. Jim and Julie are contemplating if they should go on vacation to their favorite destination. Jim argues that they cannot afford to go and Julie argues that they can afford to go. The following is a list of expected expenses for the trip: $500.00 each for airfare, $450.00 for car rental, $600.00 for a motel, and $375.00 for admission charges to events and buying memorabilia. By going on vacation Jim will not be able to work and earn his normal hourly rate of $30.00 per hour for 40 hours per week. Julie works on a salary and earns $1,200.00 per week for whatever time she spends. They both eat at restaurants exclusively. Their food expenses are normally $350.00 per week and they estimate that their food expenses for the vacation will be the same. Calculate the cost of going on vacation for Jim and Julie. Be sure to list all of the component parts in your answer.

Expected Expenses	
Airfare x2	$1000
Car Rental	$450
Motel	$600
Events/Mem.	$375
Food	$350
Total	$2775

Lost Working Wages	
Jim	$1200
Total	$1200

$3975

THE PRICE DISCOVERY MECHANISM

In the previous unit, basic economic vocabulary terms were covered. In this section, we're going to apply those concepts to graphs. We'll start slowly. By the end, the graphs will be close friends!

Supply and Demand

When we discussed buyers and sellers in the previous unit, we talked about how, in a market economy, buyers and sellers eventually agree upon a price in exchange for a good or service. How do buyers and sellers reach this price? There are some behind-the-scenes concepts that influence this process, and these concepts are best represented with a graph that uses the following axes:

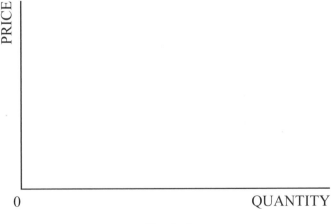

Graph A

All graphs in economics start with a vertical axis measuring price and a horizontal axis indicating quantity. Both price or cost and quantity increase as one moves away from the origin.

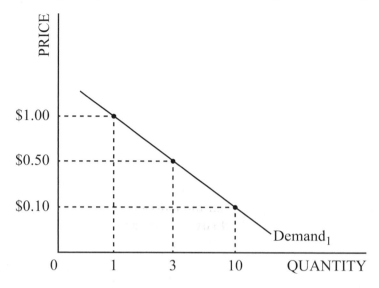

Graph B: Tom's Demand for Apples

Let's start with an example. Tom, our buyer (or **consumer** as he is officially called, as he will consume the good or service being purchased), wants to buy apples. If he can find an apple on sale for $1, he will buy one; however, if he can find apples for 50 cents each, he'll buy three. If he can find them for 10 cents each, he'll buy ten. Why these numbers at these prices? Tom has decided that these prices reflect what the apples are worth to him. Someone else may be willing to pay more, another person willing to pay less. However, as we are only concerned with Tom right now, we can connect these points, as shown in *Graph B*, and create Tom's **demand curve,** labeled Demand$_1$.

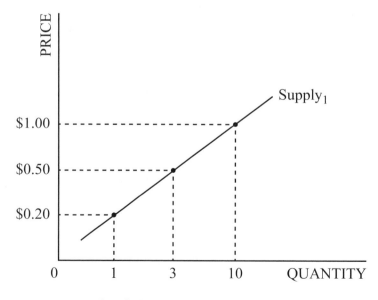

Graph C: Maria's Supply of Apples

Now, in order for Tom to purchase apples, someone has to grow apples and be willing to sell them (assume that there is no middleman here). This seller, or **producer** in economic terms (let's say her name is Maria), has decided that after all the effort of planting and tending trees, picking the apples, and bringing them to market, she is willing to sell one apple for 20 cents, three apples for 50 cents each, and ten apples for $1.50 each. Thus, Maria's **supply curve**, Supply$_1$, after connecting these price-and-quantity points, would look like *Graph C*.

You might have noticed something about Tom's demand curve and Maria's supply curve. There is one price-and-quantity combination where they agree: both are willing to exchange three apples for 50 cents apiece. This, then, is the **equilibrium**, the point where both Tom and Maria walk away from this transaction satisfied with the exchange.

If we were to plot all of the price and quantity combinations that all apple buyers would be willing to exchange in the market (that is, if we added up all the individual demand curves – Tom's plus all the rest), we would have what is called a **market demand curve**. The same is true for sellers: if we took all the apple sellers, and plotted the prices at which they are willing to sell apples, we would have a **market supply curve** (Maria's plus all the rest). It makes sense then that the equilibrium price is called the **market equilibrium**. The result is a supply and demand graph (see *Graph D*), the most basic of all economic graphs.

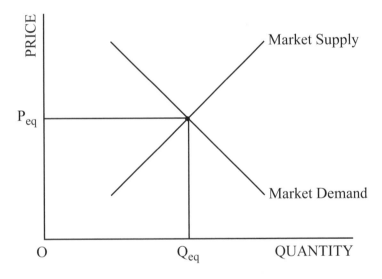

Graph D: Market for Apples

A few things to point out about this graph: if Tom had only been willing to pay 10 cents an apple, he never would have been able to purchase one since the lowest price at which Maria was willing to sell was 20 cents. Similarly, if Maria had insisted on $1.50 an apple, she'd still be sitting at the market with all of her apples, as Tom would not have purchased any of them. This movement along the curves, with buyers and sellers adjusting their respective prices is what makes the market, and the market graph, flexible and efficient.

What if all the apple buyers decide they want more apples? What if, instead of 1 apple at $1, consumers want 3 apples at $1 each? And 10 apples at 50 cents apiece? And 15 apples at 10 cents each? (A good way to keep track of these quantities and prices is to put them in a table called a **demand schedule**, on the next page).

Demand Schedule		
Price of Apples	Number of Apples (D_1)	Number of Apples (D_2)
$1.00	1	3
$.50	3	10
$.10	10	15

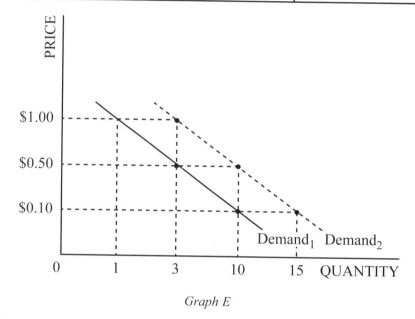

Graph E

What does this new line mean? The demand for apples has changed because consumers want more apples at every price; thus, the "demand curve has shifted." This shift is caused by what economists call **determinants of demand** (or, the things that determine where a market's demand curve lies):

Determinants of Demand	What does it mean?	Example:
Change in the number of buyers in the market	As more consumers enter the market, demand shifts to the right (increases); as consumers leave the market, demand shifts to the left (decreases).	As more people learn about the advantages of using social networking sites, the demand for those means of communication increases; as consumers use traditional mail less often, the demand for the services provided by the United States Postal Service decreases.
Change in consumer tastes and preferences	If consumers decide they want to purchase more of a good or service, demand shifts to the right (increases); if consumers want less, demand shifts to the left (decreases).	As the popularity of flat-screen TVs grows, demand for flat-screens increases and the demand for conventional TVs decreases.

Change in consumer incomes: normal and inferior goods	If consumers feel they have more money to spend, demand for "normal" goods and services increases; there is a direct relationship between the quantity purchased and income. If consumers feel they have less money to spend, demand for "inferior" goods and services increases; there is an inverse relationship between quantity purchased and income. The opposite applies in both cases: as money available to spend decreases, the demand for normal goods and services decreases and the demand for inferior goods and services increases.	As incomes increase, consumers spend more money (demand increases) on "normal goods" such as technology, haircuts, dental appointments and new cars. They spend less money (demand decreases) on "inferior goods" such as used books and instant noodles. As incomes decrease, consumers spend more money (demand increases) on "inferior goods" such as thrift-store clothing and less money (demand decreases) on "normal goods" such as fresh vegetables.
Change in the price of related goods: substitutes and complements	As the price of a good or service increases, the demand for a substitute increases. As the price of a good or a service decreases, the demand for a substitute decreases. As the price of a good or service increases, the demand for a complementary good decreases; as the price of a good or service decreases, the demand for a complementary good increases.	If the price of butter rises, quantity demanded for butter will decrease and consumers' demand for a common substitute, margarine, will increase. Why pay more for butter when margarine works just as well? If the price of peanut butter rises, the demand for its complement, jelly, will decrease. Who needs more jelly if the quantity demanded of peanut butter has decreased?
Change in expectations of the future	If consumers feel the future holds changes that will affect their income or prices, they will change their purchasing patterns accordingly.	If consumers are anxious about losing their jobs, demand falls now, as consumers will hold back on purchases in order to save money. If consumers feel prices are going to increase in the future, demand increases now, as they will want to take advantage of the current lower prices.

Two things to point out:

1) Only situations that fall under the five categories of determinants of demand can shift a curve ("**an increase [or decrease] in demand**"); and
2) If the price of a good or service ever changes, it does not shift the curve. It only causes a **movement along the curve**. A change in price might lead to an increase (or decrease) in the "**quantity demanded**" but it does not cause a change in demand. Only a shift in the demand curve by one of the five determinants can do this.

The supply of apples can shift as well. These shifts are caused by the **determinants of supply** (situations that determine where the supply curve lies).

Determinants of Supply	What does it mean?	Example:
Change in the number of sellers	As more producers enter the market, supply shifts to the right (increases); as producers leave the market, supply shifts to the left (decreases).	As tablet computers become more popular, the number of producers in the market increases, and the supply curve shifts to the right. In comparison, the leftward shift of the supply curve for medicines to treat cancer reflects the decrease in the number of producers in that market.
Change in the prices of inputs	As the prices of wages, natural resources and other inputs needed to produce a good or a service increase, producers decrease production, and supply shifts to the left (decreases). A price decrease of inputs causes an increase in supply, as producers are able to produce more output at a lower cost.	As the price of oil rose over $100 a barrel, producers of goods and services that use oil in the production process (think tractors, plastics) cut back that production, thus decreasing supply.
Change in technology	Technological advancements that make production more efficient cause the supply curve to increase; similarly, a decrease in technology would cause the supply curve to shift to the left (decreases).	As the application of automation to assembly lines increased, the amount producers were able to produce increased as well. When a widespread computer virus knocks out the ability for computers to work, production decreases.

| Change in taxes, subsidies and regulations | If a tax is applied to the production of a good or service, the cost of producing increases, and supply shifts to the left (decreases). Subsidies make the cost of production decrease, which in turn results in an increase in supply (a shift to the right). | An increase in taxes or regulations on production would limit the willingness of producers to supply. This decrease in supply will shift the curve to the left. Subsidies to corn producers, for example, increase the amount of corn farmers are willing to plant, thus shifting supply to the right. |
| Change in the price of substitutes for production | If the price of a product that involves similar production methods increases, producers will switch production to the more revenue-generating product, and the supply curve for the original product decreases. | If a farmer can just as easily raise cows as sheep, often what determines his herd is the animal that will bring in the most revenue. So, if sheep bring in more money per pound, farmers will stop raising cows and switch to sheep, and vice versa. |

The same rules apply here:

1) Only the determinants of supply can shift the curve (“**an increase [or decrease] in supply**”);
2) Any change in price is simply a **movement along the curve** (a change in “**quantity supplied**”), not a change in supply.

For example, let's say that we have the same market graph for apples as in *Graph D* on page 31. Now, something in the market changes – perhaps there is a storm that wipes out some of the apple trees. The supply of apples has just decreased (this fits under “A Change in the Price of Inputs” from the list of determinants of supply) and thus the supply curve shifts to the left, shown by Supply$_2$ in *Graph F* on page 36. Since there are fewer apples to sell, the price of each apple has increased, as shown on the new supply curve. Also notice that the equilibrium price has changed. If consumers want apples, they are going to have to pay more per apple.

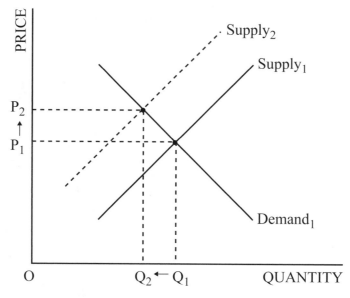

Graph F: Market for Apples

Let's assume demand changes instead of supply. Starting with the same market graph, suppose consumers plan to make many apple pies for Thanksgiving dinner. Thus, consumers need to buy more apples (this falls under "Tastes and Preferences" from the list of determinants of demand). The demand curve shifts to the right to reflect this, as shown as Demand₂ in *Graph G*, and a new equilibrium point follows.

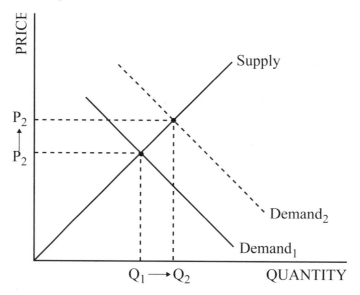

Graph G: Market for Apples

In both cases, Tom has to pay more for apples. But, of course, that is not always true. Consumers could decide they want fewer apples (a decrease in demand), and the new equilibrium price and quantity would reflect this change. Apples become cheaper because fewer consumers want them, and producers have to lower their prices to sell the product (see *Graph H* on page 37).

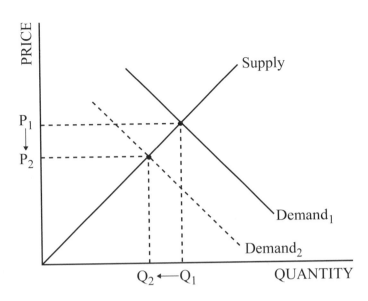

Graph H: Market for Apples

Perhaps the supply of apples increases – maybe the weather is favorable, and apple trees are especially productive this year. An increase in the supply curve shifts the equilibrium point to the right, and the price and quantity reflect this (see *Graph I*). Why would prices fall if producers have more apples? They have to sell them to the same number of buyers, so in order to get rid of the apples before they rot, the producers have to give the buyers an incentive to purchase more apples; hence, the lower price.

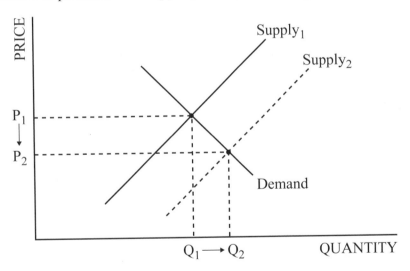

Graph I: Market for Apples

Another note about supply curves: if you look at the graph, it looks as if a shift to the left is an "increase" because the new curve is above the original supply curve; similarly, a shift to the right looks like a decrease in supply because the new curve is below the original one. However, you must remember that when we say supply increases or decreases, we are referring to the location of the curve in relation to the origin, which is zero. If you are confused, make sure to double-check the effect of any shift and its resulting new equilibrium on the quantity axis (e.g., Q_1 as compared to Q_2). If quantity has moved away from the origin, there has been an increase in supply. If quantity has moved toward the origin, there has been a decrease in supply.

Why does the demand curve have a downward slope and the supply curve an upward one?

Three ideas help determine the inverse relationship between price and quantity for demand:

1) The Substitution Effect	As price increases, consumers look for substitutes and quantity demanded of the more expensive good decreases. If the good or service in question becomes cheaper, quantity demanded increases because fewer substitutes will be purchased.
2) The Income Effect	As consumers feel wealthier because of a decrease in the price of a good or service, quantity demanded increases. If price increases, consumers feel less wealthy, and quantity demanded decreases.
3) Diminishing Marginal Utility	As more of a good or service is consumed, less satisfaction is received per unit (e.g., how good is that third double cheeseburger? It probably wasn't as enjoyable as the first one – or even the second). Thus, quantity demanded will only increase if price falls, since you receive less satisfaction from each additional unit purchased.

These three ideas are supported by the **Law of Demand**, which states that as price decreases, consumers tend to buy more of a good or service ("quantity demanded increases"), and as price increases, consumers tend to buy less of a good or service ("quantity demanded decreases"). Simply put, as consumers feel wealthier, they buy more goods and services.

Because there is a direct relationship between price and quantity from a producer's standpoint, the **Law of Supply** is straightforward: as price decreases, producers are willing to produce less of a good or service, and as price increases, producers are willing to produce more of a good or service.

A key point to remember here is that "**price**" is very different from "**cost**," and often the two terms are mistakenly interchanged. The "price" is the value that buyers and sellers agree to exchange for a good or service; the "cost" is the value of producing a good or service – the sum of the prices of the resources (labor, raw materials, entrepreneurial creativity, etc.) that go into the production of a good or service. So, the Law of Supply states that producers will be willing to increase their output as long as the price increases, which means that their total revenue (or, price x quantity) increases. However, their costs of production have not necessarily increased at the same time. Earning more revenue is sufficient motivation for suppliers to increase production.

Consumer Surplus and Producer Surplus

When the market price is the equilibrium price, both producers and consumers are happy. Economists call this happiness "surplus." Look at the following graph. There are consumers who are willing to pay more than the market price, but because the agreed-upon price is the market price, they are happy that they saved money they otherwise were willing to spend.

For example, if Lucy were willing to pay $5 for a piece of pie (she really loves pie), but the market price is $3 then her surplus is $2.

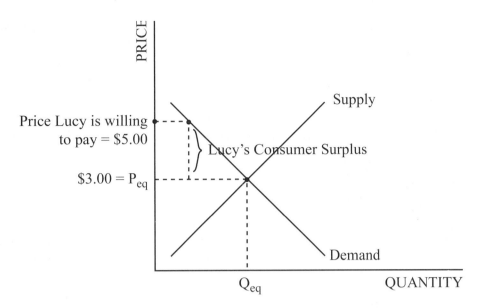

Graph J: Market for Pie

If one sums the surpluses of all the buyers in the pie market – those willing to pay even more than Lucy's $5 plus those willing to pay less than $5 but at least $3, which is the market price – this is the **consumer surplus** for the market. This area is shaded on *Graph K* as Area 1. Notice that those people who are only interested in paying less than the equilibrium price of $3 do not have any surplus, as they aren't in the market anyway. In order to have consumer surplus, one actually has to be a consumer.

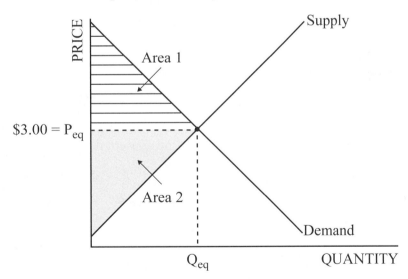

Graph K: Consumer and Producer Surplus

Producer surplus represents those prices that producers are willing to accept below the market price. However, because the market price is higher than their lowest-acceptable price, they are quite happy to receive the higher revenue. For example, if Joe makes pies, and he is willing to sell a piece for $1, his individual surplus is $2 as he is surely going to sell the piece for the market price of $3 rather than $1 if he is able to do so.

If one adds up the entire surplus all producers receive for selling their pie, this is shaded on *Graph K* as Area 2.

Remember that if a producer wants to sell his pie for more than $3, he's going to be waiting a long time for a buyer since the market price is $3 (why would a buyer pay more for pie than the market price?). This is why any price-and-quantity combination outside Areas 1 and 2 is not included in either consumer or producer surplus – these areas represent price and quantity combinations that do not exist under the current market conditions.

Price Elasticity of Demand

What if Tom's price-and-quantity combinations change, and his demand curve has a different shape? This is explained by the concept of elasticity. Elasticity measures the responsiveness of buyers to changes in prices. Specifically, how much does quantity demanded change in response to a change in price?

Price elasticity of demand (or "E_d") is calculated by determining the percentage change in quantity demanded divided by the percentage change in price, or:

$$E_d = \frac{\frac{\Delta Q}{\frac{(Q_1 + Q_2)}{2}}}{\frac{\Delta P}{\frac{(P_1 + P_2)}{2}}}$$

The numerical answer determined by using the above formula tells us how responsive demand is to a change in price.

If E_d is > 1, economists say demand is **price elastic**, meaning that consumers are quick to change quantity demanded in reaction to a change in price.

If E_d is < 1, economists say that demand is **price inelastic**, meaning that consumers are relatively unconcerned with a change in price, and tend to buy the same amount despite the change.

If E_d = 1, economists say that demand is **unit elastic**, meaning that the percentage change in price is equal to the percentage change in quantity demanded. Thus, a 10% increase in price would lead to a 10% decrease in quantity demanded.

What determines elasticity?

Determinants of demand elasticity:	What does this mean?	Example:
Number of substitutes available	If a consumer has many alternatives to a particular good or service, he will usually chose the good or service that is cheaper. If there are fewer substitutes, he has no choice but to pay the increase in price.	Cars, movies at theaters, and fresh produce tend to be price elastic. The greater the number of substitutes available, the greater the price elasticity, and vice versa.
Necessity vs. luxury	If a consumer feels he needs a particular good or service, he will be less likely to shop around for alternatives and thus will pay the higher price. Conversely, if a good is considered a luxury or expendable, he will be more likely to shop around for substitutes at a lower price.	Good examples of items that are price inelastic are insulin (a diabetic will need insulin, regardless of price), gasoline (drivers are slow to change their driving habits if gas prices fluctuate), and drugs, alcohol and cigarettes (consumers of these habit-forming products usually are not swayed by price changes). Again, the fewer the substitutes available, the greater the price inelasticity, and vice versa.
Time	The more time a consumer has to shop for a particular good or service, the more substitutes he can find. If a consumer needs a good or service right now, his demand will be price inelastic.	If the price of first class stamps increases tomorrow, and you must mail a letter, you have no choice but to pay the increased price. Demand is very inelastic. Over time, you will find substitutes – sending e-cards, paying bills online. Demand becomes more elastic as time passes.
Percentage of income	If a particular good or service costs a small percentage of one's income, buyers tend to be unresponsive to a change in price. If the good or service costs a large percentage of one's income, buyers tend to be more responsive to changes in price.	If you are buying a pair of socks, you might not pay much attention if the price changes from $5.00 to $5.50. However, if the price of a car increases from $20,000 to $22,000 you are more likely to shop around for the best price. The percent change is the same in both cases – 10% – but it is the proportion of one's income that matters.

Elasticity is reflected in the graphs by changing the slope of the curve; however, elasticity is not the same as slope.

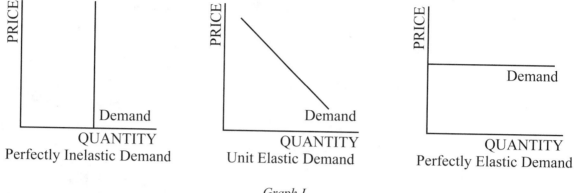

Graph L

Also, a particular curve can have different elasticities at different points along the curve. For example, fewer people want pizza when it is priced at $6 a slice; however, when it is priced at $2 a slice, quantity demanded goes up. The demand curve for pizza slices hasn't changed, but consumers' responsiveness to changes in prices has changed. This is true for all linear downward-sloping demand curves (not those that are horizontal or vertical): every curve has elastic, unit elastic and inelastic portions along its length, as shown in *Graph M*.

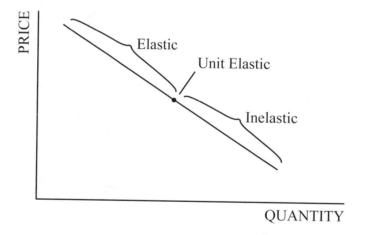

Graph M

Total Revenue Test

Another way of determining elasticity is by using the total revenue test. Think of it as an algebraic equation where you have two known quantities and you are solving for an unknown. For example, if you know price and total revenue then you can determine elasticity. If you know elasticity and total revenue, then you can figure out price.

As price increases or decreases, what happens to total revenue? (remember that $P \times Q = TR$)

If Demand is price elastic:
If P↑ then TR will ↓
If P↓ then TR will ↑

An easy way to remember this is that the arrows move in opposite directions – think of a rubber band that stretches... it is "elastic"!

If Demand is price inelastic:
If P↑ then TR will ↑
If P↓ then TR will ↓

Notice that these arrows move in the same direction (they are NOT elastic); thus demand is inelastic.

If Demand is unit elastic,
P↑ or ↓ and TR changes by the same amount.

There are other types of demand elasticity.

Cross-price elasticity of demand (or "XED") measures the degree to which a good is a substitute, a compliment or neither. It is calculated by the formula:

$$XED = \frac{\%\Delta \text{ in QD of Good X}}{\%\Delta \text{ in P of Good Y}}$$

where QD = "quantity demanded"
If the XED = positive, then the good is a substitute.
If the XED = negative, then the good is a complement.
If the XED = 0, then there is no connection.

Income elasticity of demand (or "YED") measures the degree to which goods or services are considered "normal" or "inferior". The formula is as follows:

$$YED = \frac{\%\Delta \text{ in QD}}{\%\Delta \text{ in income}}$$

If YED = positive, then the good is a normal good.
If YED = negative, then the good is an inferior good.

Price elasticity of supply (or "E_s") measures the responsiveness of producers to changes in prices.

E_s = percentage change in quantity supplied/percentage change in price. The formula is:

$$E_S = \frac{\dfrac{\Delta Q}{(Q_1 + Q_2)/2}}{\dfrac{\Delta P}{(P_1 + P_2)/2}}$$

Determinant of supply elasticity:	What does this mean?	Example:
Time	The amount of time producers have to respond to a change in product price will affect elasticity – the longer the time, the greater the elasticity of supply.	In the market for cars: is the supply elastic or inelastic? It depends. Is the question asking about the immediate market period, the short-run or the long-run? In the immediate market period (say, today), the supply is inelastic because there are few substitutes. The dealer has the cars on his lot, and he is unable to obtain any more. In the short-run, the dealer will be able to obtain cars from another dealer, but his supply is limited to dealerships within a certain mileage. In the long-run, though, the dealer can purchase any car he wants from any dealership or even from the factory itself. Thus, in the long-run, there are lots of substitutes and supply is elastic.

There is not a total revenue test for price elasticity of supply. Since the supply curve is always upsloping, price and total revenue always move together.

Price Floors and Ceilings

Even though the market equilibrium price is located at that point where consumers and producers agree to exchange goods or services, there are times when the equilibrium price does not always apply. In this case, a third party might lobby the government to enact an artificial price.

This artificial price set above equilibrium is called a **price floor**. Price floors usually occur when sellers feel the market equilibrium price is too low. Despite its misleading name (why would a "floor" be placed above the equilibrium?), it makes sense when you realize that the artificial price is the lowest that the price can fall – hence, it represents the minimum, or floor. Producers prefer this situation, as they see an opportunity to increase their revenue. *Graph N* shows a price floor.

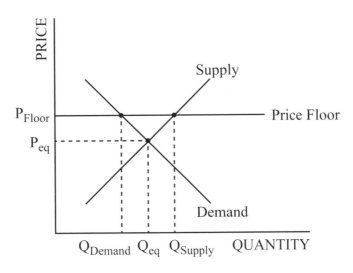

Graph N: Price Floor

An artificial price set below equilibrium is called a **price ceiling**, as shown in *Graph O*. Again, at first glance the name might seem confusing, but remember that it represents the maximum, or the ceiling, price that can be exchanged in this particular market. Price ceilings benefit consumers the most. When a price ceiling is in place, consumers are able to purchase the good or service for a lower price.

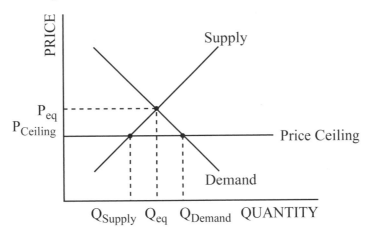

Graph O: Price Ceiling

Notice how consumer surplus and producer surplus change with the existence of a price ceiling or floor. See *Graphs P* and *Q* on the next page.

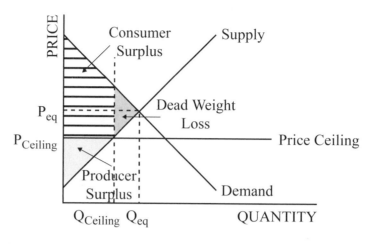

Graph P: Price Ceiling

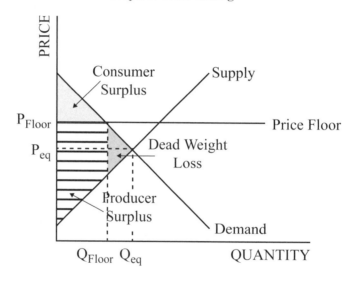

Graph Q: Price Floor

Consumer surplus increases significantly with a price ceiling, as consumers are now able to purchase a good or a service at a lower price. This increased surplus is shown by comparing consumer surplus in *Graph K* on page 39 to that in *Graph P*.

Producers obviously benefit from price floors, as shown by the increase in producer surplus from that shown in *Graph K* to the producer surplus seen in *Graph Q*.

Notice that both *Graphs P* and *Q* show an area designated "**deadweight loss.**" This is the result of the intervention in the market by the establishment of a price ceiling or a price floor. Movement away from the market equilibrium price and quantity means that the market is no longer economically efficient. The market essentially loses the output and revenue equal to the area of the triangle shown as deadweight loss. Thus, when **total surplus** (consumer surplus + producer surplus) is maximized, there is no dead weight loss and the market is considered efficient (as in *Graph K*). Anything less is inefficient.

Price ceilings and floors do more to the market than alter consumer and producer surpluses. These artificial prices send signals to consumers and producers to either buy more or produce more, respectively, than they would in a market free of interference. These unintended consequences are **shortages and surpluses**.

Take the example of a price ceiling: according to the law of demand, consumers purchase more of a good or service as prices decrease. As a price ceiling represents a lower price than equilibrium, the quantity demanded will increase. However, according to the law of supply, producers produce less of a good or service when prices fall. Thus, quantity supplied will decrease. This is a problem because now we have a **shortage** – quantity demanded is greater than quantity supplied ($Q_D > Q_S$) as shown in *Graph R*.

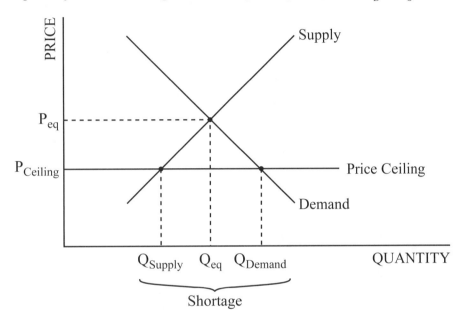

Graph R: Price Ceiling

What happens when there is a shortage? The most common result is a black market, where consumers are willing to pay more than the artificial maximum in order to obtain the good or service in question. During World War II, products like meat, tires, and penicillin were needed for the soldiers. Due to this, they were in short supply at home in the U.S. and black markets for these goods flourished. Scalping is also a common result of price floors – for example, tickets for concerts are often bought for more than face value by fans who could not buy tickets through traditional means (e.g., online or standing in line).

With price floors, the unintended result is a **surplus**. This often shows up in the case of price supports for agricultural goods. When farmers feel they are having a difficult time making a living growing their crops, the government then decrees a minimum price that is above the equilibrium price. The artificial price leads producers to produce more than they otherwise would because the anticipated increase in revenue is very enticing. However, fewer consumers want to pay the higher price, so quantity supplied is greater than quantity demanded ($Q_s > Q_D$) as shown in *Graph S* on page 48.

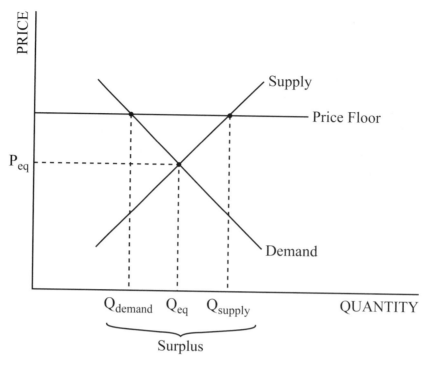

Graph S: Price Floor

In the next unit, we'll move away from the discussion of prices to a discussion of costs and how those costs affect producers and their decision-making.

Important terms:

- Supply
- Demand
- Consumer
- Demand curve
- Producer
- Supply curve
- Equilibrium
- Determinants of Demand
- Inferior and Normal goods
- Substitutes and Compliments
- Quantity demanded vs. Demand
- Quantity supplied vs. Supply
- Substitution Effect
- Income Effect
- Diminishing Marginal Utility

- Law of Supply
- Law of Demand
- Price vs. Cost
- Consumer surplus
- Producer surplus
- Total surplus
- Price elasticity of demand
- Price elasticity of supply
- Total Revenue Test
- Cross-price elasticity of demand
- Income elasticity of demand
- Price floor
- Price ceiling
- Shortage vs. Surplus
- Deadweight loss

MICROECONOMICS: UNIT II

MULTIPLE-CHOICE QUESTIONS

1. The various quantities of a good that consumers are willing to purchase at each possible price defines

    (A) demand.
    (B) quantity demanded.
    (C) supply.
    (D) quantity supplied.
    (E) equilibrium.

2. If the marginal utility associated with additional units of a good were constant, then

    (A) the demand curve would be downward sloping.
    (B) the demand curve would be upward sloping.
    (C) the demand curve would be horizontal.
    (D) the demand curve would be vertical.
    (E) the demand curve would not exist.

3. Using the figure below, what is the effect of the government setting a price ceiling at P₃?

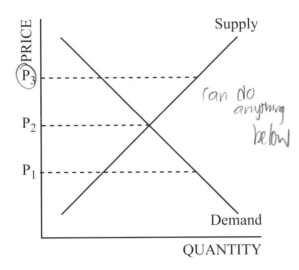

can do anything below

(A) It would have no effect.
(B) It would create a surplus.
(C) It would create a shortage.
(D) It would create an equilibrium.
(E) It would create a deficit.

4. What is true about an effective price floor?

(A) It is set above the equilibrium price.
(B) It is set below the equilibrium price.
(C) It is set at the equilibrium price.
(D) It creates a larger consumer surplus.
(E) It produces an efficient allocation of resources.

5. A rise in the price of peanut butter, a complementary good for jelly, will

(A) increase the demand for jelly.
(B) increase the demand for peanut butter.
(C) decrease the demand for jelly.
(D) decrease the demand for peanut butter.
(E) decrease the price of jelly.

6. A good is classified as inferior if the demand for it decreases when

   (A) its price increases.
   (B) its price decreases.
   (C) consumers' incomes increase.
   (D) consumers' incomes decrease.
   (E) the price of a substitute increases.

7. Which of the following is most likely to decrease the demand for David Colander economics textbooks?

   Price doesn't shift curve

   (A) a rise in the price of David Colander textbooks
   (B) a decrease in the price of David Colander textbooks
   (C) a rise in the incomes of textbook consumers
   (D) the introduction of the new J. Charles Chasey economics textbook
   (E) news that using David Colander's text improves student scores on the AP Economics examination

8. In the absence of externalities, market prices will create

   (A) greater consumer surplus.
   (B) greater producer surplus.
   (C) greater total surplus.
   (D) a less efficient output.
   (E) a surplus of goods on the market.

Questions 9-10 are based on the graphs below:

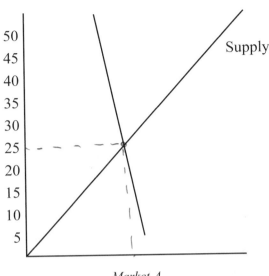

Market A   *Market B*

9. If the government were to impose a per unit tax of $10.00 on producers, the result would be

   (A) more revenue collected by the government in Market A than in Market B.
   (B) more revenue collected by the government in Market B than in Market A.
   (C) a greater reduction in equilibrium quantity in Market A.
   (D) a greater increase in equilibrium price in Market B.
   (E) the same changes in revenue, quantity and price in both markets.

10. The new price that would result from the $10.00 tax is

   (A) $25.00 in Market A and $25.00 in Market B.
   (B) $30.00 in Market A and $30.00 in Market B.
   (C) $25.00 in Market A and $30.00 in Market B.
   (D) higher in Market A than in Market B.
   (E) higher in Market B than in Market A.

11. What is the effect on equilibrium price and equilibrium quantity of an increase in both supply and demand?

   (A) Price will be indeterminate, quantity will increase.
   (B) Price will be indeterminate, quantity will decrease.
   (C) Price will be indeterminate, quantity will be indeterminate.
   (D) Price will increase, quantity will decrease.
   (E) Price will increase, quantity will be indeterminate.

12. Changes in which of the following will affect the demand for economics workbooks?

 Supply
(A) the cost of producing economics workbooks
(B) the price of economics workbooks
(C) expectations of future price increases in the economics workbook market
(D) a corporate tax on economics workbooks
(E) the price of paper changing

Questions 13-14 are based on the graph below:

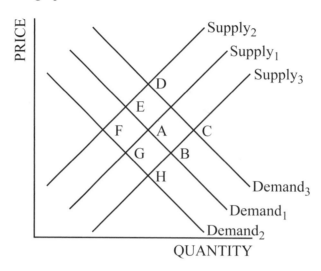

13. Movement from A to B could be caused by

(A) an increase in the price of the good.
(B) a decrease in the cost of production of the good.
(C) a decrease in the price of a substitute good.
(D) an increase in the price of a complementary good.
(E) a decrease in the number of suppliers of the good.

14. Beginning at point A, movement to point H could be caused by

(A) a decrease in the price of the good.
(B) an increase in production cost and a decrease in the popularity of the good.
(C) an increase in production cost and an increase in the price of a substitute good.
(D) an increase in production cost and an increase in the price of a complementary good.
(E) a decrease in production cost and an increase in the price of a complementary good.

15. If the price in the graph below is currently $15, we could conclude

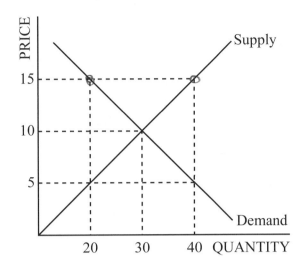

(A) there is a shortage of 20.
(B) there is a shortage of 40.
(C) there is a shortage of 10.
(D) there is a surplus of 20.
(E) there is a surplus of 30.

16. Which of the following is most likely to have a price elastic demand? ?

(A) necessities
(B) a good that constitutes a smaller share of the budget
(C) a good with many close substitutes
(D) a good for which the customer has very little time to shop
(E) a good with strong brand name recognition and extreme consumer loyalty

17. When Julie from Julie's Junque Shop put her inventory on sale, she noticed her total revenue went up. From this information, we can accurately conclude that Julie is

(A) facing an inelastic demand.
(B) facing an elastic demand.
(C) facing a unit elastic demand.
(D) selling a normal good.
(E) selling an inferior good.

P↓ →TR↑ = Elastic

Questions 18-23 refer to the graph below:

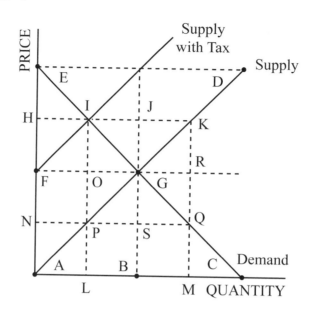

18. Consumer surplus before the tax is shown by area

    (A) A, G, F
    (B) A, B, G
    (C) F, G, E
    (D) A, G, E
    (E) A, G, C

19. Producer surplus before the tax is shown by area

    (A) A, G, F
    (B) A, B, G
    (C) F, G, E
    (D) A, G, E
    (E) A, G, C

20. Consumer surplus after the tax is shown by area

    (A) A, G, F
    (B) H, E, I
    (C) A, G, E
    (D) N, P, A
    (E) I, G, P

21. Producer surplus after the tax is shown by area

   (A) A, G, F
   (B) A, P, I, F
   (C) A, G, I, F
   (D) N, P, A
   (E) A, G, E

22. The amount of government revenue generated by the imposition of the tax is shown by area

   (A) N, P, I, H
   (B) N, P, O, F
   (C) F, O, I, H
   (D) I, G, P
   (E) A, G, E

23. The deadweight loss that results from the tax is shown by area

   (A) I, G, P
   (B) P, G, Q
   (C) I, K, G
   (D) G, K, Q
   (E) A, G, E

---

24. If it is true that as consumers' incomes increase, they tend to purchase less used clothing, then we can conclude that used clothing is

   (A) a good that validates the law of downward sloping demand.
   (B) an independent good.
   (C) a normal good.
   (D) an inferior good.
   (E) a luxury good.

Questions 25-27 refer to the graph below:

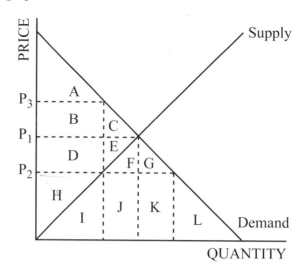

25. At a price of P_1 consumer surplus would be described by area

(A) A
(B) A & B
(C) A, B, & C
(D) A, B, C, D, E, & H
(E) A–L

26. If a price of P_2 were to be administered by the government, the result would be

	Consumer Surplus	Producer Surplus	Deadweight Loss
(A)	A + B + C	D + E + H	F + G
(B)	A + B + C + D + E	H	F + G
(C)	A	F + I + J	C + E
(D)	A + B + D	H	C + E
(E)	A + B + D	C + E + H	F + G

27. As a result of P_3 being administered by the government, we could conclude that, as compared to P_1

(A) consumer surplus increases and producer surplus increases.
(B) consumer surplus decreases and producer surplus decreases.
(C) consumer surplus increases and producer surplus decreases.
(D) consumer surplus decreases and producer surplus increases.
(E) consumer surplus and producer surplus remain unchanged.

28. A good with positive cross-price elasticity is considered to be a/an

   (A) normal good.
   (B) inferior good.
   (C) substitute good.
   (D) complementary good.
   (E) independent good.

29. A good that has an income elasticity of less than 1 is considered to be a/an

   (A) normal good.
   (B) inferior good.
   (C) luxury.
   (D) necessity.
   (E) independent good.

30. Chewing gum is a normal good. Which of the following would increase the demand for chewing gum?

   (A) an increase in the price of chewing gum
   (B) an increase in the number of chewing gum consumers in the market
   (C) a decrease in the price of chewing gum
   (D) a decrease in the cost of producing chewing gum
   (E) a decrease in the incomes of gum consumers

MICROECONOMICS: UNIT II

FREE-RESPONSE QUESTIONS

1. Using a correctly labeled graph for the Econ T-Shirts market, complete each of the following:

   (a) Identify the equilibrium price and equilibrium quantity for Econ T-Shirts.
   (b) Shade in (or numerically calculate) the consumer surplus that results from the equilibrium price.
   (c) Shade in (or numerically calculate) the producer surplus that results from the equilibrium price.
   (d) Shade in (or numerically calculate) the total surplus that results from the equilibrium price.
   (e) Assume that the government imposes a price ceiling on Econ T-Shirts. On a new graph, complete each of the following:
      i. Indicate where the price ceiling is in order to be binding.
      ii. Explain what would happen to consumer surplus as result of the price ceiling.
      iii. Explain what would happen to producer surplus as a result of the price ceiling.
      iv. Explain what would happen to total surplus as a result of the price ceiling.

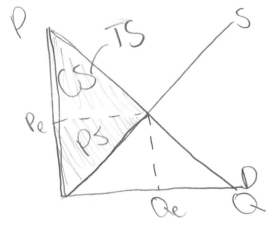 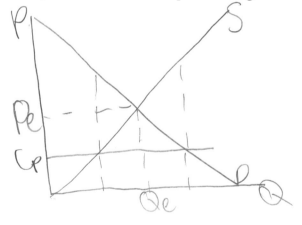

ii. Increase

iii. Decrease

iv. Decrease

2. Assume that Brown Soda and Yellow Soda are substitute goods. The government decides to <u>tax brown</u> dye, an <u>ingredient found only in Brown Soda.</u>

   (a) Using a correctly labeled graph, show the effect of the tax on brown dye for each of the following:
      i. The Brown Soda market
     ii. The Yellow Soda market

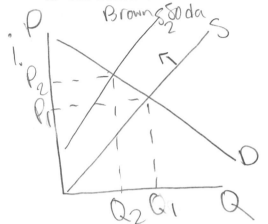

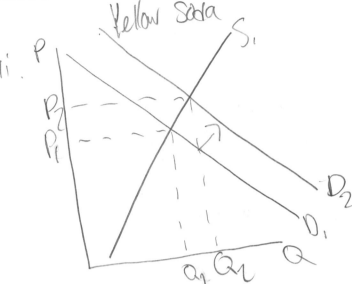

3. Explain the effect of each of the following on a typical market that is currently in equilibrium:

   (a) a reduction in the price of a complementary good
   (b) an increase in the price of a substitute good
   (c) the effect of an increase in the incomes of the consumers in this market on normal goods
   (d) the belief of consumers that in the future the price of this product will be much higher
   (e) the introduction of a new law that sets a minimum age to buy this product
   (f) ingredients used in the manufacturing of the product increase in price

a. Demand ↑, P↑, Q↑

b. Demand ↑, P↑, Q↑

c. Demand for normal ↑

d. Demand ↑

e. Demand ↓

f. Supply ↓

COST OF PRODUCTION & THEORY OF THE FIRM

One of the concepts mentioned in both Units I and II was **profit** and its components, **total cost** and **total revenue**. In this unit, costs and revenue will be explored in more detail, and then graphed to show relationships. The goal is to find the profit-maximizing output for a variety of market structures. What does that mean? It means, how does a company know what price to charge and what quantity to produce? It produces at the profit-maximizing output, of course!

In Unit I, we organized an ice cream factory according to the factors of production. This time, let's separate it according to types of costs. Look at the examples and try to predict the definition of each type of cost.

63

To review: **total revenue** is calculated by multiplying price and quantity. Calculating revenue means little, though, without comparing it to costs. **Total cost** is found by multiplying cost per unit and quantity.

Total Cost can be calculated this way, as well; Fixed Cost plus Variable Cost, or **TC = FC + VC**.

Type of cost:	Examples of factor/resource/ input costs for an ice cream factory:	Definition:
Variable Cost	cream, fruit, chocolate, nuts, sugar, advertising expenses, workers' wages, shipping charges, electricity, etc.	Costs that change according to the amount produced – if more ice cream is produced, more of these variable resources will be needed.
Fixed Cost	factory, freezers, mixing bowls, insurance, real estate taxes, executive salaries, etc.	Costs that are fixed regardless of the amount produced – if a lot of ice cream is produced, these costs will stay the same; if no ice cream is produced, these costs will stay the same.

Often, it is more important to find out the average cost per unit produced. Finding an average is simply dividing by quantity:

Average Fixed Cost ("AFC") = FC/Q
Average Variable Cost ("AVC") = VC/Q
Average Total Cost ("ATC") = TC/Q or AFC+AVC

In order to see the relationships between these costs, it helps to fill out a table. See if you can do it:

Output (or Quantity)	Fixed Cost	Variable Cost	Total Cost	Average Fixed Cost	Average Variable Cost	Average Total Cost
0		0	$10.00			
1		$10.00				
2		17.5				
3		22.5				
4		25				
5		26				
6		27.5				
7		32.5				
8		40				
9		50				
10		70				

Here are the answers. Refer back to the formulas in the previous paragraphs if you are unsure as to how to calculate the numbers.

Output (or Quantity)	Fixed Cost	Variable Cost	Total Cost	Average Fixed Cost	Average Variable Cost	Average Total Cost
0	$10.00	$0.00	$10.00	$0.00	$0.00	$0.00
1	10	$10.00	20	$10.00	$10.00	$20.00
2	10	17.5	27.5	5	8.75	13.75
3	10	22.5	32.5	3.33	7.5	10.83
4	10	25	35	2.5	6.25	8.75
5	10	26	36	2	5.2	7.2
6	10	27.5	37.5	1.66	4.58	6.25
7	10	32.5	42.5	1.42	4.64	6.07
8	10	40	50	1.25	5	6.25
9	10	50	60	1.11	5.55	6.66
10	10	70	80	1	7	8

Important concepts to recognize:

1) Fixed costs stay the same regardless of the quantity produced.
2) Variable costs increase as quantity produced increases.
3) Total costs increase as quantity produced increases.
4) The difference between total cost and variable cost is always fixed cost.

It is easier to see these relationships on a graph. Plotting the points using quantity on the X axis and price or cost on the Y axis, you will see the shaded data above drawn as cost curves on *Graph A*.

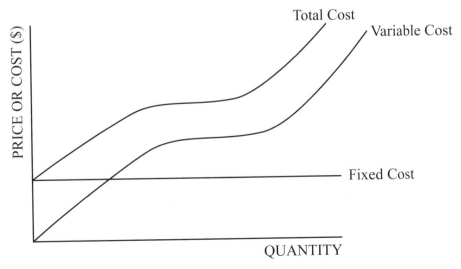

Graph A: Cost Curves

Plotting the numbers from the remainder of the chart (the non-shaded part) using quantity on the X axis and price on the Y axis, you will see the following cost curves:

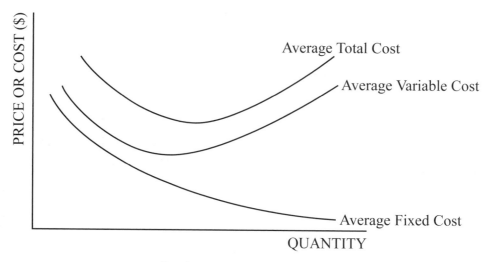

Graph B: Average Cost Curves

Some more important concepts to recognize:

5) Average fixed costs become increasingly smaller as quantity increases, but never reach zero.
6) Average variable costs grow smaller, then larger.
7) Average total costs grow smaller, then larger.
8) The difference between average total costs and average variable costs starts out large, but grows smaller as quantity produced increases; this difference is the average fixed cost.
9) The AVC and ATC curves are u-shaped due to diminishing marginal returns.

Regardless of the numbers used, the curves in *Graphs A* and *B* will always have the same shapes and relationships.

There is another cost that needs to be included in the chart for it to be complete. **Marginal Cost (or MC)** is the <u>additional</u> cost that is incurred by producing an <u>additional</u> unit. It is calculated by dividing the change in total cost by the change in quantity, or

$$MC = \frac{\Delta TC}{\Delta Q}$$

Using the table on page 65, if we add a column for marginal cost, it would look like this:

Output (or Quantity)	Fixed Cost	Variable Cost	Total Cost	Average Fixed Cost	Average Variable Cost	Average Total Cost	Marginal Cost
0	$10.00	$0.00	$10.00	$0.00	$0.00	$0.00	$0.00
1	10	$10.00	20	$10.00	$10.00	$20.00	10
2	10	17.5	27.5	5	8.75	13.75	7.5
3	10	22.5	32.5	3.33	7.5	10.83	5
4	10	25	35	2.5	6.25	8.75	2.5
5	10	26	36	2	5.2	7.2	1
6	10	27.5	37.5	1.66	4.58	6.25	1.5
7	10	32.5	42.5	1.42	4.64	6.07	5
8	10	40	50	1.25	5	6.25	7.5
9	10	50	60	1.11	5.55	6.66	10
10	10	70	80	1	7	8	20

Again, here is *Graph B* but now with the MC curve included:

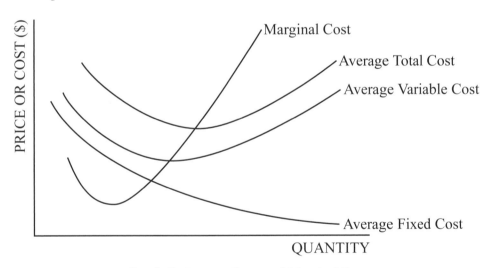

Graph C: Average Costs and Marginal Cost

Additional important concepts to recognize:

10) Marginal cost reflects the change in cost between the current unit and the previous unit. For example, producing a second unit costs an additional $7.50, while adding the third unit costs an additional $5.00.
11) The MC curve starts high, then drops to a minimum before increasing again.
12) The MC curve always intersects the AVC and ATC curves at their lowest points.
13) Because MC reflects a *change* in the cost schedules, MC is only affected by variable cost; fixed cost plays no role in calculating MC. To prove this, change the fixed cost number in the table about to $20.00 and re-calculate MC. What happens? Your marginal cost is still the same.

Why is marginal cost important? A smart producer wants to know exactly how much it costs to produce each unit of output. That way, he can determine the exact point when he should cease production: that moment when the benefit of producing (the marginal benefit, or MB) is less than the cost (the marginal cost, or MC). Using the idea of marginal analysis from Unit I, marginal cost reflects the **diminishing returns** obtained from adding variable costs to at least one, if not more, fixed costs. Translated, this means that as another worker is added to the ice cream factory, eventually the cost to hire that worker outweighs the benefit of his output. The factory is only so big and there is only so much machinery that can be used at one time (economists call this "fixed capital stock"). When marginal benefits are less than marginal costs, production needs to decrease (and perhaps workers are laid off) until the point where marginal benefits again equal marginal costs.

In order to determine where **MB = MC**, we need to find MB. Considering the production of ice cream, the benefit for the producer is the revenue he receives from selling ice cream. **Marginal Revenue** (or MR) is the <u>additional</u> revenue he receives for selling an <u>additional</u> unit of ice cream, or

$$MR = \frac{\Delta TR}{\Delta Q} \text{ or } \frac{\Delta (P \times Q)}{\Delta Q}$$

Assume the ice cream producer sells his ice cream in large containers for $7.50 apiece. Thus, using the above formula, his MR for each unit is also $7.50.

As stated earlier, costs and revenues by themselves do not mean much. We need to have both revenue and cost information in one place in order to compare. We do this by plotting MR on *Graph D*. The plotted line is horizontal because the factory can sell as much ice cream as it can produce at $7.50 per container.

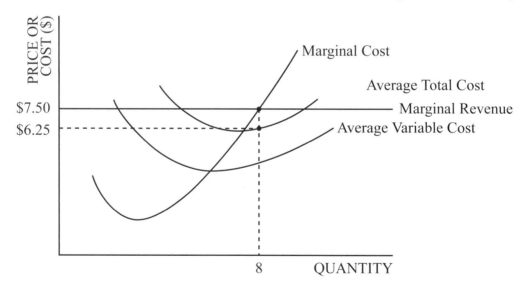

Graph D: Profit-maximizing Output

Notice that MC and MR intersect at a price of $7.50 and a quantity of 8. This intersection is one of the most important relationships in Microeconomics: economists call it the **profit-maximizing output** (do you hear the fireworks exploding? That's how important this concept is.) This is the quantity the producer should produce – no more, no less. If she produces less, where MR>MC, she will be leaving potential revenue on the table by not selling as many containers of ice cream as possible. If she sells more, where MR<MC, well, that

is never a good thing. No one wants costs to be greater than revenue, neither in the short-run nor the long-run. Thus, MR=MC is the best possible place to produce.

Profit (or total revenue – total cost), can be determined at the profit-maximizing output by calculating it one of two ways:

$$(P \times Q) - (ATC \times Q) = (\$7.50 \times 8 \text{ units}) - (\$6.25 \times 8 \text{ units}) = \$60 - \$50 = \$10$$

or

$$\$7.50 - \$6.25 = \$1.25 \text{ per unit profit}; \$1.25 \times 8 \text{ units} = \$10$$

If the price of ice cream – the MR – falls below $6.07 but stays above $4.58, that is, between the AVC and the ATC curves respectively (if you are unsure where these numbers come from, refer back to the table on page 67), then the producer is losing money in the short-run. That means she can stay in business for a short while, perhaps by dipping into her savings, but eventually her savings will run out. She also could try to cut costs by laying off workers or paying less for her factors of production. However, unless prices rise or costs fall, she will not be able to sustain her business in the long-run.

If prices fall even further, say below $4.58 – below the AVC curve – she will have to shut down production, as she can no longer cover even her fixed costs, those she has to pay regardless of how much she produces.

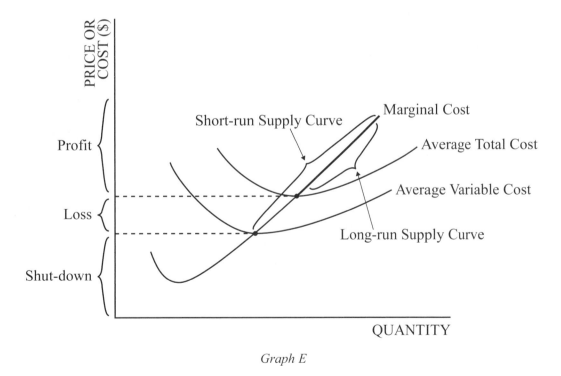

Graph E

And if prices rise? Her profits will grow (assuming costs do not change) and she will be one happy entrepreneur.

Notice in the previous examples we determined the cut-off points by looking at where the MC crossed the ATC and AVC curves (their lowest points). These points are important not only because they determine the points where the producer loses money in the short-run or shuts down production, but also because they determine the producer's supply curve. As the producer will not produce below the point where MC = AVC, the **firm's short-run supply curve** is that part of the MC curve above AVC. The **firm's demand curve** is the MR curve. As long as she charges this price, buyers will buy as much of her output as she is willing to sell.

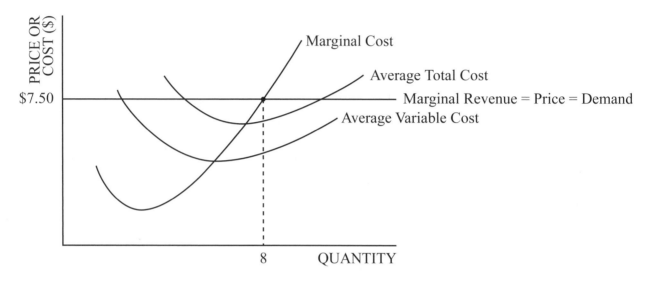

Graph F: Firm's Supply and Demand

Even more important concepts to recognize:

14) In the long-run, average total cost is usually designated as **long-run average cost**, or LRAC. This is to distinguish it from the short-run, when costs are both fixed and variable. In the long run, all costs are variable, as the long-run represents that time when everything is changeable – leases can be renegotiated, orders can be changed, new equipment can be purchased, etc. The short-run, if you remember from Unit I, is that period where at least one factor of production is fixed.

15) Long-run cost curves are the sum of many short-run cost curves. The long-run curve has three distinct parts: that part where costs are falling due to **economies of scale**, that part where costs are constant ("**constant returns to scale**"), and that part where costs are rising due to **diseconomies of scale**. *Graph G* shows this concept.

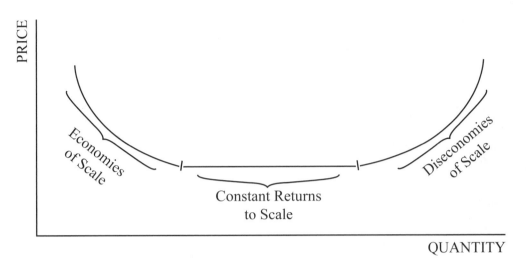

Graph G: Long-Run Average Cost

16) In the long-run, the point where MC = MR takes on new meaning. Unlike in the short-run where production can continue temporarily if a business is losing money, in the long-run, if MR falls below ATC, the company will go out of business. Thus, the firm's supply curve is that part of the MR curve above ATC. Since a producer cannot lose money in the long run, his **long-run supply curve** is that part of the MC curve where profits are always earned (see *Graph E*).

17) Cost curves are mirror images of product curves. In economic vocabulary, "product" means output. Due to increasing returns, costs fall as production increases, but only up to a point. Eventually, due to diminishing returns, costs will increase and production will fall. This is reflected in the production curve by the fact that output increases as workers become more experienced and specialization takes place. Eventually those benefits are exhausted, and production decreases. *Graph H* shows this relationship.

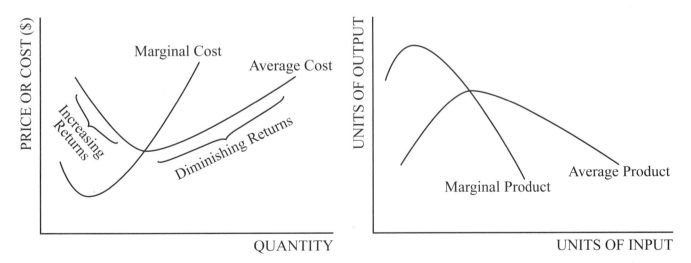

Graph H: Cost Curves and Product Curves

The previous information is useful for all types of businesses, not just ice cream factories. Economists categorize businesses into four market structures. Each market structure has its own set of characteristics, as shown in the following chart:

Market Structure Characteristic:	Perfect Competition	Monopolistic Competition	Oligopoly	Monopoly
Example	agricultural products	retail stores, restaurants	phone companies, airlines, car makers	utilities
Type of product	homogeneous	differentiated	differentiated or homogeneous	unique
Number of firms in the market/industry	thousands	hundreds	2 to 100	1
Percentage of market share	very small	small to large	large enough for market power	100.00%
Barriers to entry	none	some	many	many
Non-price competition	no	yes	yes	no
Number of substitutes	infinite	many	few	none
Slope of the demand curve	perfectly elastic (horizontal)	relatively inelastic (downward sloping)	not applicable	more inelastic (downward sloping)
Profit-maximizing price	P = MC = MR	P > MC = MR	not applicable	P > MC = MR
Price is determined by	the market ("price-taker")	the firm ("price-maker")	the firm ("price-maker")	the firm ("price-maker")
Long-run economic profits	zero	zero	yes	yes
Relationship between MR and D curves	MR = D	MR < D	not applicable	MR < D (except price-discriminating monopoly, where MR = D)
Consumer and producer surplus	at their maximums and equal	producer surplus > consumer surplus	not applicable	producer surplus > consumer surplus; (no consumer surplus in a perfectly price-discriminating monopoly)

Deadweight loss	none	yes	not applicable	yes (except price-discriminating monopoly)
Productive efficiency (P = minimum ATC)	yes	no	no	no
Allocative efficiency (P = MC)	yes	no	no	(except price-discriminating monopoly)

What does all of this mean?

First, notice that perfect competition and monopoly are at two ends of the spectrum, and that monopolistic competition and oligopoly fall somewhere in between.

Second, each of these market structures has a graph (except oligopoly) that helps describe and explain it.

Perfect Competition

The set of graphs for perfect competition should look familiar:

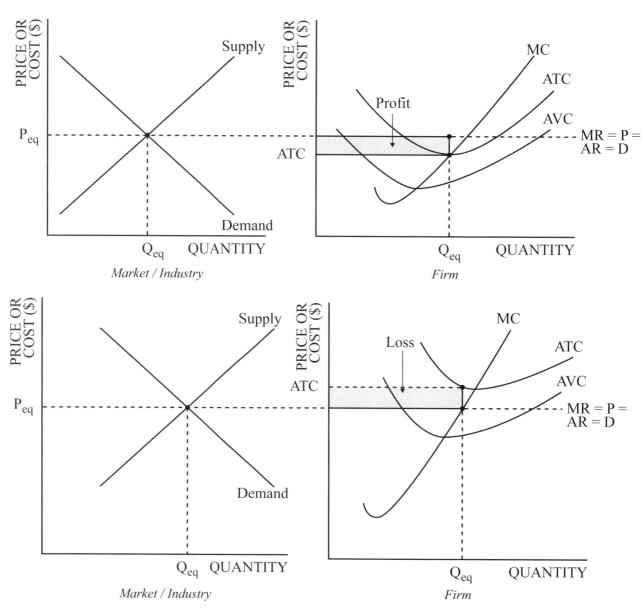

Graph I: Perfect Competition in the Short-Run

It is the combination of two graphs already discussed: the supply and demand graph from Unit II and the cost curves graph discussed previously in this unit. The supply and demand graph illustrates the market; the cost curves graph illustrates an individual firm (one of thousands) in this market. The price and quantity equilibrium in the market graph determines the price this individual firm and all others must charge, as the firms are price takers. Each firm's influence in the marketplace is so small that it must take the market price or risk pricing itself out of the market, since other firms produce homogeneous products that are perfectly substitutable. Consumers will be quick to purchase goods from other firms if the product is not priced correctly.

The concept of perfect substitutability is an important one because it defines the types of goods sold in a perfectly competitive market. The best examples are agricultural products, as it is difficult to determine the difference between one firm's output and another's. One farmer's ear of corn is indistinguishable from another's – they are homogeneous. Thus, the demand curve is perfectly elastic.

For perfect competition, $D = P = AR = MR$ because:

Quantity	Price	Total Revenue	Average Revenue	Marginal Revenue
		$TR = P \times Q$	$AR = TR/Q$	$MR = \Delta TR/\Delta Q$
0	$2.00	0	0	0
1	2	2	2	2
2	2	4	2	2
3	2	6	2	2
4	2	8	2	2

As supply and demand shift according to their respective determinants in the market, the firm's demand curve changes as well. Prices go up, prices come down, and firms enter and exit the market accordingly. This entry and exit stops as the market finds its long-run equilibrium, that point at which economic profits are zero and the firm is both allocatively and productively efficient. Because the existence of these efficiencies means that the market is now economically efficient, perfect competition is considered the ideal market structure. Consumer and producer surpluses are at their maximum, and deadweight loss does not exist.

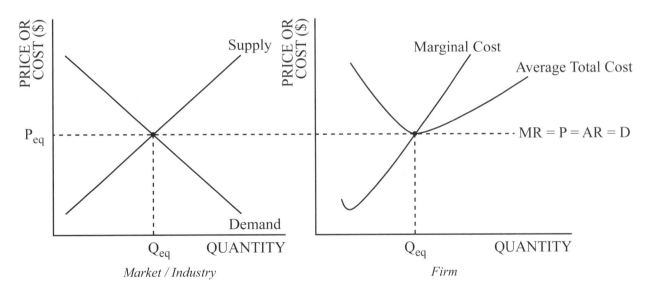

Graph J: Perfect Competition in Long-Run Equilibrium

Monopoly

The opposite of this perfection is monopoly. A firm that is a monopoly faces no competition due to the existence of **barriers to entry**. Since perfectly competitive firms make up such a small part of the market, these firms are not able to keep other competitors from joining the market. If a person wants to become a farmer, all he/she needs to do is plant some seeds. On the other hand, those firms that control a large portion of the marketplace generally do so because they benefit from these barriers that keep <u>other</u> firms out, thus lessening competition. Examples of barriers to entry are economies of scale, control over natural resources, legal barriers such as patents and licenses, pricing strategies such as underbidding or dumping, brand loyalty, mergers and/or takeovers, and the ability to conduct research and development.

The result of this lack of competition is that a monopoly is able to charge a price greater than MC = MR, as shown in *Graph K*.

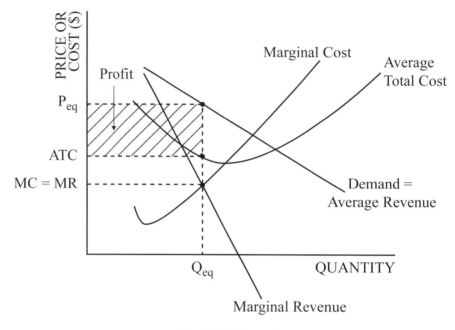

Graph K: Monopoly

Notice that profit is determined the same way as in perfect competition and that the cost curves are the same shape. However, there are some important differences between the graphs of the two market structures.

1) For a monopoly, the demand and marginal revenue curves are downward sloping, as opposed to horizontal for a perfectly competitive firm. This is due to the fact that there are fewer substitutes for a monopoly's product, and thus the curves are more inelastic. The result of this is that if the monopoly wants to sell a greater quantity than the profit-maximizing output, the monopolist will have to lower his price. This is shown in the price column of the table on the next page.
2) Unlike in perfect competition, the demand and marginal revenue curves are separate, and the marginal revenue curve has a steeper slope than the demand curve. This is proven mathematically in the table on the next page.

For monopoly, $D = AR = P$ but is $> MR$ because:

Quantity	Price	Total Revenue	Average Revenue	Marginal Revenue
0	0	0	0	0
1	10	10	10	10
2	8	16	8	6
3	6	18	6	2
4	4	16	4	-2

3) Marginal revenue can actually be negative, as shown by the marginal revenue curve falling below the X axis. Monopolists will not produce beyond this point voluntarily, as they will lose money on each unit produced.

4) There are occasions when monopolists will produce beyond where marginal revenue = 0. This is usually the result of government regulation – the government feels the monopolist's product is important enough that more consumers should benefit from increased output at a lower price. If this mandated level of output causes the monopolist to lose money, the government will often subsidize the production of the good.

5) Regulated monopolies face two possible price-and-output combinations, depending on the goal of the regulation. The first is called the "**socially optimal point**" and occurs where $P = MC = D$. This point is the closest a monopoly can get to operating like a perfectly competitive firm. A "**fair return**" or "break even" price occurs where $P = ATC = D$. Here, the firm is making zero economic profits.

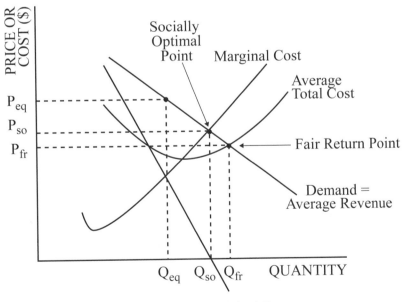

Graph L: Monopoly

6) At the point where MR = 0 (where marginal revenue crosses the X axis), total revenue is at its greatest level.

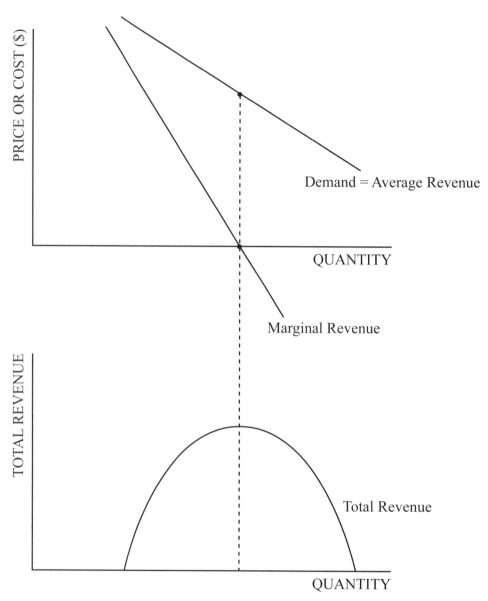

Graph M: Marginal vs. Total Revenue

Also, MR = 0 is a significant point in that this is where the demand curve changes its elasticity. Above the point where MR = 0, that portion of the demand curve is elastic; below MR = 0, demand is inelastic. The exact point where MR = 0 is unit elastic. *Graph N* shows these concepts.

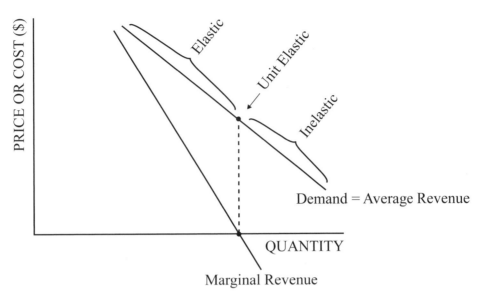

Graph N: Monopoly and Elasticity

Another type of monopoly is a price-discriminating monopoly. The main advantage a **price-discriminating monopolist** has over a **single-priced, non-regulated monopolist** is the opportunity to earn greater profits. Price-discriminating monopolists are called such because they are able to discriminate between prices that different customers are willing to pay and charge them accordingly. Consumers who are willing to pay more, do; those who want to pay less, do so as well. This is possible for three reasons:

1) The firm has monopoly power: it can determine the price it charges.
2) Elasticity of demand: the firm can identify its customers' elasticity of demand and is able to segment the market accordingly.
3) In order to ensure its market power, resale of its good or service is difficult.

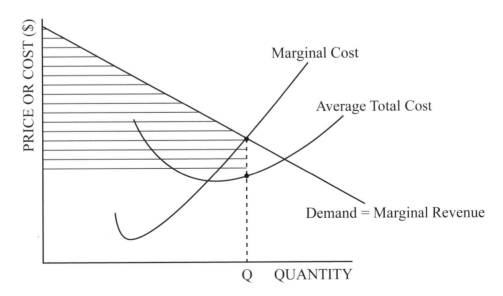

Graph O: Price-Discriminary Monopoly

Notice that in *Graph O*, the demand and marginal revenue curves are the same. For a price-discriminating monopoly, D = MR = P but not AR because:

Quantity	Price	Total Revenue	Average Revenue	Marginal Revenue
0	0	0	0	0
1	10	10	10	10
2	10 + 8	18	9	8
3	10 + 8 + 6	24	8	6
4	10 + 8 + 6 + 4	28	7	4

Total revenue reflects the fact that each consumer pays his own price (thus, P still equals demand). Thus, as in the table on page 77, in order to sell an additional unit, the monopolist must lower his price. However, he does not have to lower his price for <u>all</u> buyers; because he is able to segment his market, each consumer pays according to his own assessment of what the good or service is worth.

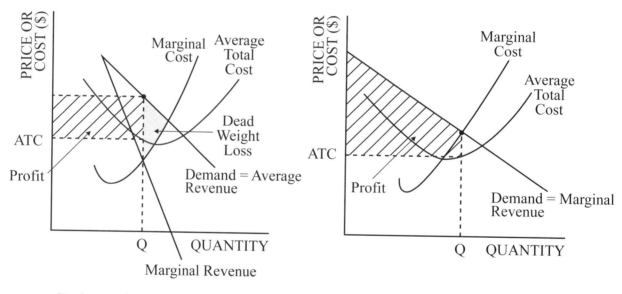

Single-priced Non-regulated Monopoly   Price Discriminating Monopoly

Graph P: Comparing Profit

Also note the comparisons of profit earned by a single price, non-regulated monopolist and a price-discriminating monopolist. The areas shaded in *Graph P* show this difference.

A **natural monopoly** is one that benefits from economies of scale, and its average total cost curve reflects that. Often, these are public utilities that benefit from economies of scale. For example, it makes little sense to have competing electric companies provide service to the same market area. This would result in each company's wires being strung all over town, which is cumbersome and aesthetically undesirable. The same used to be true for telephone companies; however, the proliferation of wireless phones has made the telephone industry more competitive. *Graph Q* shows a natural monopoly.

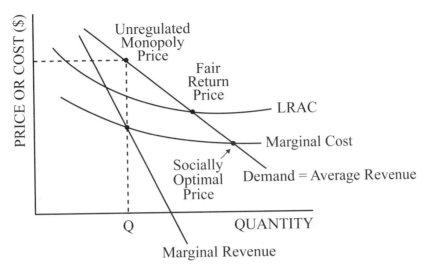

Graph Q: Natural Monopoly

The concepts of consumer surplus and deadweight loss affect the monopoly graph differently depending on whether it is a price-discriminating monopoly or a single price, non-regulated monopoly.

Because P > MC = MR in a single price, non-regulated monopoly, the consumer surplus that existed under perfect competition is mostly transferred to the producer, who benefits from the fact that he has price-setting power. This higher price and lower quantity sold means that there is deadweight loss, as the market is inefficient compared to a perfectly competitive one. In a price-discriminating monopoly, however, each consumer is paying his preferred price, which means that there is no consumer surplus – it is all transferred to the producer – and there is no deadweight loss, as quantity sold is determined where P = MC. See *Graph R* for an illustration of this difference.

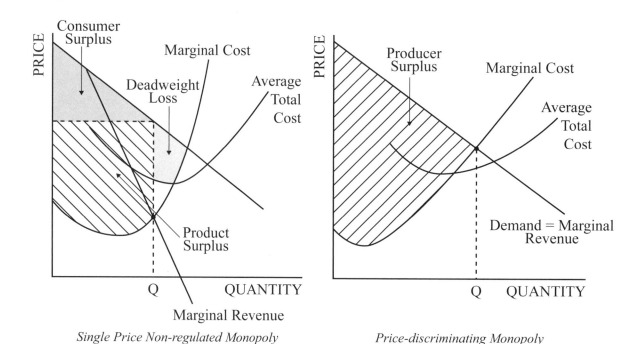

Single Price Non-regulated Monopoly   *Price-discriminating Monopoly*

Graph R: Comparing Surplus

Oligopoly

Oligopolies are similar to monopolies in terms of price-setting power and the ability to price-discriminate. However, because there is some degree of competition, an oligopoly's market behavior is interdependent – it must watch and react to its competitors in order to maintain (or, at least not lose) its market share. This, at times, leads to **collusion**, where oligopolistic firms agree to charge similar prices with the hope of gaining monopoly power. Such **cartels** are illegal since this behavior harms the consumer. Collusion is easiest when the product is homogeneous. Oligopolies, though, spend much time and effort attempting to differentiate their products from their competitors' through non-price competition.

There is no agreed-upon graph for an oligopoly. Unique to oligopoly, though, is the concept of **game theory**, which illustrates firms' interdependence and helps predict outcomes given another firm's pricing strategy. Game theory uses a matrix that shows two players' payoffs given certain behaviors.

Assume we have two airlines, Ski Airlines and Air Snowboard. Both airlines fly to the best alpine ski destinations, and both are interdependent because they must take into consideration their competitor's price when setting their own – since there are two airlines that provide similar service, consumers can chose their preferred airline based on price. The table below shows the resulting profits from each ticket price (profits are in thousands).

(In the table below the first number is for Air Snowboard and the second number is for Ski Airlines)

		Ski Airlines	
		$140 per ticket	$135 per ticket
Air Snowboard	$140 per ticket	$65/$62	$64/$64
	$135 per ticket	$74/$55	$63/$60

Notice that a **dominant strategy** exists – that place where the payoff is largest, regardless of what the other competitor does. If Air Snowboard charges $140 per ticket, Ski Airlines should charge $135 because it will earn $64,000 in profits rather than $62,000. If Air Snowboard charges $135 a ticket, Ski Airlines will make the most profit by charging $135 a ticket ($60,000 vs. $55,000). Thus, Ski Airlines' dominant strategy is $135.

Air Snowboard does not have a dominant strategy, however. If Ski Airlines charges $140, Air Snowboard should charge $135 ($74,000 vs. $65,000); however, if Ski Airlines charges $135, then Air Snowboard should charge $140 ($64,000 vs. $60,000). This means Air Snowboard's pricing strategy is always dependent on that of Ski Airlines.

Both firms might be tempted to collude by charging $140 a ticket. This would guarantee both airlines a higher profit ($65,000 rather than $64,000 for Air Snowboard, and $62,000 rather than $60,000 for Ski Airlines). However, the temptation to cheat and secretly charge $135 – and thus steal customers – while the other is honoring the $140 price is too great. This is why cartels usually fail.

Pareto Efficiency occurs when resources are allocated efficiently, and changing the allocation of resources would cause harm to one or more participants. A **Nash Equilibrium** exists when no participant has an incentive to change his behavior after considering his opponent's strategy – he would be no better off than he is currently and thus a dominant strategy does not exist.

Monopolistic competition

Monopolistic competition is the most common market structure, as most retail businesses fall into this category. Due to the large number of competitors, monopolistically competitive firms, like oligopolies, are focused on product differentiation via non-price competition. One of the preferred types of non-price competition is advertising, where the goal is to develop brand loyalty and gain a market niche.

In the short-run, this non-price competition allows for economic profit. In the long-run, though, due to competition and the fact that each firm's products are almost homogeneous, economic profits equal zero. An example would be a clothing store – it might sell trendy clothing, but in the long-run it is really only selling jeans, which can be bought elsewhere are various prices. *Graph S* on page 84 shows the profit, loss, and long-run situations of monopolistic competition.

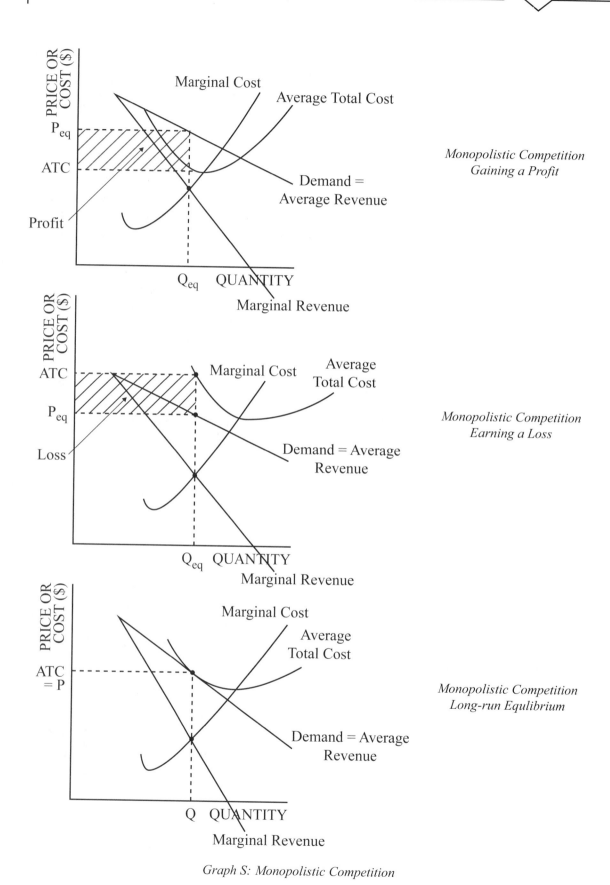

Monopolistic Competition
Gaining a Profit

Monopolistic Competition
Earning a Loss

Monopolistic Competition
Long-run Equilibrium

Graph S: Monopolistic Competition

Notice that monopolistic competition and single-price monopoly graphs look very similar. However, unlike a monopoly, because there are few barriers to entry, the result is a long-run graph that shows no economic profit as firms enter and leave the market.

Types of Business Ownership

These market structures can exist as one of three types of entities; a **sole proprietorship**, where the owner receives all the profits but also is responsible for all risks and liabilities; a **partnership**, where one or more individuals work together and share both profits and losses; or a third, a **corporation**, where a state-registered charter creates a legal entity that has limited liability – individuals work for the corporation, but the individuals are not held liable for any losses if the corporation is sued.

In the next unit, we'll graph the factors of production that make it possible for these market structures to exist.

New Terms

- Profit
- Total revenue
- Total cost
- Fixed cost
- Variable cost
- Total cost
- Average fixed cost
- Average variable cost
- Average total cost
- Marginal cost
- Profit-maximizing output
- Economies of scale
- Constant returns to scale
- Diseconomies of scale
- Long-run average cost
- Perfect competition
- Monopoly
- Monopolistic competition
- Oligopoly
- Barriers to entry
- Non-price competition
- Natural monopoly
- Price-discriminating monopoly
- Fair return price
- Socially optimal price
- Game theory
- Dominant strategy
- Pareto Efficiency
- Nash Equilibrium
- Sole proprietorship
- Partnership
- Corporation

MULTIPLE-CHOICE QUESTIONS

1. A firm that decides to shut-down but is still in business would find which of the following to be true of its fixed and variable cost?

	Fixed Cost	Variable Cost
(A)	$0	$0
(B)	$0	positive
(C)	positive	$0
(D)	positive	positive
(E)	positive	negative

(C) is circled

Questions 2-6 refer to the table below:

Output	Total Revenue	Variable Cost	Fixed Cost	Total Cost
0	0	0	200	200
1	100	50	100	___
2	200	70	100	___
3	$300	85	200	285
4	400	95	200	295
5	___	105	200	305
6	___	130		___
7	___	210		___
8	___	410		___

2. Based on the information in the table above, the total cost of producing 5 units of output is:

(A) 105
(B) 200
(C) 305
(D) 330
(E) 410

(C) is circled

3. Based on the information in the table, the marginal cost of producing the 4th unit of output is:

(A) 10
(B) 15
(C) 20
(D) 75
(E) 175

4. Based on the information in the table, the price of the product this firm is selling is:

(A) $20
(B) $40
(C) $100
(D) $120
(E) Not able to be determined from the information given.

5. Based on the information in the table, the average fixed cost of producing 5 units of output is:

(A) 200
(B) 100
(C) 95
(D) 40
(E) 20

$$AFC = \frac{TFC}{Q}$$

6. Based on the information in the table, the profit-maximizing level of output for this firm is:

(A) 8
(B) 7
(C) 6
(D) 5
(E) 0

7. Which set of cost curves in the figures below is correctly drawn?

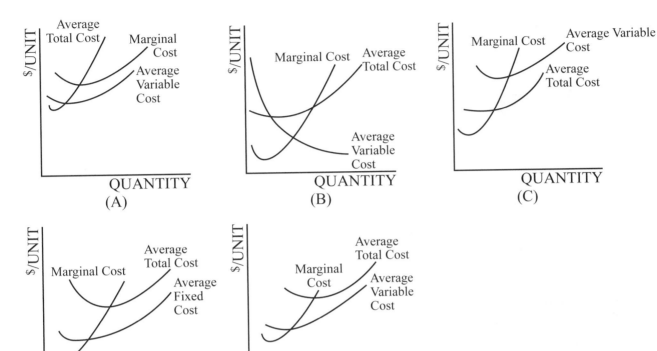

(A) A
(B) B
(C) C
(D) D
(E) E

8. The firm depicted in the graph below is

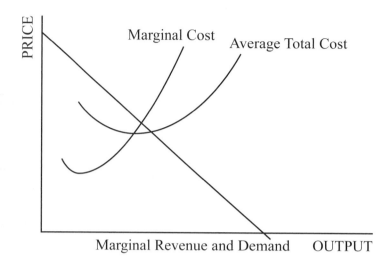

(A) a perfectly competitive firm.
(B) a perfectly price discriminating monopoly.
(C) a single price monopoly.
(D) an oligopoly in the long-run.
(E) a monopolistically competitive firm in the long-run.

Questions 9-11 refer to the table below:

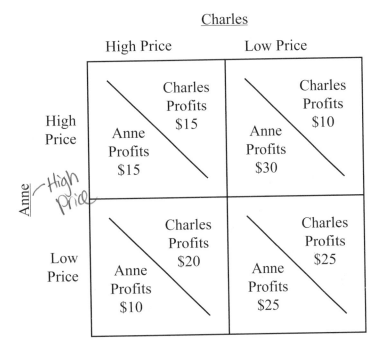

9. Based on the information in the payoff matrix box depicted above, we can conclude that in the absence of collusion

   (A) Charles and Anne will each charge a low price.
   (B) Charles and Anne will each charge a high price.
   (C) Charles will charge a high price and Anne will charge a low price.
   (D) Charles will charge a low price and Anne will charge a high price.
   (E) no conclusion can be accurately drawn from the information given.

10. Based on the information in the payoff matrix box depicted above, we can conclude that

   (A) Charles has a dominant strategy and Anne does not.
   (B) Charles and Anne both have a dominant strategy.
   (C) Charles and Anne do not have a dominant strategy.
   (D) Charles does not have a dominant strategy but Anne does.
   (E) no conclusion can be accurately made from the information given in regards to dominant and non-dominant strategy.

11. If Charles and Anne can successfully collude and agree to a binding enforceable agreement, what would be Anne's profit?

(A) 10
(B) 15
(C) 20
(D) 25
(E) 30

12. The three basic forms of business organization are

(A) proprietorship, partnership, monopoly.
(B) proprietorship, partnership, competition.
(C) proprietorship, partnership, corporation.
(D) proprietorship, monopoly, competition.
(E) monopoly, competition, oligopoly.

13. Firms in all market structures seek to

(A) maximize price and therefore maximize profit.
(B) minimize cost and therefore maximize profit.
(C) operate where MC = MR and are therefore guaranteed a profit.
(D) maximize profit.
(E) no conclusion can be accurately drawn for firms in all market structures in regard to profit maximizing behavior.

14. If fixed costs for a firm operating under conditions of perfect competition increased, but not enough to lead the firm to shut down, how would that change in fixed cost affect output, profit, and price of the firm?

	Output	Profit	Price
(A)	no change	no change	no change
(B)	no change	decrease	no change
(C)	no change	decrease	increase
(D)	decrease	decrease	increase
(E)	decrease	decrease	no change

15. Based on the graph below, this is a firm facing which combination of events?

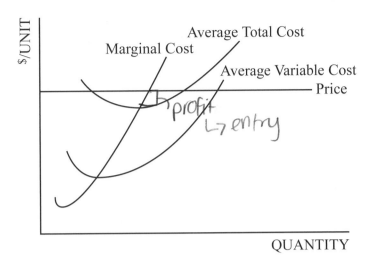

	Profits	Entry or exit of firms to this market
(A)	Positive	Firms entering the market in the long-run
(B)	Positive	Firms exiting the market in the long-run
(C)	Normal	Firms stable in the market in the long-run
(D)	Negative	Firms entering the market in the long-run
(E)	Negative	Firms exiting the market in the long-run

16. Marginal cost is calculated by

(A) adding total cost at two consecutive units of output.
(B) subtracting total cost at two consecutive units of output.
(C) adding fixed and variable cost.
(D) subtracting fixed cost from total cost.
(E) subtracting variable cost from total cost.

17. Which of the following correctly ranks market structures from least to most competitive?

(A) monopoly, oligopoly, monopolistic competition, perfect competition
(B) monopoly, monopolistic competition, oligopoly, perfect competition
(C) perfect competition, oligopoly, monopolistic competition, monopoly
(D) perfect competition, monopoly, oligopoly, monopolistic competition
(E) perfect competition, monopolistic competition, oligopoly, monopoly

18. Which of the following is/are necessary for a firm to be able to engage in price discrimination?

    I. Subdivide the market
    II. Prevent resale
    III. Monopoly power

    (A) III only
    (B) I and II only
    (C) I and III only
    (D) II and III only
    (E) I, II, and III

19. Based on the graph in the figure below, the monopoly price, break-even price, and socially optimum price are (respectively):

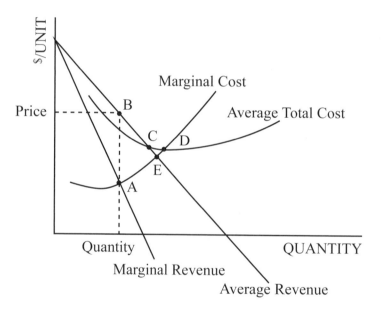

	Profit Maximizing Point	Fair Return, or Break-Even Point	Socially Optimum Point
(A)	A	B	C
(B)	E	C	B
(C)	C	D	E
(D)	B	C	D
(E)	B	C	E

20. Which of the following is true for both a perfect competitor and a monopolistic competitor in long-run equilibrium?

	Perfect Competitor	Monopolistic Competitor
(A)	Earns normal profits	Earns normal profits
(B)	Is allocatively efficient	Is allocatively efficient
(C)	Is productively efficient	Is productively efficient
(D)	Produces at P = MC	Produces at P = MC
(E)	Produces at min. ATC	Produces at min. ATC

21. Based on the table below, which of the following is true?

dominant

Karen

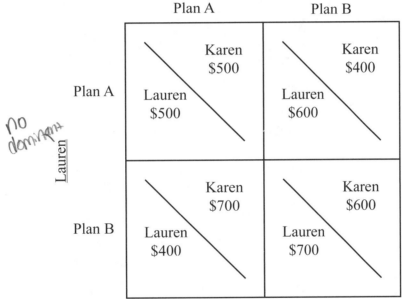

no dominant

Lauren

Plan A

Plan B

Plan A
Karen $500
Lauren $500

Karen $400
Lauren $600

Plan B
Karen $700
Lauren $400

Karen $600
Lauren $700

(A) Karen has a dominant strategy but Lauren does not.
(B) Lauren has a dominant strategy but Karen does not.
(C) Karen and Lauren both have a dominant strategy.
(D) Neither Karen nor Lauren has a dominant strategy.
(E) No conclusion can be made in regard to dominant strategy from the information given.

Questions 22-25 refer to the figure below:

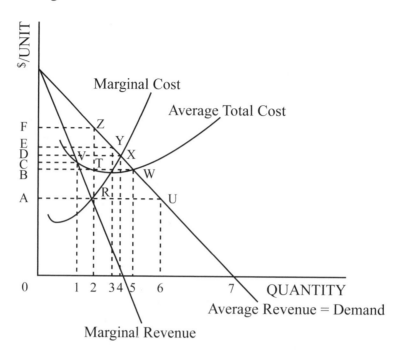

22. What area in the figure above describes total revenue at the profit maximizing level of output?

    (A) A, R, 2, 0
    (B) F, Z, 2, 0
    (C) B, W, 5 0
    (D) C, X, 4, 0
    (E) A, U, 6, 0

23. What area in the figure above describes total cost at the profit maximizing level of output?

    (A) A, R, 2, 0
    (B) F, Z, 2, 0
    (C) C, X, 4, 0
    (D) B, T, 2, 0
    (E) B, W, 5, 0

24. What area in the figure above represents profit or loss at the profit maximizing level of output?

    (A) A loss of A, R, 2, 0
    (B) A profit of F, Z, 2, 0
    (C) A profit of F, Z, R, A
    (D) A loss of F, Z, T, B
    (E) A profit of F, Z, T, B

25. If the government imposes a lump-sum tax on the monopolist in the figure, what will be the effect on the profit maximizing level of output?

    (A) It will decrease to 0.
    (B) It will decrease to 1.
    (C) It will remain at 2.
    (D) It will increase to 3.
    (E) It will increase to 5.

Questions 26-27 refer to the figure below:

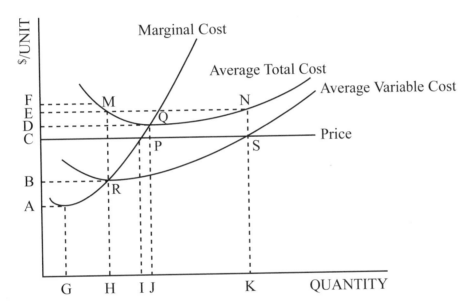

26. In the figure above, at what level of output are average costs minimized?

    min point on ATC

    (A) G
    (B) H
    (C) I
    (D) J
    (E) K

27. Based on the information in the figure above, total fixed cost is equal to

    (A) F, M, H, 0
    (B) B, R, H, 0
    (C) C, S, K, 0
    (D) D, Q, J, 0
    (E) E, N, S, C

Questions 28-32 refer to the figure below:

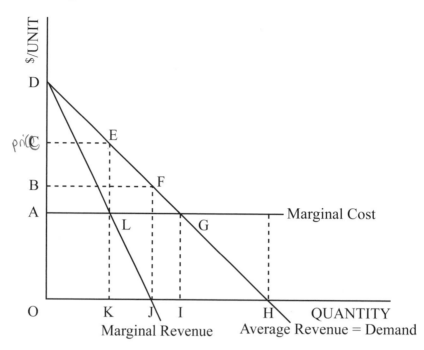

28. Based on the information in the figure above, consumer surplus is represented by the area:

(A) D, H, 0
(B) D, E, C
(C) D, J, 0
(D) C, E, L, A
(E) A, L, K, 0

29. Based on the information in the figure above, the amount of profit is represented by the area:

(A) D, H, 0
(B) D, E, C
(C) D, J, 0
(D) C, E, L, A
(E) A, L, K, 0

30. Based on the information in the figure above, the amount of deadweight loss due to monopoly is represented by the area:

(A) D, H, 0
(B) D, E, C
(C) D, J, 0
(D) E, G, L
(E) C, E, L, A

31. If the monopolist shown in the figure is able to perfectly price discriminate, the maximum profit output is:

(A) O
(B) K
(C) J
(D) I
(E) H

32. If the monopolist shown in the figure is able to perfectly price discriminate, consumer surplus is:

(A) DHO
(B) DEC
(C) DJO
(D) CELA
(E) Zero

Questions 33-34 refer to the figure below:

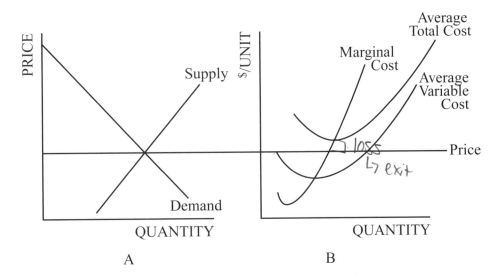

33. Based on the information in the figure above, which of the following is correct?

(A) Graph A is for the market and graph B is for the firm.
(B) Graph A is the short-run market and graph B is the long-run market.
(C) Graph A is the long-run market and graph B is the short-run market.
(D) Graph A is for the firm and graph B is for the market.
(E) Graph A is for a perfectly competitive firm and graph B is for a monopoly.

34. Based on the information in the figure, which of the following is correct?

    (A) Firms will enter the market and drive the price down.
    (B) Firms will enter the market and drive the price up.
    (C) Firms will exit the market and drive the price up.
    (D) Firms will exit the market and drive the price down.
    (E) Firms will neither enter nor exit the market and the price will remain stable.

35. Which of the following is true if a monopolist is operating in the elastic portion of the demand curve?

    (A) Marginal revenue is positive.
    (B) Marginal revenue is negative.
    (C) Marginal revenue is zero.
    (D) Marginal cost is negative.
    (E) Marginal cost is zero.

FREE-RESPONSE QUESTIONS

1. Create side-by-side graphs for a perfectly competitive firm earning short-run economic profits.

   (a) Is the short-run economic profit sustainable in the long-run? Explain.
   (b) Redraw the graph you drew to demonstrate the long-run equilibrium position for the firm and the market.
   (c) Identify the allocatively efficient level of output on the graph you drew for part (b).

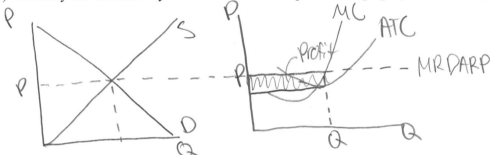

a) No because new firms will enter the market and lower the price, leading to zero economic profits

b)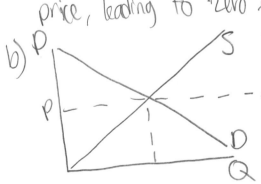

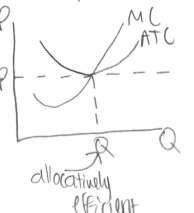

allocatively efficient

2.

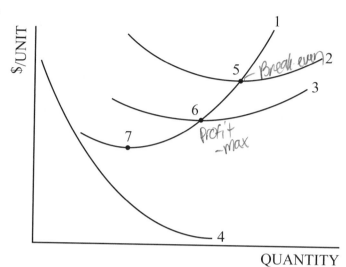

(a) On the graph above, correctly identify curves 1, 2, 3, and 4.
(b) Identify the market structure in which this firm is operating.
(c) If this firm is operating in a perfectly competitive market, identify a price that could exist only in short-run equilibrium.
(d) If this firm is operating in a perfectly competitive market, identify a price that could exist only in long-run equilibrium.

a) 1= MC
   2= ATC
   3= AVC
   4= AFC

b) Can't identify, need revenue curves

c) PL = Point 6

d) PL= Point 5

3.

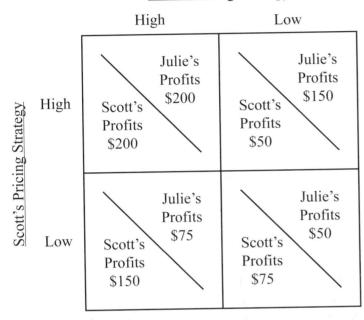

Julie's Pricing Strategy

Julie and Scott each own a firm operating in a local market. They face no other competition, they sell a slightly differentiated product, and they face significant barriers to entry. Based on this information, and the information in the figure above, answer each of the following:

(a) In what market structure do Julie and Scott operate? Explain.
(b) Does Julie have a dominant strategy? Explain.
(c) Does Scott have a dominant strategy? Explain.
(d) In the absence of collusion, what pricing strategy will prevail in this market?

a) Oligopoly because there are multiple firms with no competition, and their prices are interdependent

b) Yes, go high because she gets the most profit based on either of Scott's decisions

c) No because if Julie goes high, Scott goes high, but if Julie goes low, Scott should go low

d) Both high

NO TESTING MATERIAL ON THIS PAGE

MICROECONOMICS: UNIT IV

FACTOR MARKETS

In Unit I, the circular flow diagram was discussed. The main components of the circular flow diagram are the product market and the factor market. Unit III focused on the product market. This unit will discuss the **factor market**.

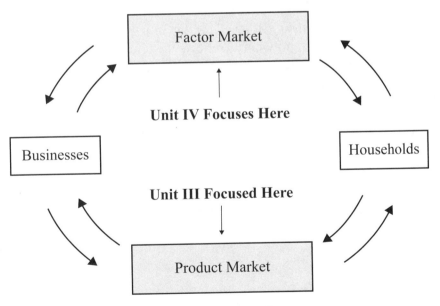

Graph A: Circular Flow Diagram

Remember that the factor market includes the **factors of production** – labor, natural resources (or land), capital and entrepreneurship – and their respective payments: wages, rent, interest and profit.

Of course, the factor market has its own graphs. The market/industry graph is a supply/demand graph, just as in the product market. However, the labels are different.

Labels for Product Market Graphs:	Labels for Factor Market Graphs:
Price	Price of Labor (or, Wages) or Price of Capital (or, Interest, i) or Price of Natural Resources (or, Rent)
Quantity	Quantity of Labor or Quantity of Capital or Quantity of Natural Resources
Supply	Marginal Resource Cost (MRC)
Demand	Marginal Revenue Product (MRP)

Labor Market

In the labor market, the consumers of the factors of production are employers, those who hire the labor. The demand curve for labor reflects the inverse relationship between wages and the quantity of labor. When wages are high, employers want to hire fewer workers; when wages fall, employers' cost of production falls, and they are willing to hire more workers. In addition, employers are concerned with the revenue that is created by their employees. Thus, **marginal revenue product** measures the revenue that each additional worker adds to total revenue. As employees add more revenue relative to their costs, the quantity demanded for these employees increases. This is why the demand curve is labeled "Demand = MRP."

The suppliers in the labor market are the workers themselves. Their main focus is the wages they earn in exchange for the production created by their efforts. Thus, the **marginal resource cost** is the additional wage (or "cost") paid to each worker. As the supply curve reflects the number of workers willing and able to work at various wage rates, economists label the supply curve in a perfectly competitive labor market as "Supply = MRC."

As in the product market, graphs are useful to determine the profit-maximizing output for a particular firm. The product market graph determines how many units should be produced; the factor market graph tells the employer how many workers he should hire. Just as the profit-maximizing output in the product market was determined by finding MC = MR, the profit-maximizing output in the factor market is determined by finding **MRC = MRP**. This is where the cost of hiring an additional worker (the MRC, or the wage rate) is equal to the revenue created by that worker's output (the MRP). This equilibrium is shown on the labor market graph, *Graph B*.

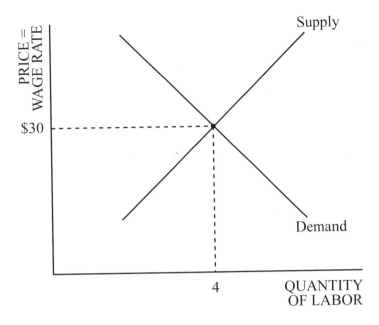

Graph B: Labor Market

Let's go back to our ice cream factory. The product market price in Unit III was $7.50 per gallon, so that is the price in this table. The wage rate is determined by the factor market equilibrium; in this case, let's say it is $30.

Quantity of Inputs	Quantity of Outputs (Total Product)	Marginal Product	Price	MRP	MRC
Workers	Gallons of ice cream	How much additional ice cream does each worker produce?	Price per gallon – set by the equilibrium in the product market	Price x Marginal Product	Wage rate
0	0	0	$7.50	0	$0
1	5	5	$7.50	$37.50	$30
2	12	7	$7.50	$52.50	$30
3	20	8	$7.50	$60.00	$30
4	26	6	$7.50	$45.00	$30
5	29	3	$7.50	$22.50	$30
6	24	-5	$7.50	-$37.50	$30

Remembering that the goal is to determine how many workers should be hired given the above price and wage information, we find where MRC = MRP (or, at least where MRC is less than or equal to MRP).

Each worker in the preceding schedule brings in more money than he is paid – his MRP > MRC – except for the fifth and sixth workers. The fifth brings in $22.50 in revenue, but the factory has to pay him $30. Thus, the ice cream factory will hire four workers, but not five (and certainly not six).

You might say, "Why doesn't the factory stop hiring after the third worker, as it is clear the MRP declines with the addition of the fourth worker?" This is true, and is the essence of the **Law of Diminishing Marginal Returns**. The total product graph shown in *Graph C* (and introduced in Unit III) illustrates this concept and gives the demand curve its downward slope. The first three workers add an increasing amount of output (gallons of ice cream) to production and the product curve has a positive slope that reflects this. This is called **increasing marginal returns**. Marginal product declines with the fourth and fifth workers. It becomes negative with the sixth worker, resulting in a negative slope and **decreasing marginal returns**. The Law of Diminishing Returns reflects the declining efficiency that occurs as more workers are added without a similar increase in other factors of production; that is, workers are being added but factory space ("capital") remains the same.

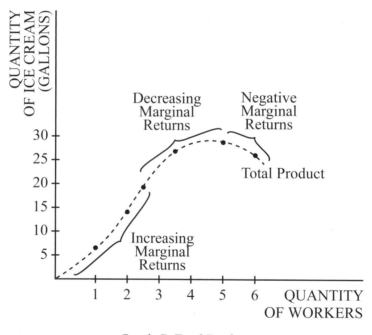

Graph C: Total Product

It is worthwhile to hire the fourth worker even though he does not create as much revenue for the factory as the previous worker. This is because the fourth worker's MRP is still greater than his MRC.

Factor market curves have determinants as well – situations that cause the curves to shift.

Determinants of Labor Demand:	Example:
Derived demand	If there is a demand for apples, there will be a demand for apple pickers. Thus, the market for apple pickers (the factor market) is "derived" from the market for apples (the product market).
Change in productivity	As apple pickers become more productive, the employers would like to hire more of them; thus, demand for apple pickers increases. The opposite is true also.
Change in the number of buyers	More apple orchards mean an increased demand for apple pickers, and vice versa.
Change in the price of related resources	If a complimentary good helps apple pickers become more productive, then the demand for apple pickers will increase. If using a substitute good results in fewer apple pickers needed, then the demand for apple pickers will fall.

Determinants of Labor Supply:	Example:
Change in tastes and preferences	If workers are unwilling to stand out in the hot sun and pick apples, then the supply of labor for the apple picking market will decrease. If workers decide that they enjoy the fresh air and vigorous activity involved in the picking of apples, the supply of labor will increase.
Change in the number of suppliers	If the labor market grows – say, due to immigration – then the number of workers willing and able to work increases. If the labor market decreases – caused by an increased number of retirees, for example – then the number of workers available for hire will fall.
Change in the prices of alternate opportunities	Workers might enter this industry if attracted by the incentive of higher wages and/or benefits. Conversely, if wages/benefits fall, workers might look elsewhere for employment opportunities.

Perfectly competitive labor markets have two graphs, just like perfectly competitive product markets. The existence of thousands of firms in a perfectly competitive market means that each firm hires a small portion of the labor market. Therefore, each firm cannot influence the wage rate. Instead, the wage rate is determined by the market/industry equilibrium, making the firm a "wage taker," and giving it a horizontal MRC curve.

This means that all workers must accept the market wage if they want to work. The concept is illustrated in *Graph D*.

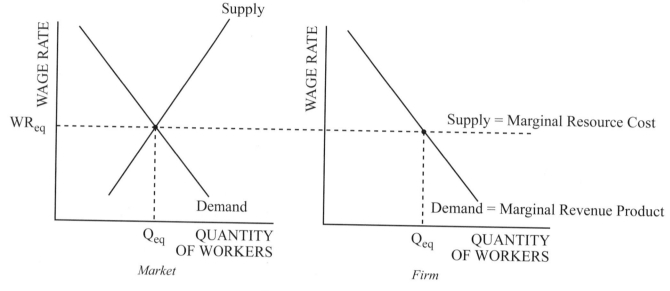

Graph D: The Labor Market

The firm's profit-maximizing output is where the firm's MRC = MRP.

There are situations where interference in the market changes the wage rate. The institution of a **minimum wage** is essentially the addition of a price floor, as it is intended to raise the wage rate above the equilibrium rate. The result is higher wages for those who have jobs.

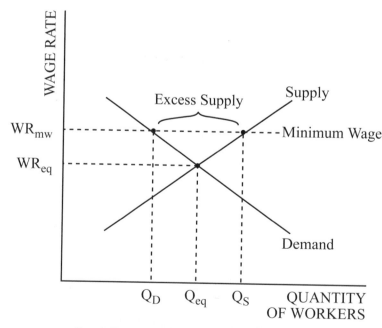

Graph E: Labor Market with Minimum Wage

Notice, however, that *Graph E* shows an excess supply (or surplus) is created. The number of potential workers increases, attracted by the higher wage rate, but employers will want to hire fewer workers as a result of the increased cost.

Also, **unions** can raise the wage rate by restricting the supply of labor. This is done by limiting access to jobs via licensing and certification. Increasing the demand for labor is another way unions can raise the wage rate. Mandating that only union members can be hired for government jobs is an example of this. Notice that the wage rate increases in each of the scenarios illustrated in *Graph F*.

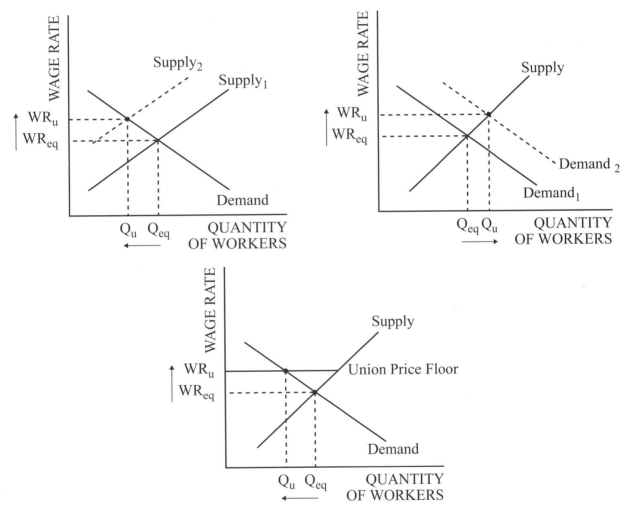

Graph F: Labor Market with Union Influance

Adding a price floor to the wage rate often shows the impact of unions on the labor market graph. Without the floor, a firm would hire more workers at a lower wage. However, with the floor, the supply is restricted and wages are increased. Again a surplus of labor is created, as more workers are willing to work at the higher wage rate.

In the ice cream factory scenario, MRP = MRC was determined based on the idea that the ice cream factory sold its product in a perfectly competitive market. What if, though, the product market were imperfect – say monopolistically competitive, or even an oligopoly or monopoly? How would that change the labor market?

The answer can be found in the following table. The key difference between an imperfect product market and a perfect one is the price. Perfect competitors can sell as much as they want at the market price – thus the price stays constant ($7.50 in the table on page 107). In an imperfect market, in order to sell more, the firm must lower its price.

Quantity of Inputs	Quantity of Outputs (Total Product)	Marginal Product	Price	MRP	MRC
Workers	Gallons of ice cream	How much additional ice cream does each worker produce?	Price per gallon – set by the product market	Price x Marginal Product	Wage Rate
0	0	0	$7.50	0	$0
1	5	5	$7.50	$37.50	$30
2	12	7	$6.00	$42.00	$30
3	20	8	$5.00	$40.00	$30
4	26	6	$4.00	$24.00	$30
5	29	3	$3.00	$9.00	$30
6	24	-5	$2.00	-$10.50	$30

The impact of this price change is that the MRP changes, and thus the place where MRC = MRP (or, in this case, MRC < MRP) is different. In this situation, only three workers will be hired; the fact that the ice cream factory now earns less money for its output means that it hires fewer workers. The "Demand = MRP" curve reflects this, and its negative slope is determined by this fact, as well as the declining marginal product.

Monopsonies

A classic case of imperfect competition in the labor market itself is the monopsony, where there is one buyer of labor who, as a result of his market power, can single-handedly affect the wage rate. A monopsony is similar to the monopoly found in a product market in the sense that it controls the price of its output; the monopsony is a "wage maker" just as a monopoly is a "price maker."

Examples of monopsonies are easily found. Monopsonies exist in company towns where one factory might employ – either directly or indirectly – the town's working population. Another example of a monopsony is a technology giant that controls the supply chain for its computer parts, either because of technological advances or access to natural resources, or both. If one wants to play professional football, there are few preferable choices other than the National Football League.

The main assumption underlying the concept of a monopsony is that it hires all the available workers it wants. Due to the fact that it is the only employer, it does not have to compete for these workers, and thus can pay them less than if it faced competition for their labor. Thus, the supply curve for a monopsonist is a representation of those who are available for employment at a given wage rate. However, it does not mean the workers will be paid according to the supply curve. The wage rate is determined by the MRC curve, which is separate from the supply curve. This is, of course, different from the "Supply = MRC" curve for a perfectly competitive labor market. The graph for a monopsonist is shown in *Graph G.*

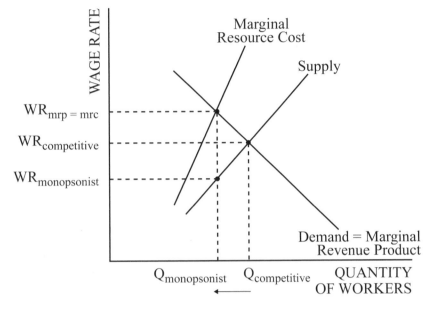

Graph G: Monopsony

Notice the WR$_c$ and Q$_c$, which would be the competitive wage rate and quantity hired. A monopsonist ignores this equilibrium, because this is not where MRP = MRC. Under competitive market conditions, the MRP = MRC equilibrium would be used to determine the wage rate. Under a monopsony, however, the wage MRC = MRP reflects the fact that if it wants to hire more workers, the monopsony will have to pay a higher wage than the competitive wage. Since it already employs all the workers available in a particular area, it will have to entice additional workers to move to the factory's location by paying higher wages. However, the monopsonist does not pay this wage rate, either. Instead, it pays only W$_m$, because it can. This is the benefit of its monopsony power – if workers do not want to accept the monopsony's wages, they will have to move elsewhere to look for work. The monopsonist is betting workers will not do this and will accept the lower pay rate.

Market for Natural Resources (Land)

When economists graph the market for natural resources, **rent** is used as the label on the Y-axis. Rent is the payment that makes the development of a particular resource worthwhile, and ensures each resource is used in its most productive manner.

Economic rent is determined by the demand for the resource, which, in turn, is affected by the:

a)   the price of the product produced;
b)   the productivity of the resource; and
c)   the prices of other resources, be they substitutes or complements.

Graph H illustrates the market for natural resources. As there is a finite amount of resources available, the supply curve is perfectly inelastic.

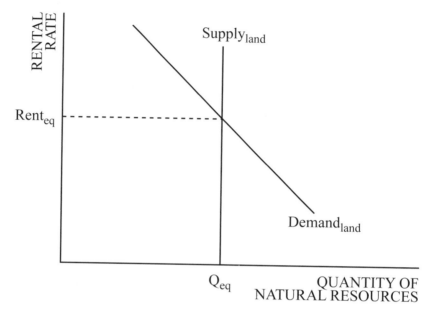

Graph H: Market for Natural Resources

As the demand curve shifts to the right or the left, the price of the resource – the rent – increases or decreases as well. It makes sense, then, that land in a dry, arid region where little grows will not be worth much. However, if natural gas is found under that ground, the price of the land increases dramatically as the demand for that increases.

Market for Capital

Interest is the price of borrowing money to invest in capital. Interest is determined by:
a)   the perceived risk of lending to a particular borrower;
b)   the size of the loan in question;
c)   the duration of the loan;
d)   competition with other banks for the borrower's business; and
e)   taxability.

All of these work to ensure that only the most efficient investment opportunities are funded. *Graph I* illustrates this market (which is known as the Loanable Funds market – more on that in the Macroeconomics section).

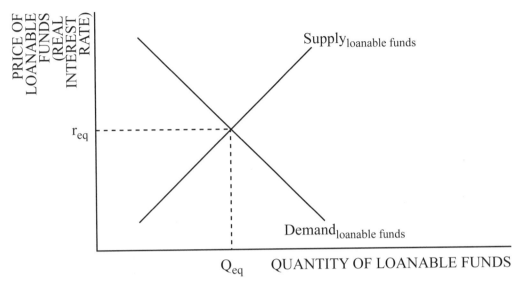

Graph I: Loanable Funds Market

Market for the Entrepreneur

Profit is the payment to the entrepreneur. It is the reward for risk, and is the entrepreneur's incentive for going into business in the first place.

Units III and IV explained the circular flow of the economy when it is operating efficiently. However, there are times when markets are inefficient. These instances are explained in Unit V.

Important Terms:

- ‣ Factor market
- ‣ Factors of production
- ‣ Land/Natural Resources
- ‣ Labor
- ‣ Capital
- ‣ Entrepreneur
- ‣ Marginal revenue product
- ‣ Marginal resource cost
- ‣ Total product
- ‣ Marginal product

- ‣ Law of Diminishing Marginal Returns
- ‣ Increasing marginal returns
- ‣ Decreasing marginal returns
- ‣ Negative returns
- ‣ Wage taker vs. wage maker
- ‣ Monopsony
- ‣ Economic rent
- ‣ Interest
- ‣ Profit

MICROECONOMICS: UNIT IV

MULTIPLE-CHOICE QUESTIONS

1. In a simple circular flow diagram there are

   (A) resource markets and product markets.
   (B) supply markets and demand markets.
   (C) perfectly competitive markets and imperfectly competitive markets.
   (D) oligopolistic markets and monopolistically competitive markets.
   (E) private markets and government markets.

Questions 2-5 refer to the figure below:

Labor Input	Total Output
0	0
1	20
2	45
3	75
4	110
5	135
6	135
7	130

2. Using the information in the figure above, the total product of 4 workers is:

   (A) 20
   (B) 35
   (C) 75
   (D) 110
   (E) 135

3. Using the information in the figure, the marginal product of the 6th worker is:

(A) 0
(B) 130
(C) 135
(D) 385
(E) 520

4. Using the information in the figure, diminishing returns set in with the addition of which worker?

(A) 3rd
(B) 4th
(C) 5th
(D) 6th
(E) 7th

5. Using the information in the figure, if workers can be hired at $90 per day and the product sells for $5 each, a firm would hire how many workers to maximize profits?

(A) 3
(B) 4
(C) 5
(D) 6
(E) 7

6. If an unlimited number of workers can be hired at $90 per day and the product sells for $5 each, this product is being produced in a/an

(A) monopoly resource market.
(B) monopsonist resource market.
(C) oligopolist resource market.
(D) mixed resource market.
(E) perfectly competitive resource market.

7. The demand for a resource is described as

(A) elastic
(B) substitute
(C) efficient
(D) derived
(E) profit-maximizing

8. A firm will continue to hire additional labor inputs as long as

   (A) MRP of labor > MRC of labor.
   (B) MRP of labor < MRC of labor.
   (C) MPP of labor > price of the product.
   (D) MPP of labor < price of the product.
   (E) MPP = MRP.

9. The firm hiring only two resources, capital and labor, will minimize costs and will hire an additional unit of labor if

   (A) MRC of labor = MRP of labor.
   (B) MPP of labor/price of labor > MPP of capital/price of capital.
   (C) MPP of labor/price of labor < MPP of capital/price of capital.
   (D) MRP of labor = MRP of capital.
   (E) MPP of labor = MPP of capital.

10. Which of the following will decrease the demand for labor?

    (A) an increase in the price of the product made by labor
    (B) an increase in the productivity of labor
    (C) an increase in the wage of labor
    (D) a decrease in the wage of labor
    (E) a decrease in the marginal physical product of labor

    Demand = MPP × P

11. Productivity is influenced by:

    I. Human capital
    II. Physical capital
    III. Technology

    (A) I only
    (B) II only
    (C) I and II only
    (D) I and III only
    (E) I, II, and III

12. Ranges A, B, and C in the figure below demonstrate:

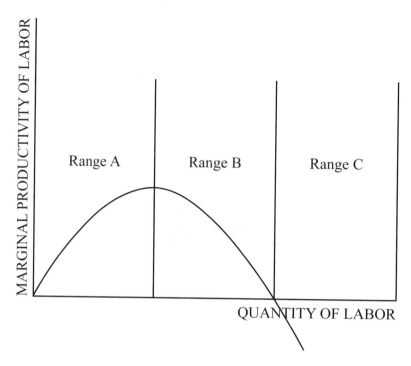

   I. Increasing marginal returns to labor
  II. Diminishing marginal returns to labor
 III. Constant marginal returns to labor
 IV. Zero marginal returns to labor
  V. Negative marginal returns to labor

(A) I, II, and III
(B) I, II, and IV
(C) I, II, and V
(D) II, III, and IV
(E) II, III, and V

Questions 13-15 refer to the figure below:

Units of Labor Input	Total Product	Marginal Physical Product	Product Price	Marginal Revenue Product
0	____		$10.00	0
1	100	0	$10.00	0
2	100	0	$10.00	0
3	260	+60	$10.00	1600
4	310	50	$10.00	500
5	340	30	$10.00	300
6	380	40	$10.00	____
7	370	-10	$10.00	____

13. Using the information in the figure, the marginal revenue product of the 5th worker is

(A) $10
(B) $50
(C) $100
(D) $300
(E) $500

14. Using the information in the figure, if the product price increases from $10 to $15

(A) the marginal physical product will increase.
(B) the marginal physical product will decrease.
(C) the marginal revenue product will increase.
(D) the marginal revenue product will decrease.
(E) the productivity of labor will decrease.

15. If a firm can hire all of the workers it wants for $10.00 per hour and sell all of the output it can produce at a price of $25.00, we can conclude that this firm is facing

(A) a perfectly competitive resource market and an imperfectly competitive product market.
(B) an imperfectly competitive resource market and an imperfectly competitive product market.
(C) an imperfectly competitive resource market and a perfectly competitive product market.
(D) a perfectly competitive resource market and a perfectly competitive product market.
(E) no accurate conclusion can be made about the product market or the resource market from the information given.

Questions 16-17 refer to the figure below:

Resource A Costs $3.00 per Unit				Resource B Costs $4.00 per Unit			
Quantity of Resource A	Total Product	Marginal Physical Product A	Marginal Revenue Product A	Quantity of Resource B	Total Product	Marginal Physical Product B	Marginal Revenue Product B
0				0			
1	30	30	90	1	40	40	160
2	51	21	63	2	82	42	164
3	89	38	114	3	96	14	56
4	84	-5	-15	4	112	16	64
5	96	12	36	5	124	12	48
6	102	6	18	6	132	8	32

16. Using the information in the figure, the least-cost combination of Resource A and Resource B to produce 102 units of output would be

(A) using all Resource A.
(B) using all Resource B.
(C) using 4 units of Resource A and 1 unit of Resource B.
(D) using 2 units of Resource A and 2 units of Resource B.
(E) using 1 unit of Resource A and 2 units of Resource B.

17. Using the information in the figure, which combination of resources would maximize profit for the firm?

(A) 6 A and 0 B
(B) 6 B and 0 A
(C) 4 A and 5 B
(D) 5 A and 4 B
(E) 5 A and 5 B

Questions 18-19 refer to the figure below:

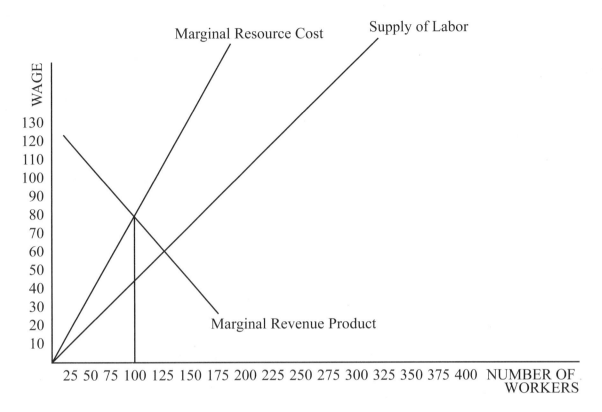

18. Using the information in the figure, which of the following correctly identifies the wage rate being paid and the number of workers hired?

   (A) wage $80, quantity hired 100
   (B) wage $60, quantity hired 150
   (C) wage $40, quantity hired 200
   (D) wage $40, quantity hired 100
   (E) wage $40, quantity hired 50

19. Using the information in the figure, this graph is for a(an)

   (A) monopoly firm.
   (B) oligopoly firm.
   (C) monopsony firm.
   (D) perfectly competitive firm.
   (E) monopolistically competitive firm.

20. If a firm must raise the wage to hire additional workers but it can sell all of the output it can produce at the existing price, we can conclude that this firm is facing

   (A) a perfectly competitive resource market and an imperfectly competitive product market.
   (B) an imperfectly competitive resource market and an imperfectly competitive product market.
   (C) an imperfectly competitive resource market and a perfectly competitive product market.
   (D) a perfectly competitive resource market and a perfectly competitive product market.
   (E) no accurate conclusion can be made about the product market or the resource market from the information given.

FREE-RESPONSE QUESTIONS

1. The following table is for a firm that can sell all of its output for $20 each and hire all of the workers it wants for $250 per day.

Workers	Output
0	0
1	25
2	55
3	90
4	120
5	140
6	150
7	150
8	145

(a) In what type of market does this firm sell its output? Explain.
(b) In what type of market does this firm hire its inputs? Explain.
(c) What is the marginal physical product of the 3rd worker?
(d) At what point (if any) do diminishing returns set in?
(e) Calculate the marginal revenue product for each worker.
(f) Calculate the marginal resource cost for each worker.
(g) Determine the profit-maximizing number of workers this firm would hire.

2. Assume that paper and labor are the only two inputs used in the Econville Links Factory. If the Econville Links Factory experiences a decrease in the demand for links, analyze what will happen to each of the following:

(a) The supply and demand of Econville Links
(b) The demand for paper
(c) The demand for Links workers
(d) Explain the process by which the change in part (a) affected your answer for parts (b) and (c)

3. Using the information in graph *A* and graph *B* in the figure below, answer the following questions:

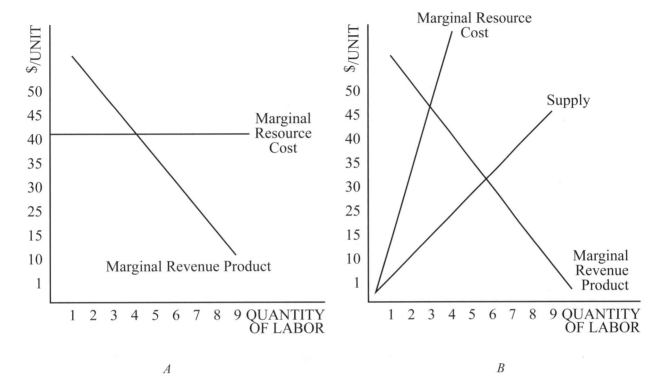

A

B

(a) What type of resource market is depicted in graph *A*?
(b) What type of resource market is depicted in graph *B*?
(c) What is the quantity of labor hired and the equilibrium wage in graph *A*?
(d) What is the quantity of labor hired and the equilibrium wage in graph *B*?

MICROECONOMICS: UNIT V

PUBLIC FINANCE

In Units I and II, we discussed why markets – guided by the concepts of supply and demand – are the most efficient way to determine resource allocation. In this unit, we identify the exceptions to market efficiency: under what circumstances might markets actually fail to efficiently allocate resources? In addition, there are instances when government intervention in the market, in an attempt to correct a perceived problem, actually causes inefficiency. This unit covers **market failures** and **government failures**, plus public policy and finance issues.

Externalities

Markets, at times, affect those who are not consumers or producers. These third-party effects are called **externalities**, as the effects are external to the market – they take place outside of the market.

A classic example of a **negative externality** is pollution. In the market for energy, producers create energy for consumers to use in their businesses and homes. The production and use of energy can also pollute the air and water. This pollution, in turn, affects people who are neither consumers nor producers. Thus, an externality exists.

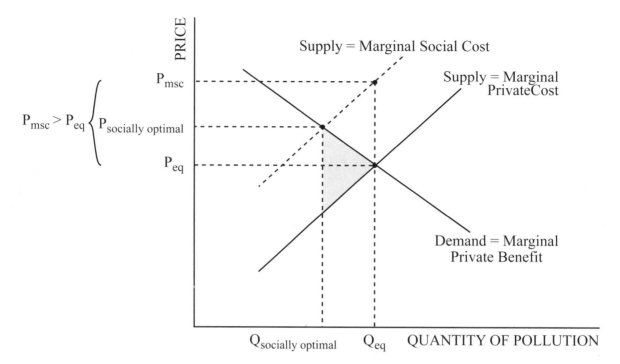

Graph A: Negative Externality

Remember that the goal of the efficient market is to produce where MSC = MPB (the **marginal private benefit**). This concept is illustrated in *Graph A*. MSC = MPB is the point where private consumers' wants do not cause harm to society (or, do not produce an excess amount of harm). When a negative externality exists, the market is OVERproducing (konwn as "**overallocation**") the good or service. Economists explain negative externalities by saying that the cost to society as a whole of producing a good or service – in this case, energy – is greater than the private benefit to the consumers and producers of this good or service. Thus, the **marginal social cost** (MSC) is greater than the **marginal private cost** (MPC).

Negotiating private compromise and enacting public policy are two ways to correct for a negative externality. Regarding the latter, the government might raise taxes or assign fines to increase the cost of production. A tax meant to correct for a negative externality is called a **Pigouvian tax.** This would shift the "supply = MRC" curve to the left, raising the cost of production and decreasing output to the point where MSC = MPB again.

When people who are external to the market benefit from the production and consumption of a good or service, economists acknowledge the existence of **positive externalities**. Think of vaccines: someone in your class might not have received the same vaccines as you, but that student is less likely to get ill simply because you and other vaccinated students are less likely to become ill. Hence, the un-vaccinated student is what economists call a "free rider" – someone who benefits without actually participating in the market.

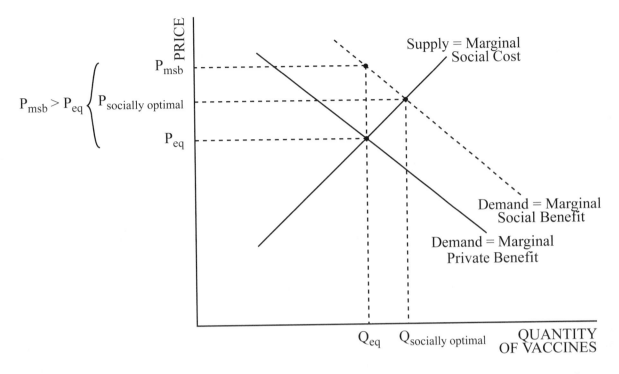

Graph B: Positive Externality

In this case, *Graph B* shows that the marginal social benefit is greater than the marginal private benefit, and the good is UNDERproduced (known as "**underallocation**"). To correct it, the government might 1) subsidize production to lower costs (and thus increase supply); 2) subsidize consumption to increase demand; or 3) mandate consumption by law. For example, children are mandated to receive vaccines before entering kindergarten, in essence raising the demand for vaccines. A few years ago, when the H1N1 flu virus was making people ill worldwide, local governments provided the proper flu vaccine at low or no cost – thus, increasing supply.

Tariffs and Quotas

A **tariff** is a tax charged to the producer of imported goods. One of the most famous tariffs is the Smoot-Hawley Tariff of 1930, which added more than 20% in taxes to goods coming into the United States.

In general, tariffs are meant to insulate domestic producers from the effects of world competition. For example, tariffs can protect domestic producers from having to compete with foreign producers and charge a lower price for their products. With a tariff in place, domestic producers receive a higher price than if they had to compete at the world price. Consumers, though, are worse off, since they must pay the tariff price rather than the lower world price.

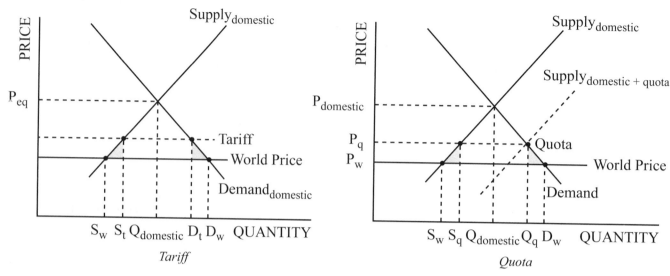

Graph C: Tariffs and Quotas

A **quota** is a restriction in the amount that can be exchanged in a market; it usually refers to limitations placed on the importation of certain goods. The result of a quota is similar to that of a tariff: domestic producers receive protection from competing against the world price equilibrium while consumers are restricted from benefiting from the world price. In an effort to help the American auto industry, President Bill Clinton placed quotas on the number of Japanese cars that could be sold in the United States. American car companies benefited from the fact that Japanese cars were now more expensive, and American consumers were faced with the choice of paying more for an imported car or buying a less expensive American-made one.

Public Goods vs. Private Goods

There are certain goods that will not be produced by the market, as there is no incentive for private companies to do so. However, these goods are important to society, so government steps in to fill the void left by the market. Economists call these goods **public goods**, as opposed to **private goods** produced by private companies. In order for a good to be considered a public good, it must meet two criteria:

1) it must be non-excludable; and
2) it must be non-rivalrous.

These terms are fancy ways of saying everyone must share these goods. For example, if a city installs a traffic signal, the city cannot keep those people who do not pay for it – those who avoid paying taxes, for instance – from using it. In addition, the use of the traffic signal by one person does not prohibit others from using it also. Parks are public goods, as are fireworks shows, national defense and lighthouses. Private goods, though, can be exclusionary and rivalrous: you can keep others from eating your hamburger if they did not help pay for it, and by eating your hamburger, you have prevented others from eating it too.

Tragedy of the Commons

Enforcing property rights for private goods takes care of a free-rider problem such as the non-taxpaying individual referred to in the previous paragraph. However, when goods are owned in common, economists believe there is little incentive to ensure the quality of the good or service being shared. For example, in medieval times, peasants put their animals to graze in the manorial pasture, called "the commons." As the lord of the manor owned the land – and the peasants did not – there was little incentive for the peasants to protect the land from overgrazing. This concept is also at the heart of open sea fishing, where it is difficult to patrol exactly how many fish are caught each day by commercial fishermen. The result is overfishing and the depletion of certain species of fish to the point where the species becomes unsustainable. Economists call this problem the **"tragedy of the commons"**. The suggested solution is assigning property rights to the individuals involved, thus avoiding the free-rider problem.

Taxes

Governments can raise taxes based on income (**the ability-to-pay principle**) or based on the use of specific goods/services (**the benefits-received principle**).

Following the ability-to-pay principle of taxation, a tax system can be either progressive or regressive. Under a **progressive tax** system, taxpayers pay a larger percentage of their income in taxes as their income increases. For example, one might pay 10% of their income in taxes if they earn $40,000, but their tax rate might increase to 20% if their income increases to $75,000. Under a **regressive tax** system, the lowest earners pay proportionally more in taxes than those who earn greater incomes – essentially, the poor pay a larger share of their income in taxes than do the wealthy.

Another example of a tax is the **proportional tax.** Sometimes called a flat tax, a proportional tax charges everyone the same rate, regardless of their income level. In a proportional tax rate system, those whose income is $20,000 and those who have an income of $200,000 will pay the same tax rate.

Excise taxes

An **excise tax** is a tax paid upon the purchase of a select good or service. This is a benefits-received tax, as only those who use the good or service pay taxes on its use.

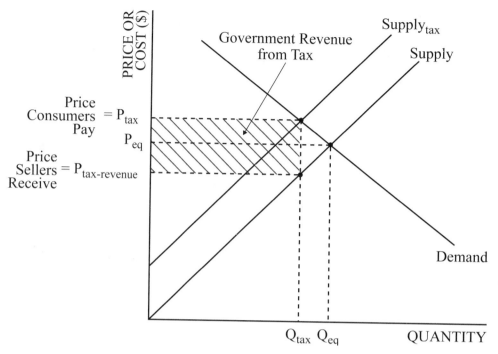

Graph D: Market with a Tax

An example of an excise tax is the tax placed on the purchase of gasoline. One of the functions of government is to maintain roads. The funds for such upkeep come from taxing the users of the roads via a tax on gasoline. This tax decreases supply (see "taxes and subsidies" in the table entitled "Determinants of Supply" in Unit II), decreases quantity demanded (because price has increased), and raises revenue for the government.

Notice in *Graph D* that consumers pay a higher price with the tax, but producers do not receive this higher price because they have to turn over the amount of the tax to the government. In fact, producers receive even less revenue than they did prior to the tax.

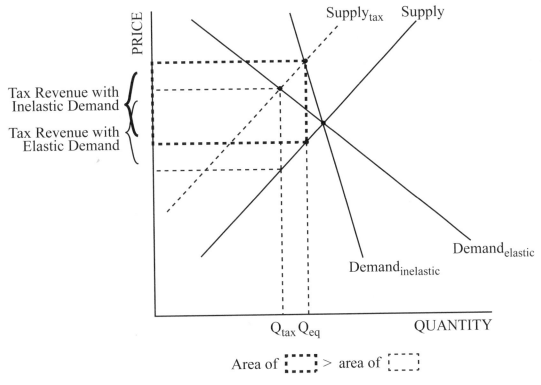

Graph E: Market for Gasoline

Excise taxes raise the most revenue when demand is relatively inelastic. In the case of gasoline, the demand for gasoline is relatively inelastic, and quantity demanded decreases less than the increase in price due to the tax. It does not make sense to tax items for which the demand is relatively elastic. Who would pay for a heavily-taxed paper clip, for example? *Graph E* illustrates this concept.

Deadweight Loss

In some of the previous graphs (*Graph C* for example), you may have noticed a shaded area. This is found between the original equilibrium price and the new equilibrium price and denotes that area where nothing is happening – no one is buying, no one is selling. Economists call this area "deadweight loss", and it represents the loss of efficiency to society by the change or interference in the market. In essence, as a market moves away from that point where MSB = MSC, deadweight loss exists. However, keep in mind that when a tax (or a subsidy) corrects a market, thus moving it closer to the optimum point of MSB = MSC, no deadweight loss is created. This is true when taxes and subsidies are used to correct for externalities.

Is this deadweight loss always a negative result? It depends. One has to weigh the marginal benefits and marginal costs. For example, in terms of a price floor, if society is better off with higher prices (think minimum wage laws), then the existence of deadweight loss is acceptable. However, if a tariff hurts the economy (by stifling trade) far more than it helps (by raising revenue in the form of taxes), then the deadweight loss truly is a loss.

Lorenz Curve and the Gini Coefficient

A question that arises when discussing taxes is "which tax rate is the most equitable?" One way to answer that question is to keep in mind income distribution. Economists often use the Lorenz Curve and the Gini Coefficient to measure income distribution.

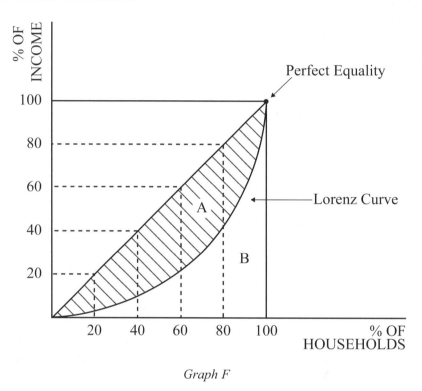

Graph F

When graphed against a straight line showing perfect equality in the distribution of income, the **Lorenz Curve** allows a comparison to be made between a country's real distribution of income to this line of perfect equality. As the curved line moves closer to the straight line, income is spread more equally between all earners. As the Lorenz Curve moves away from the straight line, income distribution becomes less equitable.

The **Gini coefficient of inequality** is the shaded area between the straight line and the Lorenz Curve, labeled "A" on the above graph. It is calculated by the formula

$$\frac{A}{(A + B)}$$

where A+B is the total area to the right of the straight line representing perfect equality.

The resulting numerical value measures income inequality, 0 meaning complete equality and 1 meaning all wealth lies in the hands of one individual. The table on the following page lists Gini coefficients for a selection of economies as of March 2013:[1]

---

[1] The World Factbook, www.cia.gov

Country:	Gini Coefficient:
Unites States	.45
China	.48
European Union	.30
Brazil	.53

Countries can have the same coefficients but different shaped Lorenz curves. For example, two countries might both have a Gini coefficient of .55, but one country's income distribution might be skewed toward the bottom while the other is skewed toward the top. Thus, the two measurements are best used together to give a clear picture of the distribution of income across a society. Gini coefficients can also be used to demonstrate inequality in market share by firms within an industry, such as those found in oligopoly market structures.

Important terms:

- Market failure
- Negative externality
- Positive externality
- Public good
- Private good
- Tariff
- Quota
- Deadweight loss
- Progressive tax
- Regressive tax
- Proportional tax
- Ability-to-pay taxation principle
- Benefits-received taxation principle
- Excise tax
- Tragedy of the commons
- Lorenz Curve
- Gini Coefficient

MULTIPLE-CHOICE QUESTIONS

1. A "flat tax" of 5% on income would be a(an)

   (A) progressive tax.
   (B) proportional tax.
   (C) regressive tax.
   (D) indirect tax.
   (E) value added tax.

2. The term "market failure" implies that the

   (A) market fails to provide the socially optimum quantity.
   (B) market does provide the socially optimum quantity.
   (C) market always over allocates resources.
   (D) market always under allocates resources.
   (E) market always efficiently allocates resources.

3. Purely public goods, like police protection, are

   (A) rival and excludable.
   (B) rival and non-excludable.
   (C) non-rival and excludable.
   (D) non-rival and non-excludable.
   (E) either excludable or non-excludable but only rival.

4. When some of the costs associated with an action are paid not by the producer or the consumer of the good but instead by the general public, we say that a(an)

   (A) equilibrium exists.
   (B) surplus exists.
   (C) shortage exists.
   (D) positive externality exists.
   (E) negative externality exists.

5. When some of the benefits associated with an action are received not by the producer or the consumer of the good but instead by the general public, we say that a(an)

(A) equilibrium exists.
(B) surplus exists.
(C) shortage exists.
(D) positive externality exists.
(E) negative externality exists.

6. In the absence of any government intervention, resources would be over-allocated to the production of a good if

(A) negative externalities existed.
(B) positive externalities existed.
(C) negative externalities equaled positive externalities.
(D) neither negative nor positive externalities existed.
(E) all of the externalities were internalized.

7. A 9% sales tax on food would be classified as

(A) progressive and direct.
(B) progressive and indirect.
(C) regressive and direct.
(D) regressive and indirect.
(E) proportional and direct.

8. Using marginal analysis, the government might adopt which of the following recycling programs?

	Total Benefit	Total Cost
Program A	0	0
Program B	100	30
Program C	175	80
Program D	225	150
Program E	250	240

(A) A
(B) B
(C) C
(D) D
(E) E

9. Sources of government failure stem from:

    I. Bureaucracy
   II. Special-interest effects
  III. Unintended consequences

   (A) I only
   (B) II only
   (C) I and II only
   (D) II and III only
   (E) I, II, and III

Questions 10–12 are based on the figure below:

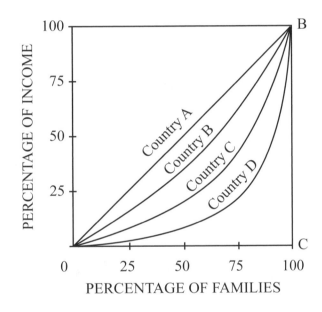

10. Based on the information in the figure, we can conclude that this graph is a

   (A) marginal utility curve.
   (B) marginal product curve.
   (C) marginal cost curve.
   (D) Lorenz curve.
   (E) Gini curve.

11. Based on the information in the figure, which curve represents the greatest degree of income equality?

   (A) A
   (B) B
   (C) C
   (D) D
   (E) They all have the same degree of income equality.

12. Using the information in the figure, if a country adopted a system of progressive taxes and initiated a system of transfer payments, the combined effect of these two measures would move that country

   (A) from a curve like A to a curve like B.
   (B) from a curve like A to a curve like D.
   (C) from a curve like C to a curve like B.
   (D) from a curve like B to a curve like C.
   (E) from a curve like C to a curve like D.

   _____

13. Purely private goods, like the purchase of a cell phone, are

   (A) rival and excludable.
   (B) rival and non-excludable.
   (C) non-rival and excludable.
   (D) non-rival and non-excludable.
   (E) either rival or non-rival but only non-excludable.

14. The statement "only those who use a government service should ultimately pay taxes for that service," is in agreement with which of the following?

   (A) the ability-to-pay principle of taxation
   (B) the ability-to-receive principle of taxation
   (C) benefits of collection principle
   (D) benefits-received principle of taxation
   (E) nominal vs. Real principle of taxation

15. Using the information in the figure below, if wealth is more unequally distributed than income then:

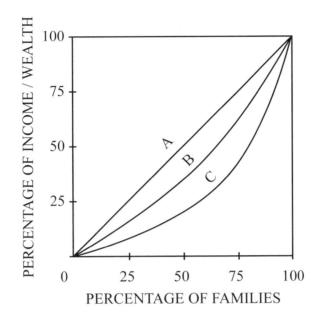

(A) Curve C is income distribution and curve B is wealth distribution.
(B) Curve B is income distribution and curve A is wealth distribution.
(C) Curve A is both wealth and income distribution.
(D) Curve C is wealth distribution and curve B is income distribution.
(E) Curve C is both income and wealth distribution.

16. The Gini coefficient could range from

(A) zero, in a society in which income is perfectly distributed, to 1, in a society in which income is the most imperfectly distributed.
(B) 1, in a society in which income is perfectly distributed, to zero, in a society in which income is the most imperfectly distributed.
(C) zero, in a society in which income is perfectly distributed, to infinity, in a society in which income is the most imperfectly distributed.
(D) infinity, in a society in which income is perfectly distributed, to zero, in a society in which income is the most imperfectly distributed.
(E) zero, in a society in which income is perfectly distributed, to 100, in a society in which income is the most imperfectly distributed.

17. A tax that is levied at a set dollar amount for every taxpayer would be classified as:

   (A) nominal
   (B) real
   (C) regressive
   (D) proportional
   (E) progressive

18. The older couple on your street who constantly improve the landscaping in their yard, trim their bushes, paint their house, and plant trees and flowers in the common areas of your neighborhood are creating

   (A) a consumer surplus for your neighborhood.
   (B) a producer surplus for themselves.
   (C) positive externalities.
   (D) negative externalities.
   (E) a pure public good.

19. Which of the following comes the closest to providing an example of the "tragedy of the commons"?

   (A) a farmer using too much fertilizer on his own land
   (B) sports fans paying extremely high prices to see their favorite team play
   (C) professional athletes making extremely high salaries
   (D) commercial fishers over-fishing the open waters
   (E) hunters paying to hunt on private land

20. The incidence (or burden) of an excise tax on producers is more easily shifted to consumers

   (A) when demand is more inelastic and supply is more elastic.
   (B) when demand is more elastic and supply is more elastic.
   (C) when demand is more elastic and supply is more inelastic.
   (D) when demand is more inelastic and supply is more inelastic.
   (E) when both supply and demand are perfectly inelastic

Questions 21–24 are based on the figure below:

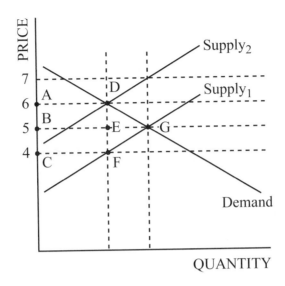

21. Using the information in the figure above, a tax of what size would shift the supply curve from Supply$_1$ to Supply$_2$?

(A) $7
(B) $6
(C) $5
(D) $2
(E) $1

22. Using the information in the figure above, the total amount of tax paid to the government would be represented by the area

(A) A, B, E, D
(B) B, C, F, E
(C) C, D, G, F
(D) A, C, F, D
(E) A, D, G, F, C

23. Using the information in the figure above, the total amount of tax paid by consumers would be represented by the area

(A) A, B, E, D
(B) B, C, F, E
(C) C, D, G, F
(D) A, C, F, D
(E) A, D, G, F, C

24. Using the information in the figure, the deadweight loss due to the tax would be represented by the area

   (A) D, E, G
   (B) E, F, G
   (C) D, F, G
   (D) A, D, G, F, C
   (E) A, D, G, B

---

25. Analyze the information in the figure below and then select the statement that best describes graphs A and B.

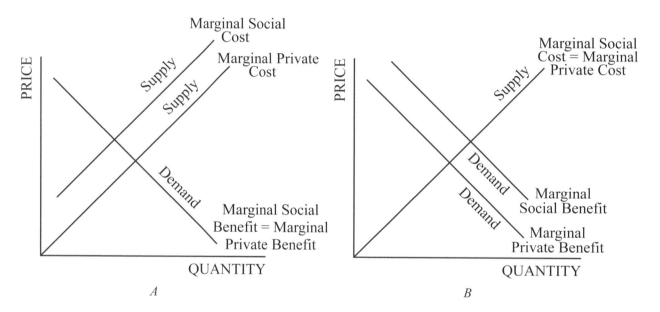

A   B

   (A) Graph A demonstrates a positive externality and graph B demonstrates a negative externality.
   (B) Graph B demonstrates a positive externality and graph A demonstrates a negative externality.
   (C) Graph A and graph B demonstrate a negative externality.
   (D) Graph A and graph B demonstrate a positive externality.
   (E) Neither graph A nor graph B demonstrates a positive or a negative externality.

FREE-RESPONSE QUESTIONS

1. The supply and demand for TINSTAAFL T-Shirts is shown in the following graph:

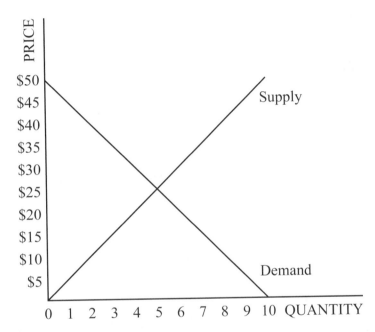

(a) Identify the equilibrium price as P_1 and the equilibrium quantity as Q_1.
(b) Calculate the size of consumer surplus at equilibrium.
(c) Calculate the size of producer surplus at equilibrium.
(d) Calculate the size of total surplus at equilibrium.
(e) If the government imposes a tax of $20 on each TINSTAAFL T-Shirt, identify the new equilibrium price and equilibrium quantity.
(f) Calculate the amount of government revenue raised by the tax.
(g) Calculate the size of consumer surplus at the new equilibrium.
(h) Calculate the size of producer surplus at the new equilibrium.
(i) Calculate the size of total surplus at the new equilibrium.
(j) Is there any deadweight loss that results from the tax? If yes, determine the size of the deadweight loss, if no, explain why not.

2. Use the graph provided below to complete each of the following:

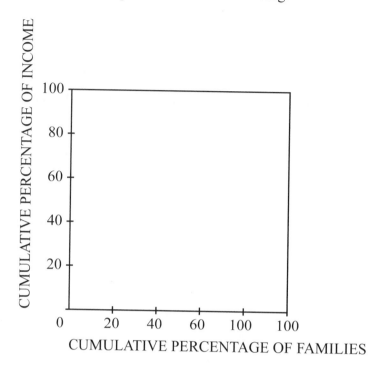

(a) Draw a Lorenz curve that represents a perfectly equitable distribution of income and label it A.
(b) Draw a Lorenz curve that represents a perfectly inequitable distribution of income and label it B.
(c) Draw a Lorenz curve for each of the following countries and label them Country C and Country D.

Quintile	Percentage of Total Income for Country C	Percentage of Total Income for Country D
lowest 20 %	5	15
second 20%	10	15
third 20%	20	20
fourth 20%	30	25
highest 20%	35	25

(d) Which country has the highest Gini coefficient? Explain.

3. Using the information in the graph below, answer the following questions:

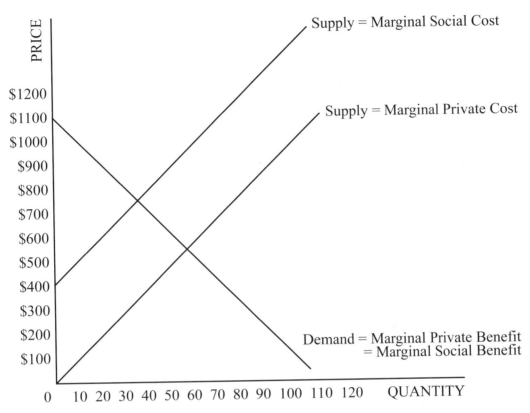

(a) Identify the market price.
(b) Identify the market quantity.
(c) Does this graph show a positive or a negative externality? Explain.
(d) Shade in the amount of deadweight loss that would result in the market if the government imposed a $400 tax on the producers of this good.

SAMPLE EXAMINATION I

1. A production possibility curve will be shifted inward (to the left) by which of the following?

   (A) an increase in the capital stock
   (B) an increase in the population
   (C) an increase in the rate of consumption of nonrenewable resources
   (D) an increase in the general level of literacy and training of the work force
   (E) an increase in the rate of scientific advancement

2. Which of the following will decrease the supply of a good?

   (A) a decrease in the demand for the good
   (B) a decrease in the price of inputs used to produce the good
   (C) a decrease in the price of the good
   (D) an increase in the price of inputs used to produce the good
   (E) an increase in the price of the good

3. Setting an effective price ceiling would

(A) raise the actual price.
(B) lower the actual price.
(C) have no effect on the actual price.
(D) create a surplus of the good on which the ceiling was set.
(E) have no effect on consumer or producer surplus.

4. Which of the following will increase consumer surplus?

(A) increasing the cost of production
(B) imposing a price floor
(C) decreasing supply
(D) increasing supply
(E) limiting on the number of producers allowed in the market

Questions 5–8 refer to the figure below:

Number of workers	Output	Price of the output
0	0	$10
1	10	$10
2	25	$10
3	45	$10
4	70	$10
5	80	$10
6	80	$10
7	79	$10

5. The table above represents production data for a perfectly competitive firm. Based on the information in the table, the marginal physical product of the 4th worker is

(A) 0
(B) 10
(C) 25
(D) 70
(E) 150

6. Based on the table, the marginal revenue product of the 5th worker is

(A) $0
(B) $10
(C) $100
(D) $700
(E) $800

7. Based on the table, the "law of diminishing returns" sets in with the addition of which worker?

(A) 1st
(B) 2nd
(C) 5th
(D) 6th
(E) 7th

8. Using the data in the table, if workers are paid $200, how many workers would a profit maximizing firm employ?

(A) 0
(B) 1
(C) 3
(D) 4
(E) 6

9. Which of the following would decrease the demand for a good?

(A) a decrease in the cost of production
(B) an increase in the price of the good
(C) a decrease in the price of the good
(D) a decrease in the price of a substitute good
(E) a decrease in the price of a complementary good

10. An increase in the Gini coefficient for the United States from 0.463 to 0.563 would indicate

(A) income in the United States has become more equally distributed.
(B) income in the United States has become less equally distributed.
(C) income levels in the United States are a fraction of what they should be.
(D) income levels in the United States have fallen.
(E) income levels in the United States have risen.

11. If a good has a negative cross-price elasticity, it is considered

(A) a luxury good.
(B) an inferior good.
(C) a normal good.
(D) a substitute good.
(E) a complementary good.

Questions 12–16 refer to the figure below:

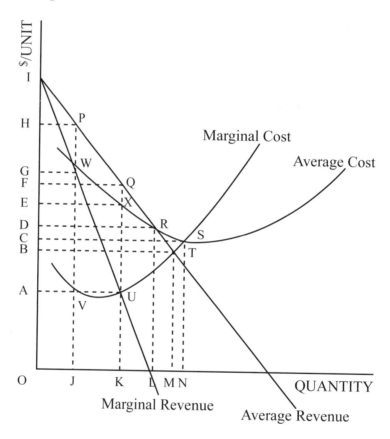

12. The Cooper Company is the sole provider of "Antler Chew Toys." Cost and revenue information is shown in the graph above. To maximize profits, the Cooper Company should set the price of "Antler Chew Toys" at

(A) A
(B) B
(C) C
(D) F
(E) H

13. In the graph, the Cooper Company would maximize profits by producing a quantity of

(A) J
(B) K
(C) L
(D) M
(E) N

14. In the graph, at the profit maximizing level of output, the Cooper Company will have a total revenue of

(A) OHPJ
(B) OAUK
(C) OAVJ
(D) OCSN
(E) OFQK

15. In the graph, at the profit maximizing level of output, the Cooper Company will have a total cost of

(A) OHPJ
(B) OCSN
(C) ODRL
(D) OEXK
(E) AFQU

16. In the graph, at the profit maximizing level of output, the Cooper Company will earn a profit of

(A) EFQX
(B) GHPW
(C) AFQU
(D) OAUK
(E) OCSN

_____

17. A utility maximizing consumer will purchase goods that

(A) provide the highest total utility.
(B) cost the least amount.
(C) have the lowest marginal utility.
(D) have the highest marginal utility.
(E) have the highest marginal utility per dollar spent.

18. Imagine a production possibilities curve for two goods with different production requirements. Each good requires different specialized land, labor, and capital in its production.

(A) The graph would be a straight line sloping downward and to the right.
(B) The graph would be a straight line sloping upward and to the right.
(C) The graph would be a curved line convex to the origin sloping downward and to the right.
(D) The graph would be a curved line concave to the origin sloping downward and to the right.
(E) The graph would be graphed as a point rather than a curve.

19. The economic advantage that is associated with a market-based economy, as compared to other systems of resource allocation, is

(A) a more equitable distribution of income and wealth.
(B) a greater ability to eliminate positive and negative externalities.
(C) a lower level of on-the-job stress that comes from rapid technological change.
(D) economic efficiency.
(E) sustainability of resources.

20. If a legal price ceiling is established on a good below the existing equilibrium price, it would

(A) raise the price of the good and raise the quantity purchased.
(B) lower the price of the good and raise the quantity purchased.
(C) lower the price of the good and lower the quantity purchased.
(D) raise the price of the good and lower the quantity purchased.
(E) have no effect on the actual price and quantity.

21. If supply and demand both decrease, we can correctly conclude that the

I. equilibrium price will rise.
II. equilibrium price will fall.
III. equilibrium price is indeterminate.
IV. equilibrium quantity is indeterminate.
V. equilibrium quantity will fall.

(A) I only
(B) I and V only
(C) II and IV only
(D) III and IV only
(E) III and V only

22. The rule that a rational consumer would follow in deciding how to spend money and maximize satisfaction when shopping for two goods is expressed by which of the following?

(A) MR = MC
(B) $MU_A/P_A = MU_B/P_B$
(C) $MRP_A/P_A = MRP_B/P_B$
(D) Supply of A = Demand for A
(E) Demand for A = Demand for B

23. The situation in the graph below shows a firm in:

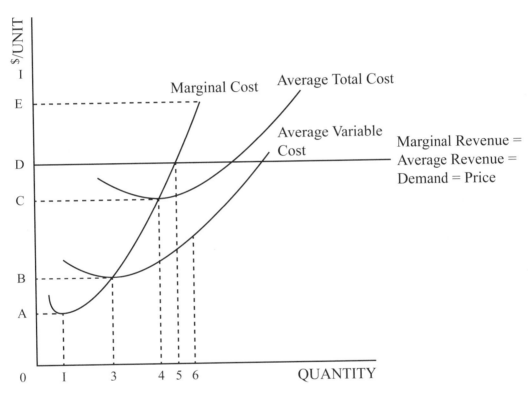

(A) a perfectly competitive market experiencing economic profits.
(B) a perfectly competitive market experiencing economic losses.
(C) a perfectly competitive market breaking even.
(D) an imperfectly competitive market experiencing economic profits.
(E) an imperfectly competitive market experiencing economic losses.

24. The firm shown in the graph would shut down in the short-run if the price fell below

(A) A
(B) B
(C) C
(D) D
(E) E

25. The profit maximizing rule for all firms, regardless of market structure, is

(A) AR = AC
(B) TR = TC
(C) P = minimum ATC
(D) MR = MC
(E) P = MC

26. If producing a good creates costs that accrue to neither the producer nor the consumer of the good, we can accurately conclude that

(A) the market is efficient and correctly allocating resources.
(B) the market is inefficient and will over-allocate resources to the production of that good.
(C) the market is inefficient and will under-allocate resources to the production of that good.
(D) the market is efficient, but will over-allocate resources to the production of that good.
(E) the market is efficient, but will under-allocate resources to the production of that good.

27. Which of the following would definitely raise the equilibrium price of a good?

(A) increased raw material costs and increased popularity of the product
(B) increased raw material costs and decreased popularity of the product
(C) more producers and fewer consumers
(D) fewer producers and fewer consumers
(E) more producers and an increase in the price of a complementary good

Questions 28-29 refer to the figure below:

	U.S.	T.H.E.M.
Cars	2 hours	4 hours
Computers	8 hours	6 hours

28. The table above shows the total labor hours needed to produce one car and one computer for U.S. and T.H.E.M. Which country has an absolute advantage in cars?

(A) Both countries have an absolute advantage in cars.
(B) Neither country has an absolute advantage in cars.
(C) U.S. has an absolute advantage in cars.
(D) T.H.E.M. has an absolute advantage in cars.
(E) Absolute advantage cannot be determined without output levels being given.

29. The table above shows the total labor hours needed to produce one car and one computer for U.S. and T.H.E.M. Which country has a comparative advantage in computers?

(A) Both countries have a comparative advantage in computers.
(B) Neither country has a comparative advantage in computers.
(C) U.S. has a comparative advantage in computers.
(D) T.H.E.M. has a comparative advantage in computers.
(E) Comparative advantage cannot be determined without output levels being given.

Questions 30–31 refer to the figure below:

30. Based on the information in the figure below:

Karen's Pricing Strategy

	High	Low
High	Karen's Profits $75 / Steve's Profits $75	Karen's Profits $100 / Steve's Profits $75
Low	Karen's Profits $40 / Steve's Profits $100	Karen's Profits $50 / Steve's Profits $50

Steve's Pricing Strategy

(A) Steve has a dominant strategy and Karen does not.
(B) Karen has a dominant strategy and Steve does not.
(C) Neither Karen nor Steve has a dominant strategy.
(D) Both Karen and Steve have a dominant strategy.
(E) No conclusion can be accurately made about strategic decision making based on the information in the figure above.

31. Based on the information in the figure above, in the absence of collusion

(A) Steve and Karen will both pursue a high price strategy.
(B) Steve and Karen will both pursue a low price strategy.
(C) Karen will pursue a high price strategy while Steve will pursue a low price strategy.
(D) Steve will pursue a high price strategy while Karen will pursue a low price strategy.
(E) No accurate conclusion can be made about pricing strategy from the information given.

32. Which of the graphs below correctly shows the demand and marginal revenue facing a price discriminating monopolist?

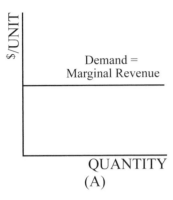

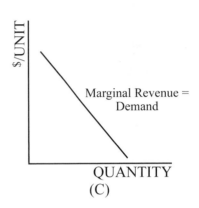

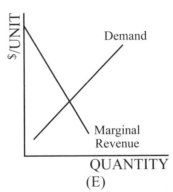

(A) A
(B) B
(C) C
(D) D
(D) E

33. A firm wishing to use the least-cost combination of labor and land to produce a given output would be guided by which of the following?

(A) marginal product of labor/price of labor = marginal product of land/price of land
(B) marginal revenue product of labor/price of labor = marginal revenue product of land/price of land
(C) marginal revenue of labor/price of labor = marginal cost of land/price of land
(D) marginal revenue product = marginal resource cost
(E) marginal revenue product/price = marginal resource cost/price

34. If your firm is charged an additional lump-sum tax by the government, which of the following combinations correctly describes the effect this will have?

	Average Total Cost	Average Variable Cost	Marginal Cost
(A)	No Change	No Change	No Change
(B)	Increase	Increase	No Change
(C)	Increase	No Change	No Change
(D)	Increase	Increase	Increase
(E)	No Change	Increase	Increase

35. If a decrease in the price of one good increases the demand for another good, then these two goods are

(A) normal goods.
(B) inferior goods.
(C) public goods.
(D) complementary goods.
(E) substitute goods.

36. Imperfect competitors are said to be inefficient because, unlike perfect competitors, for them

(A) $P > MC$
(B) $P = MC$
(C) $P < MC$
(D) $MR = MC$
(E) $MR > MC$

37. If the product being sold by a firm in a perfectly competitive industry becomes more popular with consumers, which of the following combinations will result for that firm?

	Price	Quantity	Profit
(A)	decrease	decrease	decrease
(B)	decrease	increase	increase
(C)	no change	decrease	increase
(D)	no change	increase	increase
(E)	increase	increase	increase

38. Which of the following is the best example of a private good?

    (A) a city providing police and fire protection
    (B) a business purchasing a new computer
    (C) the federal government buying a new aircraft carrier
    (D) a village government installing new street lights
    (E) a student attending a public high school

39. If two competing firms are jointly concerned about the pricing strategy of the other firm in determining their own profit maximizing price and output, they are most likely competing in which of the following market structures?

    (A) perfect competition
    (B) monopolistic competition
    (C) oligopoly
    (D) single price monopoly
    (E) price discriminating monopoly

Questions 40–43 refer to the table below:

Output	Variable Cost	Fixed Cost	Total Cost
0	_____	_____	120
1	20	_____	_____
2	30	_____	_____
3	35	_____	_____
4	70	_____	_____
5	130	_____	_____

40. Based on the information in the table above, the average fixed cost of producing the 4th unit of output is

    (A) 30
    (B) 40
    (C) 65
    (D) 70
    (E) 160

41. Based on the information in the table, the marginal cost of producing the 4th unit of output is

    (A) 20
    (B) 40
    (C) 35
    (D) 70
    (E) 120

42. Based on the information in the table, if product price is $30.00, to maximize profits this firm will produce

    (A) zero, the firm will lose money by producing any level of output.
    (B) zero in the short-run, but 3 in the long-run.
    (C) zero in the long-run, but 3 in the short-run.
    (D) 4 in the short-run, and 5 in the long-run.
    (E) 4 in the long-run, and 4 in the short-run.

43. Based on the information in the table, if product price increases to $50, what will this firm do?

    (A) It will produce in the short-run but not the long-run.
    (B) It will produce in the long-run but not the short-run.
    (C) It will produce in both the short-run and the long-run.
    (D) It will produce in neither the short-run nor the long-run.
    (E) It will shut-down in the short-run, but produce in the long-run.

    _____

44. A business would continue to hire new workers as long as which of the following conditions is met?

    (A) MR = MC
    (B) MRP > MRC
    (C) MRP < MRC
    (D) MPP L = MPP K
    (E) MPP L/P L = MPP K/P K

45. If the demand for a product is price inelastic and a government imposes an excise tax on that product, relative to the situation with an elastic demand curve, which of the following is most likely to result?

(A) There will be a relatively large decrease in use and a relatively large increase in government revenue.
(B) There will be a relatively large decrease in use and a relatively small increase in government revenue.
(C) There will be a relatively small decrease in use and a relatively large increase in government revenue.
(D) There will be a relatively small decrease in use and a relatively small increase in government revenue.
(E) There will be a relatively large increase in use and a relatively large decrease in government revenue.

46. In the resource (or factor) market, what would be the most likely result of an increase in worker productivity and, at the same time, a decrease in the price of the product?

(A) There would be an increase in the demand for labor.
(B) There would be a decrease in the demand for labor.
(C) There would be an increase in both the demand for labor and the supply of labor.
(D) There would be a decrease in the supply of labor.
(E) There would be an indeterminate effect on the demand for labor.

Questions 47–48 refer to the graph below:

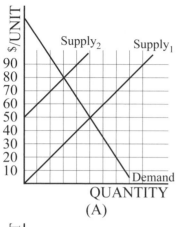

(A)

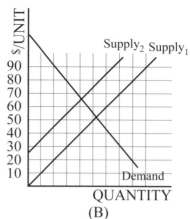

(B)

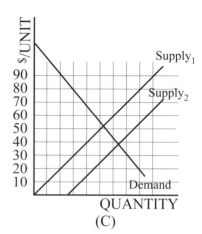

(C)

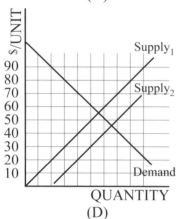

(D)

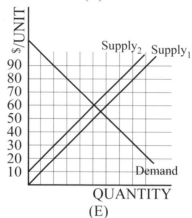

(E)

47. Which graph above correctly demonstrates the effect of the government imposing a $10 tax on the production of this good?

(A) A
(B) B
(C) C
(D) D
(E) E

48. Based on the information in the graph, which of the following is correct?

(A) The consumer will pay most of the tax.
(B) The producer will pay most of the tax.
(C) Consumers and producers will share equally in paying the tax.
(D) The equilibrium price will increase by more than the tax.
(E) The government will pay the tax.

49. A single-price monopolist, unlike a price discriminating monopolist, has a price

   (A) equal to its marginal revenue.
   (B) greater than its marginal revenue.
   (C) less than its marginal revenue.
   (D) greater than its marginal cost.
   (E) less than its marginal cost.

50. The numbers in the table below are for a firm that has a production process characterized by

Labor

		0	1	2	3
	1		100	200	300
Capital	2		200	300	400
	3		300	400	500

(Figures in the table represent output.)

   (A) decreasing returns to labor.
   (B) constant returns to labor.
   (C) increasing returns to labor.
   (D) increasing returns to capital.
   (E) constant returns to scale.

51. If a business experiences an increase in a per-unit tax, what will be the effect on production costs?

   (A) Only fixed cost will increase.
   (B) Only marginal cost will increase.
   (C) Only variable cost will increase.
   (D) Marginal cost and variable cost will increase.
   (E) Marginal cost and fixed cost will increase.

52. The long-run average cost curve in the graph below demonstrates

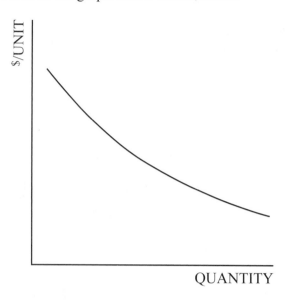

(A) economies of scale.
(B) diseconomies of scale.
(C) constant returns to scale.
(D) opportunity cost.
(E) increasing returns to labor.

53. Based on the information in the table below, I LOVE ECONOMICS bumper stickers are considered

Income of bumper sticker consumers	Quantity demanded of bumper stickers
$50,000	500
75,000	400
100,000	300
125,000	200
250,000	100

(A) normal goods.
(B) inferior goods.
(C) superior goods.
(D) positive goods.
(E) negative goods.

54. Based on the graph below, which of the following combinations is correct?

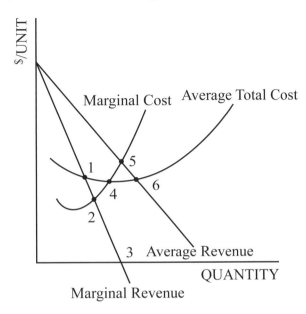

	Allocatively Efficient Point	Productively Efficient Point	Break-even Point
(A)	1	2	4
(B)	4	5	6
(C)	1	4	6
(D)	2	4	5
(E)	5	4	6

55. Which of the following is true for a monopolistic competitor in long-run equilibrium?

   I. Zero economic profits
  II. Allocatively efficient
 III. Productively (technically) efficient

(A) I only
(B) II only
(C) III only
(D) I and II only
(E) I, II, and III

Questions <u>56–58</u> refer to the graph below:

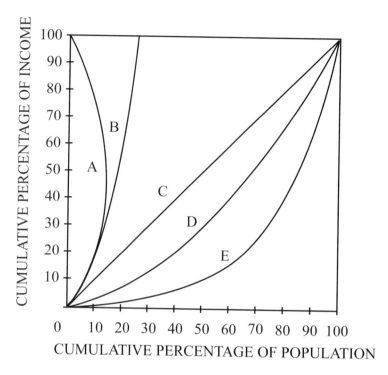

56. The graph above is a(an)

(A) Lorenz curve.
(B) Laffer curve.
(C) Gini curve.
(D) Production possibilities curve.
(E) Marginal revenue product curve.

57. Using the information in the graph above, the most equitable distribution of income is demonstrated on curve

(A) A
(B) B
(C) C
(D) D
(E) E

58. Using the information in the graph, establishing a system of government transfer payments and changing income taxes from a flat rate to a progressive rate system would move a country from

(A) curve C to curve D.
(B) curve D to curve E.
(C) curve C to curve E.
(D) curve A to curve C.
(E) curve E to curve D.

Questions 59–60 refer to the graph below:

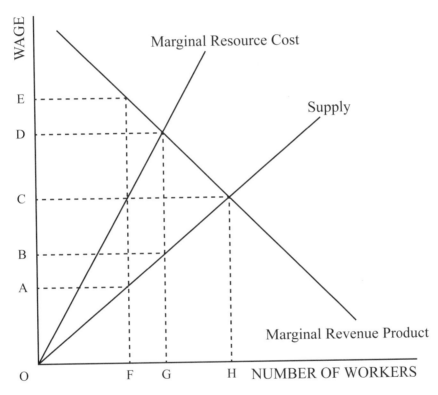

59. The graph above is for a/an

(A) perfectly competitive product market.
(B) imperfectly competitive product market.
(C) perfectly competitive resource market.
(D) imperfectly competitive resource market.
(E) monopoly firm maximizing revenue.

60. Using the information in the graph, the wage and the quantity of labor hired are

   (A) A and F.
   (B) D and G.
   (C) C and H.
   (D) E and F.
   (E) B and G.

FREE-RESPONSE QUESTIONS

1. The Hemphill J. Company is a firm operating in a perfectly competitive market producing widgets. This firm is presently in short-run equilibrium earning economic profits in a constant-cost industry. Using side-by-side graphs for the firm and the industry:

   (a) Draw a correctly labeled graph for the widget market.
   (b) Draw a correctly labeled graph for the Hemphill J. Company.
       i. On your graph, identify the price that the Hemphill J. Company will charge.
       ii. On your graph, identify the quantity that the Hemphill J. company will produce.
       iii. On your graph, shade in the amount of economic profit.
   (c) Demonstrate how the graphs you drew for parts (a) and (b) would change in the long-run.

2. Identify each of the following using the letters and numbers in the graph below.

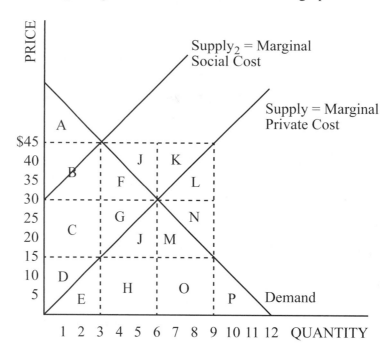

(a) Identify the private market price and quantity.
(b) At the private market price, identify:
   i. Consumer surplus
   ii. Producer surplus
(c) Does this graph portray a positive externality, negative externality, or no externality? Explain.
(d) If the government imposes a $30 tax, identify:
   i. The new equilibrium price
   ii. The new equilibrium quantity
   iii. The new consumer surplus
   iv. The new producer surplus
   v. The amount of deadweight loss that will result from the tax

3. The following is a production function for the Jimmy Charles Company. The Jimmy Charles Company can hire all of the workers it wants for $200 per day and can sell all it can produce for $30 each.

Number of workers	Output per day
0	0
1	6
2	13
3	21
4	30
5	38
6	40
7	40
8	39

(a) Calculate the marginal physical product of the 3rd worker.
(b) Calculate the marginal revenue product of the 7th worker.
(c) Calculate the marginal revenue the Jimmy Charles Company will receive.
(d) At what point (if any) does the law of diminishing returns set in? Explain.
(e) Calculate the profit-maximizing number of workers for the Jimmy Charles Company to hire.
(f) In what type of market does the Jimmy Charles Company sell its product? Explain.
(g) In what type of market does the Jimmy Charles Company hire its workers? Explain.

SAMPLE EXAMINATION II

1. In a particular market, if all firms are producing where the price equals the marginal cost then

   (A) this market is imperfectly competitive.
   (B) revenue is being maximized.
   (C) costs are being minimized.
   (D) the maximum profit output is being produced.
   (E) the allocatively efficient level of output is being produced.

2. The supply curve for a perfectly competitive firm is

   (A) equal to the falling and rising sections of the marginal cost curve.
   (B) equal to the rising part of the marginal cost curve above average total cost.
   (C) equal to the rising part of the marginal cost curve above the average variable cost curve.
   (D) equal to the rising part of the average total cost curve.
   (E) equal to the rising part of the average variable cost curve.

3. The concept of derived demand is demonstrated by which of the following?

    (A) Demand creates its own supply.
    (B) Supply creates its own demand.
    (C) The demand for a product is determined by the demand for the resource.
    (D) The demand for a resource is determined by the demand for the product.
    (E) The supply of a resource is determined by the supply of the product.

4. Setting a price floor below equilibrium would

    (A) create a surplus of the good.
    (B) lower the actual price and the actual quantity of the good.
    (C) restore equilibrium.
    (D) raise the actual price.
    (E) have no effect on the actual price.

Questions 5–7 refer to the figure below:

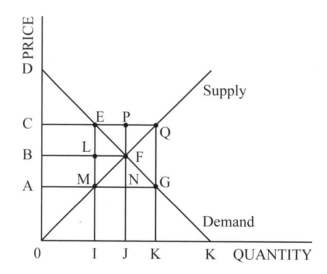

5. Based on the information in the graph above, the producer surplus that would result from a competitive equilibrium would be represented by the area

    (A) ODF
    (B) ODH
    (C) OBF
    (D) MEF
    (E) BDF

6. Using the information in the graph, the result of an effective price floor set at C would be a

   (A) shortage of K-I.
   (B) shortage of I-O.
   (C) shortage of J-I.
   (D) surplus of K-I.
   (E) surplus of I-O.

7. Using the information in the graph, the efficiency loss that would result from a price ceiling set at A would be represented by the area

   (A) ODF
   (B) OBF
   (C) MEF
   (D) MFG
   (E) EFQ

8. Which of the graphs shown below demonstrates the correct shape of a production possibilities curve for two goods with land, labor, and capital requirements that involve a high degree of specialization?

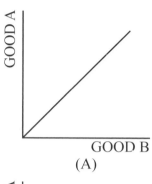

(A)

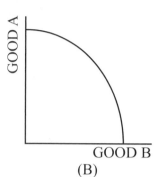

(B)

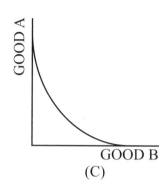

(C)

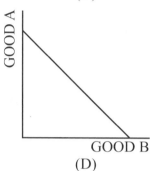

(D)

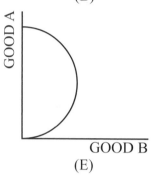

(E)

(A) A
(B) B
(C) C
(D) D
(E) E

9. A profit-maximizing single-price monopolist and a profit-maximizing price-discriminating monopolist have which of the following in common?

(A) The size of consumer surplus.
(B) The size of producer surplus.
(C) The amount of profit.
(D) They are operating at a level of output where price = marginal cost.
(E) They are operating at a level of output where marginal cost = marginal revenue.

10. If supply decreases and demand increases, we can correctly conclude that

    I. equilibrium price will rise.
    II. equilibrium price will fall.
    III. equilibrium price is indeterminate.
    IV. equilibrium quantity is indeterminate.
    V. equilibrium quantity will rise.

    (A) I only
    (B) I and IV only
    (C) II and IV only
    (D) III and IV only
    (E) III and V only

Questions 11-12 refer to the figure below:

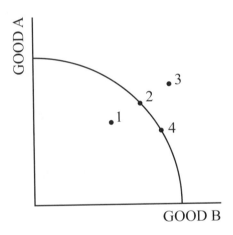

11. Based on the information in the figure above, the result of an economy entering a period of increased unemployment, lowered levels of production, and closing of factories would result in movement from point

    (A) 1–2
    (B) 3–2
    (C) 2–4
    (D) 4–2
    (E) 2–1

12. Based on the information in the figure, assume that the economy is currently using all of its scarce resources efficiently and Good B becomes more popular with consumers. As a result, producers increase production of Good B. The economy would experience a movement from

(A) 1–2
(B) 1–4
(C) 2–3
(D) 2–4
(E) 3–4

Questions 13–15 refer to the table below:

Quantity of Output	Average Variable Cost	Average Fixed Cost	Average Total Cost
0			
1	$30	$100	___
2	$25	___	___
3	$30	___	___
4	$40	___	___
5	$50	___	___
6	$60	___	___

13. The total cost of producing 4 units is

(A) $40
(B) $65
(C) $90
(D) $260
(E) $460

14. The marginal cost of producing the 5th unit is

(A) $10
(B) $20
(C) $65
(D) $90
(E) $350

15. If product price is $40, to maximize profits this firm will produce

(A) zero, the firm will lose money by producing any level of output.
(B) zero in the short-run, but 2 in the long-run.
(C) 3 in the short-run, but zero in the long-run.
(D) 3 in the short-run, and 4 in the long-run.
(E) 5 in the short-run, and 3 in the long-run.

Questions 16–17 refer to the table below:

	Everystan	Pluribus
Bicycle	4 hours	8 hours
Scooter	16 hours	12 hours

16. The information above shows the total labor hours needed to produce one bicycle and one scooter for Everystan and Pluribus. Which country has an absolute advantage in bicycles?

(A) Both countries have an absolute advantage in bicycles.
(B) Neither country has an absolute advantage in bicycles.
(C) Everystan has an absolute advantage in bicycles.
(D) Pluribus has an absolute advantage in bicycles.
(E) Absolute advantage cannot be determined without output levels being given.

17. The information above shows the total labor hours needed to produce one bicycle and one scooter for Everystan and Pluribus. Which country has a comparative advantage in scooters?

(A) Both countries have a comparative advantage in scooters.
(B) Neither country has a comparative advantage in scooters.
(C) Everystan has a comparative advantage in scooters.
(D) Pluribus has a comparative advantage in scooters.
(E) Comparative advantage cannot be determined without output levels being given.

18. As used in economics, the term economic rent means

(A) a monthly payment for an apartment.
(B) the return for the resource, land.
(C) monetary payment of a royalty.
(D) a return to a factor of production above the minimum payment necessary to employ that resource.
(E) an inefficient output level.

Question 19 refers to the figures below:

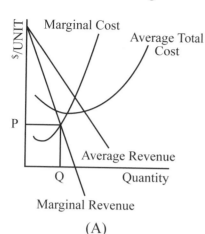

(A)

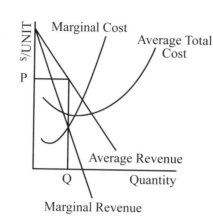

(B)

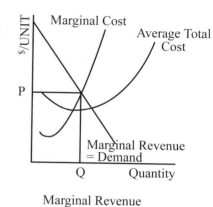

(C)

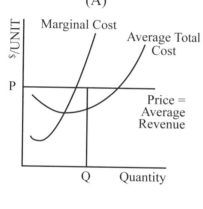

(D)

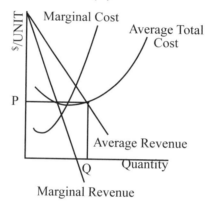

(E)

19. Which of the graphs above correctly shows the profit-maximizing price and output for a price-discriminating monopolist?

(A) A
(B) B
(C) C
(D) D
(E) E

20. If an increase in the price of one good increases the demand for another good, then these two goods are

(A) normal goods.
(B) inferior goods.
(C) public goods.
(D) complementary goods.
(E) substitute goods.

21. If the demand for a product is price elastic and a government imposes an excise tax on that product, which of the following is most likely to result?

    (A) a relatively large decrease in use and a relatively large increase in government revenue
    (B) a relatively large decrease in use and a relatively small increase in government revenue
    (C) a relatively small decrease in use and a relatively large increase in government revenue
    (D) a relatively small decrease in use and a relatively small increase in government revenue
    (E) a relatively large increase in use and a relatively large decrease in government revenue

Questions 22–25 refer to the table below:

Number of Workers	Output
0	0
1	15
2	35
3	60
4	90
5	110
6	110
7	100

22. The table above represents production data for a perfectly competitive firm. Based on the information in the table, the marginal physical product of the 6th worker is

    (A) 0
    (B) 20
    (C) 100
    (D) 110
    (E) 200

23. In the table above, the "law of diminishing returns" sets in with the addition of which worker?

    (A) 1st
    (B) 3rd
    (C) 4th
    (D) 5th
    (E) 7th

24. If the product being produced in the table sells for $10, the marginal revenue product of the 5th worker is

    (A) $100
    (B) $110
    (C) $200
    (D) $900
    (E) $1,100

25. Using the data in the table, if workers are paid $150 and the product being produced sells for $10, how many workers would a profit maximizing firm employ?

    (A) 3
    (B) 4
    (C) 5
    (D) 6
    (E) 7

26. All forms of imperfect competition are considered to be inefficient because they operate at a point where

    (A) P > MC
    (B) P = MC
    (C) P < MC
    (D) P > MR
    (E) P = MR

27. Which of the following best describes the characteristics of a pure public good?

    (A) a good that is nonexclusive and nonrival
    (B) a good that is neither nonexclusive nor nonrival
    (C) a good that is nonexclusive but is rival
    (D) a good that is nonrival but is exclusive
    (E) a good that has both positive and negative externalities

Questions <u>28–32</u> refer to the figure below:

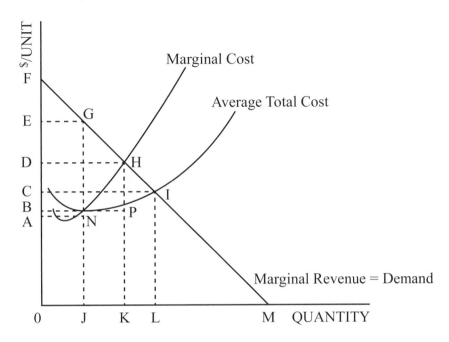

28. The George and Violet Company has cost and revenue data as shown in the graph above. Based on this information, the George and Violet Company is a

   (A) perfect competitor in long-run equilibrium.
   (B) perfect competitor in short-run equilibrium.
   (C) price-discriminating monopolist.
   (D) single-price monopolist.
   (E) monopolistic competitor in long-run equilibrium.

29. In the graph above, the George and Violet Company will maximize profits by producing a quantity of

   (A) O
   (B) M
   (C) J
   (D) K
   (E) L

30. In the graph, the George and Violet Company will have a total revenue equal to the area described by

   (A) OANJ
   (B) OFHK
   (C) OFM
   (D) OCIL
   (E) ODHK

31. In the graph, the George and Violet Company will have a total cost equal to the area described by

    (A) OBPK
    (B) OANJ
    (C) OEGJ
    (D) DHPB
    (E) OCIL

32. In the graph, the George and Violet Company will earn a profit equal to the area described by

    (A) OANJ
    (B) BFHP
    (C) OEGJ
    (D) OCIL
    (E) ODHK

---

33. Which of the following is most likely to decrease the demand for widget makers?

    (A) an increase in the wages of widget makers
    (B) a decrease in the wages of widget makers
    (C) a decrease in the supply of widget makers
    (D) an increase in the price of widgets
    (E) a decrease in the price of widgets

34. If a perfectly competitive market experiences a decrease in demand, what will happen to price, quantity produced, and profits of a single firm in that market in the short-run?

	Price	Quantity	Profit
(A)	decrease	decrease	decrease
(B)	decrease	increase	increase
(C)	no change	decrease	increase
(D)	no change	increase	increase
(E)	increase	increase	increase

35. In which market structure are there few firms competing, significant barriers to entry, and interdependent pricing and output decisions?

(A) perfect competition
(B) monopolistic competition
(C) oligopoly
(D) single-price monopoly
(E) price-discriminating monopoly

Questions 36–38 refer to the figure below:

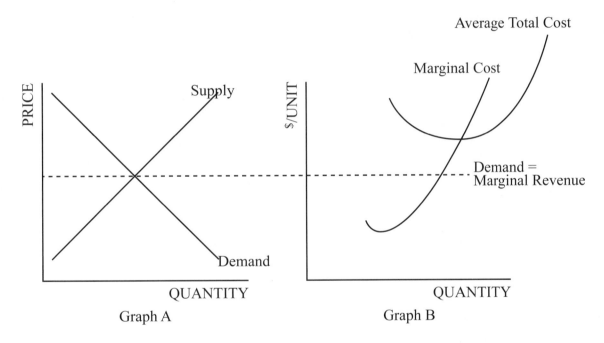

Graph A   Graph B

36. The situation in the graphs above shows

(A) a market in Graph A and a firm earning economic profits in Graph B.
(B) a market in Graph A and a firm breaking even in Graph B.
(C) a market in Graph A and a firm earning economic losses in Graph B.
(D) a firm in Graph A and a market in long-run equilibrium in Graph B.
(E) a firm in Graph A and a market in short-run equilibrium in Graph B.

37. The firm shown in the graph above is a(an)

(A) perfect competitor.
(B) monopolistic competitor.
(C) oligopoly.
(D) single-price monopoly.
(E) price-discriminating monopoly.

38. Based on the information in the graph, in the long-run we would expect to find

(A) economic profits to exist.
(B) economic losses to exist.
(C) no change from the short-run equilibrium shown.
(D) new firm entering the market.
(E) some existing firms exiting the market.

39. A market demand curve is

(A) the horizontal sum of the individual demand curves.
(B) the same as the market supply curve.
(C) the vertical sum of the individual demand curves.
(D) the sum of the equilibrium prices and quantities for all firms in the market.
(E) the sum of consumer and producer surplus.

40. A nation that adopts a system of transfer payments and a progressive tax system would find its Gini coefficient

(A) getting closer to zero.
(B) getting closer to 1.
(C) rising above 1.
(D) falling below zero.
(E) not changing.

41. If the company that supplies raw materials for your production process decreases the price they charge and the fuel to run your machinery in that production process also decreases in price, which of the following correctly shows the effect on your average total cost, average variable cost, and marginal cost?

	Average Total Cost	Average Variable Cost	Marginal Cost
(A)	No Change	No Change	No Change
(B)	Increase	Increase	Increase
(C)	Decrease	No Change	No Change
(D)	Decrease	Decrease	Decrease
(E)	Decrease	Decrease	No Change

42. Which of the following would lower the current equilibrium price of a good?

    (A) an expectation on the part of consumers that future prices will be lower than present prices
    (B) an expectation on the part of consumers that future prices will be higher than present prices
    (C) more consumers and fewer producers in the market
    (D) a decrease in the price of a complementary good
    (E) an increase in the price of a substitute good

43. During the last recession, when consumers experienced a decline in income, the Econville grocery store noticed that sales of T-Bone steak declined and the sales of Up-Chuck steak increased. From this information we can conclude that

    (A) Up-Chuck steak is an inferior good.
    (B) Up-Chuck steak is a normal good.
    (C) the demand for Up-Chuck steak is price elastic.
    (D) the demand for Up-Chuck steak is price inelastic.
    (E) T-Bone steak is an inferior good.

Questions 44–46 refer to the figure below:

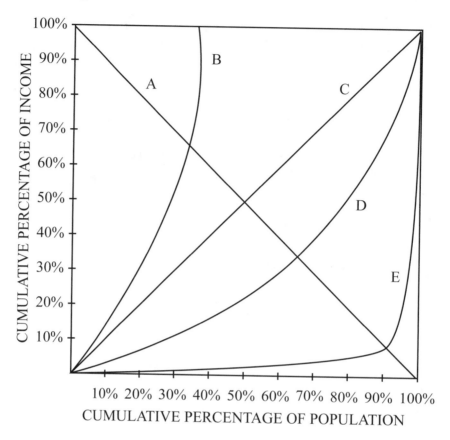

44. The graph above is a

    (A) Lorenz curve.
    (B) Laffer curve.
    (C) production possibilities curve.
    (D) marginal revenue product curve.
    (E) efficiency loss curve.

45. Using the information in the graph, the most unequal distribution of income is demonstrated on curve

    (A) A
    (B) B
    (C) C
    (D) D
    (E) E

46. The Gini coefficient would be zero if income were distributed as shown by curve

(A) A
(B) B
(C) C
(D) D
(E) E

Questions 47–48 refer to the figure below:

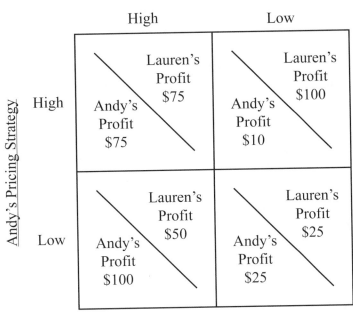

Lauren's Pricing Strategy

47. Based on the information in the figure above

(A) Lauren has a dominant strategy and Andy does not.
(B) Andy has a dominant strategy and Lauren does not.
(C) neither Lauren nor Andy has a dominant strategy.
(D) both Lauren and Andy have a dominant strategy.
(E) no conclusion can be accurately made about strategic decision making based on the information in the figure above.

48. Based on the information in the figure above, in the absence of collusion,

   (A) Lauren and Andy will both pursue a high price strategy.
   (B) Lauren and Andy will both pursue a low price strategy.
   (C) Lauren will pursue a high price strategy while Andy will pursue a low price strategy.
   (D) Andy will pursue a high price strategy while Lauren will pursue a low price strategy.
   (E) No accurate conclusion can be made about pricing strategy from the information given.

49. In the resource (or factor) market, what would be the most likely result of an increase in worker productivity and, at the same time, a decrease in the price of the product?

   (A) There would be an increase in the demand for labor.
   (B) There would be a decrease in the demand for labor.
   (C) There would be an increase in both the supply and demand for labor.
   (D) There would be a decrease in the supply of labor.
   (E) There would be an indeterminate effect on the demand for labor.

50. Which of the following would decrease the supply of a good?

   (A) an increase in the price of the good
   (B) a decrease in the price of the good
   (C) an increase in the demand for the good
   (D) a decrease in the cost of producing the good
   (E) an increase in the cost of producing the good

Questions 51–52 refer to the figure below:

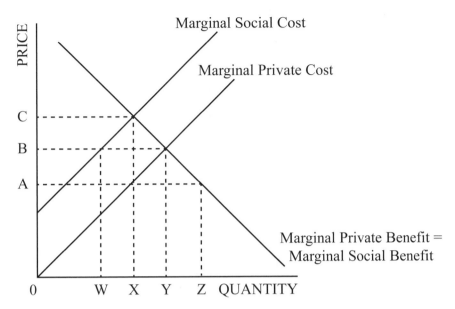

51. In the graph above, the socially optimum quantity is

(A) O
(B) W
(C) X
(D) Y
(E) Z

52. The graph shows

(A) a negative externality.
(B) a positive externality.
(C) a neutral externality.
(D) an imperfect resource market.
(E) a perfectly competitive resource market.

53. If you find that every time you hire an additional worker in your factory, while holding capital constant, output increases by 10 units of production, then you would correctly conclude that you are experiencing

(A) increasing marginal returns to labor.
(B) constant marginal returns to labor.
(C) diminishing marginal returns to labor.
(D) increasing marginal returns to scale.
(E) constant marginal returns to scale.

Questions 54–55 refer to the figure below:

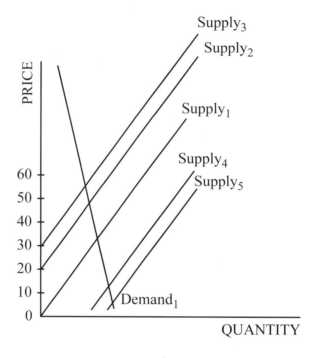

54. Refer to the graph above. The correct supply shift of the government imposing a $20 tax on the production of the good would be shown by a movement from

(A) Supply$_1$ to Supply$_2$
(B) Supply$_2$ to Supply$_1$
(C) Supply$_1$ to Supply$_3$
(D) Supply$_1$ to Supply$_4$
(E) Supply$_1$ to Supply$_5$

55. Based on the information in the graph above, which of the following is true?

(A) Consumers would pay most of the tax.
(B) Producers would pay most of the tax.
(C) Consumers and producers would share equally in paying the tax.
(D) The equilibrium price would increase by more than the tax.
(E) The government would wind up paying the tax.

Questions 56–57 refer to the figure below:

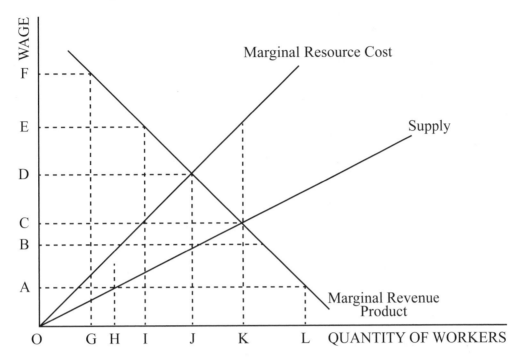

56. The graph above is for a(an)

   (A) perfectly competitive labor market.
   (B) imperfectly competitive labor market.
   (C) perfectly competitive product market.
   (D) imperfectly competitive product market.
   (E) negative externality.

57. The equilibrium wage and the quantity of labor hired in the graph above is

   (A) C and H
   (B) C and J
   (C) D and I
   (D) B and I
   (E) B and J

58. The long-run average cost curve below demonstrates

(A) economies of scale.
(B) diseconomies of scale.
(C) constant returns to scale.
(D) opportunity cost.
(E) diminishing returns.

59. Which of the following would decrease the demand for a good?

(A) an increase in the price of the good
(B) a decrease in the price of a substitute good
(C) a decrease in the price of a complementary good
(D) an increase in the price of a substitute good
(E) a decrease in the supply of the good

60. The firm in the table below has a production process characterized by

Labor

	0	1	2	3
	1	100	200	500
	2	200	300	600
	3	300	400	700

Capital

(Figures in the table represent output.)

(A) decreasing returns to labor and increasing returns to capital.
(B) constant returns to labor and constant returns to capital.
(C) increasing returns to labor and constant returns to capital.
(D) increasing returns to capital and increasing returns to labor.
(E) constant returns to scale and constant returns to labor.

FREE-RESPONSE QUESTIONS

1. The Jimshaun Company is the sole producer of widgets. Answer each of the following for the Jimshaun Company:

   (a) In what market structure does the Jimshaun Company operate? Explain.
   (b) Draw a correctly labeled graph for the Jimshaun Company to illustrate each of the following:
       i. Marginal revenue
       ii. Average revenue (demand)
       iii. Average total cost
       iv. Marginal cost
   (c) On the graph you drew for part (b), identify each of the following:
       i. Profit-maximizing level of output
       ii. Price charged
       iii. Shade in the amount of profit or loss
   (d) If the Jimshaun Company experiences an increase in a lump-sum tax, explain how that will affect each of the following:
       i. The price charged for the product
       ii. The quantity offered for sale
       iii. Profits of the Jimshaun Company

2. Peanut butter and jelly are complementary goods. There is an insect infestation that decreases only the harvest of grapes used in the production of jelly. For each of the following, draw a correctly labeled supply and demand graph to demonstrate the effect of the insect infestation on:

(a) The peanut market
(b) The jelly market
(c) The market for peanut harvesting equipment
(d) The market for workers to harvest grapes

3. Only two firms compete for business in a small lakeside resort community. The Chasey Company and the Waldron Company are both considering opening new retail outlets in this market. Each firm is considering opening on the east side or the west side of the lake. The table below lists payoffs for the Chasey Company and the Waldron Company for each possible set of locations:

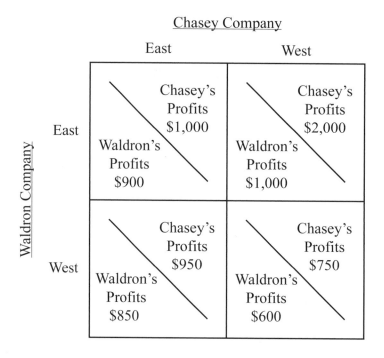

(a) Does the Chasey Company have a dominant strategy? Explain.
(b) Does the Waldron Company have a dominant strategy? Explain.
(c) If the two firms operate independently in arriving at their decision to locate east or west of the lake, where will each firm locate?
(d) Re-draw the table to show the effect of a city government plan to help improve the business climate by offering a subsidy of $500 to any firm that locates on the east side of the lake.

MACROECONOMICS: UNIT VI

BASIC CONCEPTS & MACROECONOMIC INDICATORS

In microeconomics, we looked at how individuals make choices when faced with limited resources and unlimited wants. **Macroeconomics** uses the concepts of microeconomics and applies them on both a national and international scale. Thus, the basic ideas of supply, demand, scarcity and opportunity costs discussed in Unit I are as important in macro as they are in micro.

This unit will build upon on the basic ideas presented in Unit I and discuss the major macroeconomic indicators that measure the three main goals of macroeconomic policy: economic growth, low unemployment and low inflation.

Gross Domestic Product

Economic growth is measured by calculating a nation's **gross domestic product** (its "GDP") and tracking changes in GDP over time. Gross domestic product is defined as the final market value at current market prices of all goods and services produced within a country's borders in one year. The expected rate of growth for an economy is 2-3% per year.

It is important to understand each part of this definition:

1. GDP counts the production of **goods and services.** This includes cars, haircuts, software design and tourism, to name a few examples.
2. GDP counts **production**, NOT sales. Whether or not a good or service was purchased is irrelevant; what matters is if it was produced. This is why inventories play a large role in the calculation of GDP.
3. GDP counts only **final** goods and services, NOT intermediate goods and services. This is to avoid the problem of double-counting. For example, if you were to count the production of windows to be installed in a new home as part of GDP, and then also included the new home upon its completion (the value of which includes the new windows), then the windows would be counted twice: once as a set of windows and again as a part of the new home.
4. GDP counts **market value** only; non-market activities are not included. Goods that are traded or given as gifts are not included. The market value is determined by the exchange between a willing buyer and a willing seller.
5. GDP counts only **domestic production**, meaning production within a country's borders. If an American company produces its goods in China, then it is not included in GDP (this is counted as GNP – Gross National Product); however, if a Chinese company produces goods on American soil, this IS included in GDP. Location is important, not the ownership of a company.
6. GDP measures production in **current** dollars and must therefore be adjusted for inflation to reflect real values. This is necessary to enable comparisons of GDP over time. When my grandfather tells me the cost of admission to the movies used to be a nickel ("Prices are outrageous these days!" he says), it means nothing if that nickel isn't adjusted for inflation. In 2011 dollars, that price of admission in 1920 would now be $.55. (Maybe he is on to something.)
7. GDP is an **annual measurement**, even though it is calculated quarterly. The U.S. Department of Commerce's Bureau of Economic Analysis is responsible for calculating and reporting GDP.

There are two main ways to calculate GDP: the **expenditures approach** and the **income approach**.

Method of calculating GDP:	What is included?
Expenditures approach:	Consumer Spending (C) + Investment Spending (I) + Government Spending (G) + Net Foreign Spending (or Exports [X] – Imports [M])
Income approach:	Income to Labor (or Wages) + Income to owners of Capital (or Interest) + Income to owners of Natural Resources (or Rent) + Income to Entrepreneurs (or Profit)

Remember that the circular flow diagram shows that expenditures in one sector of the economy are income for another; therefore, both approaches should equal each other, plus or minus accounting discrepancies. However, the most commonly-used approach is the expenditures approach. It is often abbreviated by writing the equation as

$$GDP = C + I + G + (X - M).$$

Category of GDP	What is included in this category?
Consumer Spending (C)	Durable goods (goods that last at least a year) Non-durable goods (goods that last less than a year) Services
Investment Spending (I)	Capital purchases, net change in inventories, new construction (including new home construction)
Government Spending (G)	Goods (both durable and nondurable) and services
Net Foreign Spending (X – M)	Exports minus imports

Of the above, investment spending (I) is the most unpredictable, and inventories are the most volatile component of investment.

Most government policy is intended to spur economic growth. Thus C, I, G and (X – M) get lots of attention from business leaders and politicians. There are two situations, though, that can slow economic growth, and thus negatively impact GDP: unemployment and inflation.

Unemployment

Unemployment occurs when individuals who are willing and able to work are unable to find a job, despite actively looking for one. The existence of unemployment means that someone who could be paying taxes and contributing to GDP growth and potential output is not doing so.

There are four categories of unemployment:

Type of unemployment:	Definition:	Example:
Structural	The most serious, it results when the skills of workers do not match the needs of employers.	As furnaces and air conditioning units become more computerized, HVAC workers without computer skills are no longer able to provide repair service to their customers.
Frictional	This type of unemployment is often voluntary.	College graduates enter the labor force when they apply for jobs; workers leave jobs in order to search for more desirable ones.
Cyclical	This type of unemployment is the result of contractions or expansions of the business cycle, and not because of any individual's skills or lack thereof.	Workers are laid off due to a recession (and are often rehired once the economy expands again).
Seasonal	This type of unemployment is a result of the change in seasons.	Carnival workers are left without a job during the winter months.

In order to be considered unemployed, one must be a member of the **labor force** – 16 years of age or older and part of the civilian, non-institutionalized population. For example, the following are <u>not</u> included in the labor force:

Students – not working and not looking for a job

Retired Persons – not working and not looking for a job

Military Personnel – working but not part of the civilian population

Homemakers – working but not for pay

Underground workforce – working but not counted because the job is illegal

Discouraged workers – not working and not currently looking for a job

Prisoners – perhaps working, but members of the institutionalized population

The "employed" includes not only people with full-time jobs but also people who work part-time (meaning at least one hour per week for pay), and the underemployed (those who have skills for a better-paying job but are working for less money; e.g., a physicist who drives a cab because he cannot find work as a physicist).

What is "**full employment**"? It does NOT mean that the unemployment rate = 0 (as would make sense). Instead, it means that all available resources are being used in order to achieve the full potential level of output for an economy. Think back to the production possibilities curve. "Full potential level of output" means that the economy is operating at a point on the curve – the best place to be. We call this the "**natural rate of unemployment**." The natural rate of unemployment occurs when cyclical unemployment = 0, but structural and frictional unemployment exist. The acceptable rate of unemployment – "the natural rate of unemployment" – is 4-6%, meaning that some structural and frictional unemployment exists, but no cyclical unemployment is occurring. The official unemployment rate is calculated by the Federal Bureau of Labor Statistics and is seasonally adjusted.

So, what is the cost of unemployment? Economists call this cost the **GDP gap** – the difference between potential GDP and actual GDP. Another way to understand it is by using **Okun's Law**, which states that each 1% increase in the unemployment rate means a 2-3% decrease in GDP (and vice versa).

Inflation

Inflation can also negatively impact economic growth. It is defined as a rise in the <u>general</u> price level over time. A 2-3% rise per year is considered acceptable; anything above this can be problematic.

There are two types of inflation. The first is **demand-pull inflation,** where total demand exceeds total supply, causing the demand curve to shift right and prices to rise. For example, after World War II American consumers, who had spent years rationing their spending and consumption, starting buying goods like crazy and producers could not keep up with demand. This caused prices to rise; hence, demand-pull inflation.

The second type of inflation is called **cost-push inflation**. When wages or other input prices increase, the marginal cost to produce goods increases. This moves the supply curve to the left, causing prices to rise. For example, when the price of oil rises, the cost of energy rises. Thus, the cost to manufacture goods increases, which shifts the supply curve to the left. This leads to higher prices – thus, cost-push inflation.

A little inflation can be a good thing...

Prices rise gradually => Higher prices increase profits so firms want to expand production => Firms hire additional workers => More people working means more money in the economy => More money leads to increased demand and higher prices. GDP rises in response.

Too much inflation, though, is not so good. High inflation means prices rise too quickly, therefore people can't buy as much => Demand for most goods starts to fall => Inventories begin to build due to lack of sales => Manufacturers reduce production and lay off workers => Higher unemployment means people have less money to spend. GDP falls.

Anticipated inflation propagates itself: if people or firms anticipate inflation occuring, they'll want to buy their goods now at the lower prices. This increases the demand for goods and services. Increased demand leads to higher prices, which may lead people to think that inflation is coming. In response, banks will charge higher rates to offset the cost of inflation or encourage adjustable rate loans. In addition, investors will favor short-term investments rather than long-term ones, as the unpredictability of the value of money in the long-run leads them to protect their portfolios.

Banks are influenced by the rate of inflation when they both make loans and pay interest on deposits. The interest rate they charge on these loans is determined, in part, by what those banks anticipate the rate of inflation will be over the life of the loan.

For example, assume that the real interest rate is 5% – this is the return the bank needs to cover expenses, make a profit, and stay in business. The bank anticipates that future inflation will be 3%. The bank will then charge the borrower 8% interest for the opportunity to take out a loan.

Nominal Interest Rate   = Real Interest Rate   + Anticipated Interest Rate

     8%   5%   3%

But what if the rise in inflation is **unanticipated?**

Whom does it <u>hurt</u>?	Whom does it <u>help?</u> (Or, at least, have no impact on)
Fixed-income receivers	Flexible-income receivers
Landlords with long-term leases	Those who receive any type of pension that is adjusted for inflation
Workers on fixed pay schedules/minimum wage/welfare	Debtors
Savers (either in banks or under mattresses)	Workers who receive cost-of-living raises
Creditors	Government (the largest debtor)

Thus, when unanticipated inflation occurs, anyone whose income or debts can adjust in the short-run is better off than those with fixed incomes or long-term contractual obligations.

A reminder – the key **Economic Indicator Benchmarks** for the United States:

GDP growth	2-3% per year
Unemployment rate	4-6% of the labor force
Inflation rate	2-3 % per year

At the beginning of the unit, we learned that economic growth is measured by calculating a nation's gross domestic product and tracking changes in GDP over time. However, it is difficult to track changes in GDP over time when inflation occurs and distorts the value of the dollar. How can one compare the GDP of 2012 to the GDP of 2010 (or any other year) when inflation has changed the purchasing power of the dollar between those years? The solution is to use the **GDP Price Deflator**, which is a price index used to adjust GDP for inflation. It is calculated using the following formula:

$$\frac{\text{Nominal GDP}}{\text{Price Index}} = \text{Real GDP}$$

For example: Let's say that GDP increased from $8 trillion in Year 1 to $9 trillion in Year 2. This increase reflects the change in **nominal GDP**. Using the raw numbers, it looks as if GDP increased 12.5%.

However, during this same period, prices increased by 10%, so the deflator increases from 100 to 110. Thus, the Price Index is 1.1.

$$\frac{\$9 \text{ Trillion}}{1.1} = \$8.18 \text{ Trillion} = \text{Real GDP}$$

Taking into account the impact of inflation on the value of the dollar gives a more accurate picture. Using the GDP deflator, the economy experienced 2.25% growth, not 12.5%. Thus, **real GDP** is gross domestic product adjusted for inflation.

The federal government's Bureau of Labor Statistics calculates the price index used in the above calculation. While the GDP price deflator looks at all the goods and services produced in the economy, the **consumer price index** (the "CPI") takes into account a stable "basket of goods" that a typical urban family would purchase and tracks the changes in price over time. The **producer price index** (the "PPI") tracks prices received by domestic producers for their output. This covers a wide variety of industries, from telecommunications to dentists to building construction to oil refining.

Another example of the difference between real and nominal numbers is shown by the **Fisher Equation** which states that:

$$\Delta\% \text{ Real Income} \approx \Delta\% \text{ Nominal Income} - \Delta\% \text{ Price Level}$$

For example, an employee gets a 5% salary increase during her review. Inflation is currently at 3%. Thus, her "**real**" income adjustment (her "real" raise) is...

$\Delta\%$ Real Income $\approx \Delta\%$ Nominal Income $- \Delta\%$ Price Level
$\Delta\%$ Real Income $\approx 5\% - 3\%$
$\Delta\%$ Real Income $\approx$ **2%**

A quick way to estimate how long it will take for prices (and other measurements) to double is calculated using the **Rule of 72**.

$$\text{Approximate \# of years} = \frac{72}{\text{annual \% increase}}$$

For example, if inflation = 3%, how long will it take for prices to double?

$$\frac{72}{3} = 24 \text{ years}$$

Thus, nominal and real values are a very important part of macroeconomics. Nominal and real GDP, nominal and real income, and nominal and real interest rates are key to understanding the health of the economy.

Some inflation-related terms:

Inflation	A sustained increase in the general price level in an economy
Disinflation	A temporary reduction in the rate of inflation
Deflation	A sustained decrease in the price level over time
Hyperinflation	A rapid increase in prices over time
Stagflation	Sluggish economic growth coupled with a high rate of both inflation and unemployment

Even after adjusting for inflation, GDP can over- or under-estimate the true health of an economy because the following are not included in its calculation:

What is left out of GDP?	Example/concern:
Underground economy	Illegal goods and services (e.g., prostitution, drug trade)
Spillovers/externalities	Costs or benefits to third parties outside the market
Allocative efficiency	Is the economy producing what society wants?
Per capita income	Is wealth distributed equitably?
Change in leisure/well-being	Is society better off?
Change in quality of products	Are the products/services produced this year of superior quality than in past years?
Some services	Stay-at-home parents, volunteer work
Environmental health	Is the environment being harmed or helped by the production of these goods/services?

Despite these issues, GDP is the best measurement we have for detailing the final production of goods and services – the quantity of the economy, if not the quality.

Important terms:

- Macroeconomics
- Gross domestic product (GDP)
- Unemployment
- Labor force
- Full employment
- Natural rate of unemployment
- GDP gap
- Okun's Law
- Structural unemployment
- Frictional unemployment
- Seasonal unemployment
- Cyclical unemployment
- Inflation
- Anticipated inflation

- Unanticipated inflation
- Economic indicator benchmarks
- GDP price deflator
- Demand-pull inflation
- Cost-push inflation
- Real vs. nominal
- Consumer price index
- Producer price index
- Fisher Equation
- Deflation
- Disinflation
- Stagflation
- Hyperinflation
- Rule of 70

MULTIPLE-CHOICE QUESTIONS

1. Which of the following would contribute to a decrease in GDP?

   (A) exports greater than imports
   (B) exports equal to imports
   (C) exports less than imports
   (D) a growing federal budget deficit
   (E) a growing national debt

2. An increase in the Consumer Price Index from 300-315 would indicate an annual rate of measured inflation of

   (A) 3%
   (B) 5%
   (C) 15%
   (D) 30%
   (E) 315%

3. Which of the following is NOT a widely recognized goal of United States economic policy?

   (A) economic growth
   (B) price stability
   (C) full employment
   (D) maximum production
   (E) minimum cost of production

4. Which of the following would be considered a macroeconomic issue as opposed to a microeconomic issue?

   (A) the calculation of deadweight loss due to a tax
   (B) the determination of a product's price
   (C) the determination of the profit-maximizing output level for a perfectly competitive firm
   (D) the determination of the full-employment level of GDP
   (E) the determination of the effect of a price ceiling

211

5. The types of unemployment include all of the following EXCEPT:

(A) frictional
(B) cyclical
(C) seasonal
(D) nominal
(E) structural

6. The "central economic problem" faced by all economies is the result of

(A) unequal distribution of income.
(B) scarcity.
(C) globalization.
(D) technological change.
(E) global warming.

7. An economy would experience a reduction in GDP if

(A) imports are less than exports.
(B) savings are less than investment.
(C) savings equal investment.
(D) savings are greater than investment.
(E) imports equal exports.

8. If actual inflation is less than anticipated inflation, which of the following groups will most certainly benefit?

(A) lenders
(B) borrowers
(C) minorities
(D) women
(E) men

Questions 9-10 refer to figure below:

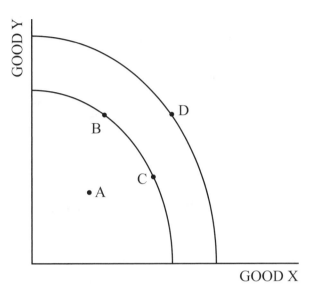

9. Based on the graph above, economic growth is shown by a movement from:

   (A) A to B
   (B) B to C
   (C) C to D
   (D) A to C
   (E) C to B

10. Based on the graph above, an economy that is experiencing a significant reduction in the availability of nonrenewable resources, a decline in entrepreneurial spirit, and a decrease in population can expect to experience a movement from:

   (A) A to C
   (B) B to C
   (C) C to D
   (D) D to B
   (E) C to A

_____

11. The type of unemployment caused when a worker loses her job due to a decline in the level of business activity is

   (A) frictional unemployment.
   (B) seasonal unemployment.
   (C) nominal unemployment.
   (D) cyclical unemployment.
   (E) structural unemployment.

12. Which of the following is recognized as a valid criticism of the current practice of measuring unemployment?

(A) Discouraged workers are counted in the total and therefore the published number overstates the actual amount of unemployment.
(B) Discouraged workers are not counted in the total and therefore the published number understates the actual amount of unemployment.
(C) Inflation is not factored in, thereby making the published number a nominal and not a real value.
(D) Inflation is figured in, thereby making the published number a real and not a nominal value.
(E) All published numbers are susceptible to variations by season.

13. United States gross domestic product (GDP) measurements include

(A) the purchase of a ticket to attend a sporting event from a scalper.
(B) the purchase of 10 shares of General Motors common stock.
(C) the purchase of U.S. Government series E savings bonds.
(D) the dollar amount of exports from the United States.
(E) a contribution to your retirement account.

14. If Marie's annual income rose from $40,000 to $44,000 per year while the consumer price index rose from 300 to 360, we could conclude that she experienced which of the following combinations of events?

	Nominal Income	Real Income
(A)	increase	increase
(B)	increase	constant
(C)	increase	decrease
(D)	constant	constant
(E)	decrease	decrease

Questions 15-18 refer to the figure below:

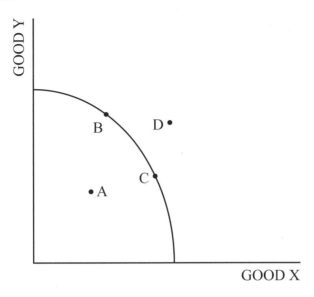

15. Based on the graph above, point A demonstrates

    (A) inflation.
    (B) stagflation.
    (C) unemployment.
    (D) a maximum attainable level of production.
    (E) the effect of globalization.

16. Based on the graph above, point D demonstrates

    (A) inflation.
    (B) stagflation.
    (C) unemployment.
    (D) an unattainable level of production.
    (E) the effect of globalization.

17. Based on the graph above, a movement from point B to point C demonstrates which of the following economic principles:

    (A) equilibrium
    (B) opportunity cost
    (C) profit maximization
    (D) inflation
    (E) unemployment

18. Based on the graph, a movement from point C to point A could be the result of

    (A) a recession.
    (B) increased rates of inflation.
    (C) increased technology.
    (D) increased discovery of resources.
    (E) increased international trade.

19. The specific name for a period of time during which the rate of inflation slows to a lower level of inflation is

    (A) inflation.
    (B) deflation.
    (C) recession.
    (D) disinflation.
    (E) hyperinflation.

20. If actual inflation, as measured by the CPI, is greater than anticipated inflation in a country then

    (A) workers will benefit.
    (B) workers will be hurt.
    (C) banks that loaned out money will benefit.
    (D) the economy will eliminate future inflationary pressures.
    (E) employers will be hurt.

21. The concept of a "full-employment unemployment rate" or a "natural rate of unemployment" would be demonstrated by which of the following statements?

    (A) Frictional unemployment is zero.
    (B) Structural unemployment is zero.
    (C) Seasonal unemployment is zero.
    (D) Cyclical unemployment is zero.
    (E) All four types of unemployment are zero.

22. Which of the following is an example of a worker who would be classified as unemployed by the Bureau of Labor Statistics?

(A) a part-time worker who wants to be employed full-time
(B) a worker who has given up looking for work during a prolonged and severe recession
(C) a worker who is out of work but refuses to take a minimum wage job
(D) an unemployed welder who is looking for work but cannot find work due, in large part, to the increase in the number of robotic welders used in factories
(E) a worker who is retired

23. Which of the following most accurately represents the "economic bias" of United States economists toward free trade?

(A) Free trade is desirable as it increases voluntary exchange.
(B) Free trade is desirable as it decreases voluntary exchange.
(C) Free trade is undesirable as it extends our production possibilities curve.
(D) Free trade is undesirable as it increases inflation.
(E) Free trade is undesirable as it restricts economic growth.

24. The combination of simultaneously high rates of unemployment and inflation is called

(A) inflation.
(B) recession.
(C) depression.
(D) stagflation.
(E) slow growth.

25. The components of GDP from an expenditure perspective include:

(A) consumption + investment + government spending + net exports
(B) consumption + investment + net exports + depreciation
(C) savings + taxes + imports + exports
(D) imports + velocity + exports + income
(E) government spending + taxes + reserve requirement + discount rate

26. Turn of the 21st century benchmarks for unemployment, inflation, and real GDP growth are respectively:

(A) 0%, 0%, 0%
(B) 2%, 3%, 4%
(C) 4-5%, 2-3%, 3-3.5%
(D) 6-7%, 3-4%, 3.5-4%
(E) 7-8%, 4-5%, 4-5%

27. Which of the following statements about unanticipated inflation is correct?

    (A) It reallocates income from one group to another.
    (B) It helps people who are in debt.
    (C) It hurts people who are on fixed incomes.
    (D) It hurts people who have loaned money to others.
    (E) All the above are correct statements about the effects of unanticipated inflation.

28. With an annual rate of inflation of 5% how many years would it take for prices to double?

    (A) 5
    (B) 10
    (C) 14
    (D) 35
    (E) 70

29. The following list of films are ranked by box office receipts. Their dates of release and the GDP deflator for those years are also listed. The top three highest grossing films for each of the following categories, respectively, would be

1.	Micromania	$100 million	1935	.10 GDP deflator
2.	Cincinnati Strangler	$600 million	1947	.50 GDP deflator
3.	Macromonster	$800 million	2012	2.0 GDP deflator

Nominal	Real
(A) 1,2,3	3,2,1
(B) 3,2,1	1,2,3
(C) 3,2,1	2,1,3
(D) 3,2,1	3,1,2
(E) 3,2,1	2,3,1

30. A car that was manufactured in the U.S. in 2012 and not sold until 2013 would

    (A) increase 2012 GDP.
    (B) increase 2013 GDP.
    (C) decrease 2012 GDP.
    (D) decrease 2013 GDP.
    (E) have no effect on 2012 GDP.

31. Which of the following will increase potential GDP over time?

    (A) an increase in inflation
    (B) an increase in unemployment
    (C) an increase in investment
    (D) an increase in consumption
    (E) an increase in government spending

FREE-RESPONSE QUESTIONS

1. Draw and correctly label a business cycle graph. On your graph, identify each of the following:

   (a) a peak, a trough, a contraction, an expansion.
   (b) the area, or point, where unemployment is most likely to be a problem.
   (c) the area, or point, where inflation is most likely to be a problem.
   (d) the area, or point, where the economy is most likely to experience "full employment."
   (e) at the point (or area) you identified in part (d), how would you define "full employment?"

2. The data in the table below shows how Super Senior spends his money.

Item	Quantity Consumed in 2012-2013	2012 Price (each)	2013 Price (each)
Books	6	$125	$150
Food	10	$10	$12
Entertainment	2	$15	$20
Recreation	3	$100	$125

Given the information in the table, complete each of the following:

(a) Construct a price index for Super Senior for 2012 and 2013.
(b) Calculate the annual rate of inflation Super Senior is experiencing from 2012 to 2013.
(c) How does the rate of inflation you calculated in part B compare to the level of inflation the U.S. would consider as acceptable?

3. There are four types (or categories) of unemployment.

    (a) List the four types of unemployment.

    (b) Is it possible for the total unemployment rate to ever be 0%? Explain.

    (c) Define the "full-employment unemployment rate."

    (d) Why is an unemployment rate greater than 7% considered unhealthy for the economy?

BUSINESS CYCLES
& FISCAL POLICY

A key concept in macroeconomics is the **business cycle**. Historically, economies tend to grow and shrink as economic conditions change; the business cycle reflects these changes as it tracks changes in gross domestic product, or GDP.

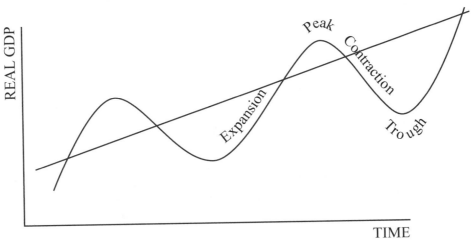

When an economy is in the expansion/growth phase, employment tends to rise (unemployment falls) and inflation is steady. However, as the economy reaches its peak, inflation tends to rise and economic growth stalls. This can lead to a contraction of the economy. As employment declines (and unemployment rises), the economy can head into a recession, or worse, a depression. Deflation can occur. Eventually, the economy finds its equilibrium and economic growth begins again.

When tracking the health of the economy, economists closely watch the **leading indicators**. Examples of these are GDP, the CPI, the Consumer Confidence Index, and the number of building permits filed. **Lagging indicators** are numbers that confirm long-term trends such as the average time people remain unemployed or the amount of outstanding loans. There are also **coincidental indicators** which help round out the picture of the economy such as the number of employees on payrolls or the amount of personal income.

The National Bureau of Economic Research, a "private, nonprofit, nonpartisan research organization dedicated to promoting a greater understanding of how the economy works," is the sole arbiter of identifying the phases of the business cycle, and "has no fixed rule to determine whether a contraction is only a short interruption of an expansion, or an expansion is only a short interruption of a contraction."[1] Thus, regardless of what the media says about the number of successive quarters of declining GDP necessary for defining a recession, a recession (or depression) does not exist unless the NBER says it does.

Two key ideas to keep in mind: one is that peaks and troughs can vary in degree. Sometimes they are very mild and other times they are particularly "exuberant"[2] or painful, respectively. The other important concept is that despite their cyclical nature, these fluctuations are not particularly worrisome as long as the path of growth continues to have an upward trend – that is, over time, on average, overall output grows at a rate of at least 2-3%.

Fiscal Policy

Governments often attempt to smooth fluctuations in the business cycle by using **fiscal policy** – changing government spending or taxes in order to treat the ailments facing the economy. In the 1930's, for example, the federal government created a number of programs such as the Works Progress Administration which built interstates, bridges, libraries and so on, providing 8 million jobs between 1935-1943 for previously-unemployed Americans. These federal programs pumped money back into a depressed economy. After World War II, federal laws were changed to ensure that full employment, full production and stable prices were priorities. The creation of the Council of Economic Advisors furthered this aim, as did the requirement that the President submit an annual economic report to Congress. In the 1960's, the opposite occurred: inflation rose from a low of 2% to a high of 5% (and even higher in the decades that followed). Increases in taxes followed in order to curb the effects of inflation. Thus, while consumers, businesses and state and local governments tend to exhibit pro-cyclical behavior – for example, when times are flush, voters tend to expect more public goods from government – it is the responsibility of the federal government to act in a counter-cyclical manner.

Fiscal policy may be achieved via **automatic stabilizers**. If GDP is increasing (the economy's business cycle is in the expansionary phase), tax revenues will increase as a result of rising incomes. This increase in tax revenues takes money out of society's hands – lowering disposable income – and helps offset the potentially inflationary effect of the increase in GDP. In the unfortunate situation of a contraction of the business cycle, GDP falls and the amount of money in circulation decreases. However, during this time transfer payments and subsidies from the government increase, which in turn increases disposable income, and thus offsets the decline in GDP.

---

[1] website, *The National Bureau of Economic Research.*

[2] To paraphrase former Federal Reserve Board Chairman Alan Greenspan, who cited "irrational exuberance" in the market during a speech entitled "The Challenge of Central Banking in a Democratic Society" before the American Enterprise Institute of Public Policy Research, December 5, 1996.

During more severe swings in the business cycle, government leaders might feel that the automatic stabilizers already in place are insufficient to address the economic problems at hand and need to be boosted by short-term **discretionary stabilizers**. These are changes in taxes and government spending that take place when Congress decides they are needed.

Problem:	Why is it a problem?	Goal:	Discretionary Stabilizer Fix:
Inflation	Too much money in circulation causes the dollar to lose value, which reduces its purchasing power.	Encourage society to spend less.	Contractionary Fiscal Policy: decrease government spending and/or increase taxes.
Unemployment	Not enough money in circulation causes spending to decrease, which leads producers to cut back production and lay off workers.	Encourage society to spend more.	Expansionary Fiscal Policy: increase government spending and/or decrease taxes.

Expansionary fiscal policy often (but not always) creates a budget deficit to combat a recession. Borrowing money to spend in order to lift the economy out of a recessionary period is called **deficit spending**. Ideally, this spending would be temporary; once the economy is back on track, the deficit would be reduced.

Fiscal policy is tricky, though, and brings with it a unique set of complications.

Problems with fiscal policy:	Explanation:
Recognition lag	Often it is difficult to identify exactly when fiscal policy is needed – the statistics used to identify stages of the business cycle are gathered after they happen. Thus, the problem might be well under way by the time it has been officially declared a problem.
Administrative lag	Legislating a change in government spending or a change in taxes can be complicated and politically divisive, and thus it takes time for fiscal policy to be enacted, maybe too much time to make it effective.
Operational lag	After changes are made by Congress to address the economic problem at hand, it takes time for the intended result of the law to become effective and show up in the economy.
Expansionary bias	It is very easy for a member of Congress to promise his or her constituents an increase in government spending or a decrease in taxes; however, no one really likes cuts in spending or tax increases. Politicians, who want to please their voters and earn re-election, often tend toward putting money in their district's coffers rather than taking it away.
Political business cycle	Because of the expansionary bias of fiscal policy, politicians tend to promise more expansionary benefits when election time rolls around.

Export effect	Net exports tend to increase with contractionary fiscal policy – an expansionary effect that offsets the economic goal of the government. The opposite is true as well; expansionary fiscal policy causes net exports to decrease, which has a contractionary effect on GDP.
Crowding-out effect	When the government uses deficit spending to finance expansionary fiscal policy, it pulls from a fixed pool of available loanable funds. This might potentially "crowd out" borrowers from the private sector. (The opposite effect is called "crowding in.")
Effectiveness of decreasing taxes	As taxes affect GDP via disposable income and then consumption (the "C" in C+I+G+[X-M]=GDP), a more direct route to expansionary policy would be increasing government spending, a direct component of GDP (the "G" in C+I+G+[X-M]=GDP).

The **Laffer Curve** represents another dilemma in fiscal policy: at what point are taxes so high that revenues actually decrease due to a decline in incentives to work? The following diagram illustrates this concept:

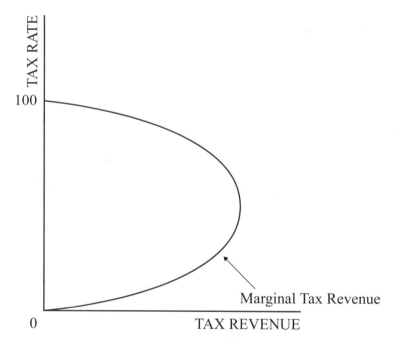

Most economists agree that this dilemma is a real one; however, the point where taxes become "too high" is one of great debate.

Economic Growth

How does a government encourage economic growth at a rate that isn't *too slow* (which leads to unemployment) or *too fast* (which leads to inflation)? Remember that the levels of output (production) and employment (of factors of production/inputs) depend directly on the level of total spending in an economy.

Since consumption makes up about 70% of GDP spending, and investment is the most volatile of the four components of GDP, policy makers target both consumption and investment to encourage economic growth (that is, the growth of GDP) at a healthy 2-3% per year. Consumption and investment are also the focus of economic growth policy because the other two components are more difficult to target: net foreign purchases [X – M] are affected by overseas policies beyond the federal government's control and government spending [G] is subject to the whims of politicians.

People tend to spend a large portion of their **disposable income** ("disposable income" = income – taxes). As one can only consume or save disposable income, the following helps determine the ratio of consumption to saving:

Determinant of Consumption/ Saving:	How it works:
Wealth	When consumers have more wealth, they tend to consume more and save less (and vice versa).
Expectations of the future	When the outlook for the future looks rosy (i.e., consumers are confident they will have a job, inflation will be stable), they tend to consume more and save less (and vice versa).
Interest Rates	When interest rates are low, consumers tend to feel comfortable taking on more debt and savings fall. Higher interest rates encourage more saving and less spending.
Taxation	An increase in taxes means less disposable income which decreases both consumption and saving (and vice versa).

The ratio of consumption to saving increases as income increases because households spend a larger proportion of a small income than of a large income – poor people save less on average than wealthy people. "**Dissaving**" takes place when consumption is greater than one's income.

The other focus of economic growth policy, investment, is very unstable because a) capital goods are "**durable**" (meaning they last more than a year or so... think appliances, cars, furniture; **non-durables** such as clothing and food need to be replaced on a regular basis); b) innovation is irregular; c) profits are unpredictable; and d) expectations change quickly.

Determinant of Investment:	How it works:
Cost of capital goods (*i*)	When interest rates are high, businesses are reluctant to borrow and investment falls (and vice versa).
Business taxes	High taxes reduce the money available for investment spending, and investment falls (and vice versa).
Technology/Innovation	Developments in technology and innovation encourage investment with promises of increased productivity. Investment increases.
Inventories/Capacity Utilization	If inventories are high (meaning goods are not being sold) or production capacity currently isn't being utilized, then investment declines (and vice versa).
Expectations/Business confidence	If business owners expect increased sales and stable economic growth, then investment increases (and vice versa).

Since Investment = investment demand (or, "planned investment") + unplanned changes in inventory, the importance of inventories cannot be discounted. Changes in inventories can be "**unplanned investment**" (inventories piling up because goods are not selling as fast as anticipated) and/ or "**unplanned disinvestment**" (inventories falling faster than anticipated because sales are more robust than expected).

When the macroeconomy is out of sync, adjustments are made. Let's say GDP is $500 billion and total spending (C + I) is $525 billion. Businesses will adjust to excess demand and increase production.

What if GDP is $500 billion, but total spending is only $480 billion?

Businesses will have unsold, unplanned inventory and will cut back. Jobs and total income will decline until the ratio of GDP to total spending reaches a new equilibrium (this could be painful in the short-run).

The Multipliers

An important tool in macroeconomics is the spending multiplier, as it helps economists understand the relationship between consumption and saving. Because any change in spending or saving affects total GDP, economists calculate the **marginal propensity to consume** to determine how a change in disposable income is likely to affect consumption, or the **marginal propensity to save** in order to determine how likely a change in disposable income is to affect saving. The relevant equations are shown below:

$$MPC = \frac{\Delta \text{consumption}}{\Delta \text{disposable income}}$$

$$MPS = \frac{\Delta \text{savings}}{\Delta \text{disposable income}}$$

where MPC + MPS = 1 (or 100%)

So, if our economy currently spent 80% of its income and saved 20%, the MPC would be .8 and the MPS = .2.

How much this affects GDP is determined by the **spending multiplier** (sometimes called the expenditures multiplier), which describes the ripple effect any change in spending has on our economy. The equation for the spending multiplier is:

$$\frac{1}{(1 - MPC)} \text{ or } \frac{1}{MPS}$$

Using the above numbers, the multiplier would be:

$$\frac{1}{MPS} \text{ or } \frac{1}{(1 - MPC)} = \frac{1}{.2} = 5$$

Thus, any change in spending would increase (or decrease) our GDP by 5 times. This is because your spending at the grocery store helps the storeowner pay for electricity and the wages of the cashier, who in turn pays his rent. His landlord then uses the rent money to pay the mortgage to the bank which, in turn, lends money to the tailor down the street to expand his business, and so on.

It does not matter if the change in spending comes from a change in consumption, investment or government spending – the equation and the effect on the multiplier are the same. If the change comes from a change in taxes, however, the multiplier is different:

$$\text{tax multiplier} = \frac{-MPC}{MPS} = -\frac{MPC}{MPS}$$

This equation is negative because an increase in taxes decreases disposable income, which then decreases both consumption and saving (and vice versa). Remember as well that taxes have an indirect effect on GDP, having to operate through consumption and/or investment to affect GDP.

The connection between the spending multipliers and fiscal policy is that in order to enact appropriate fiscal policy, the government needs to understand the MPC of consumers. If policy makers underestimate the MPC, then fiscal policy changes will add too much money to the economy, causing inflation. If MPC is overestimated, then changes to fiscal policy will not influence the economy enough to overcome the problem of unemployment.

An attempt to address the issue of deficit spending is to use the **balanced budget multiplier**. Let's say that the government wants to increase government spending to help the economy out of a recession and decides to pay for it using an increase in taxes. Thus, there will be a change in both government spending (G) and taxes (T) at the same time (that is, both an injection AND a leakage). How does this work?

Suppose G increases by $20 billion and T does the same. The MPC = .80.

First, calculate the spending multiplier for the change in G:

$$\text{spending multiplier} = \frac{1}{(1 - \text{MPC})} = \frac{1}{.2} = 5$$

Then, calculate the change in GDP caused by the change in G:

$20 million increase $\times$ 5 = $100 million

Next, calculate the tax multiplier:

$$\frac{-\text{MPC}}{\text{MPS}} = -\frac{.8}{.2} = -4$$

Now, calculate the change in GDP caused by the change in T:

$20 million increase in T $\times$ (−4) = −$80 million

Thus, the total impact of the changes in G and T on GDP is:

$100 million − $80million = $20 million

The end result is the same as the initial injection of government spending; therefore, the balanced budget multiplier is always equal to 1.

$$\text{Balanced Budget Multiplier} = \frac{1}{(1 - \text{MPC})} + \frac{-\text{MPC}}{(1 - \text{MPC})} = \frac{1 - \text{MPC}}{1 - \text{MPC}} = 1$$

One final note, since we are discussing the budget: the **deficit** (or, conversely, a surplus) is the difference between the government's revenue and its expenses within a given year. Since it is a variable concept, it is considered a "**flow**" – it is measuring change over time. The **debt** is the sum of yearly deficits over time and is a "**stock**," a measurement taken at one moment in time. Examples of other stock measurements are the housing stock (how many houses exist at any one time) or capital stock (the quantity of durable goods available for use in the production of other goods or services).

Important terms:

- Business cycle
- Leading, lagging and coincidental indicators
- Fiscal policy
- Automatic stabilizers
- Discretionary stabilizers
- Expansionary fiscal policy
- Contractionary fiscal policy
- Deficit spending
- Recognition lag
- Administrative lag
- Operational lag
- Expansionary bias
- Political business cycle
- Export effect
- Laffer Curve

- Disposable income
- Dissaving
- Durables
- Non-durables
- Unplanned investment
- Unplanned disinvestment
- Marginal propensity to consume
- Marginal propensity to save
- Spending multiplier
- Tax multiplier
- Balanced budget multiplier
- Debt
- Deficit
- Stock and flow

MACROECONOMICS: UNIT VII

MULTIPLE-CHOICE QUESTIONS

1. Which of the following would be counted as investment spending?

   (A) new home construction
   (B) stock purchase
   (C) bond purchase
   (D) a new car purchase by a consumer
   (E) purchase of a certificate of deposit

2. Net domestic product is less than gross domestic product by an amount equal to

   (A) income taxes.
   (B) indirect business taxes.
   (C) depreciation.
   (D) interest.
   (E) inflation.

3. Which of the following would be an expansionary discretionary fiscal policy measure?

   (A) increasing the reserve requirement
   (B) making more payments to the recipients of unemployment compensation
   (C) people paying higher taxes due to "bracket creep" associated with the progressive income tax
   (D) increasing the personal income tax rate
   (E) decreasing the personal income tax rate

4. Based on the graph below, A, B, and C represent a budget

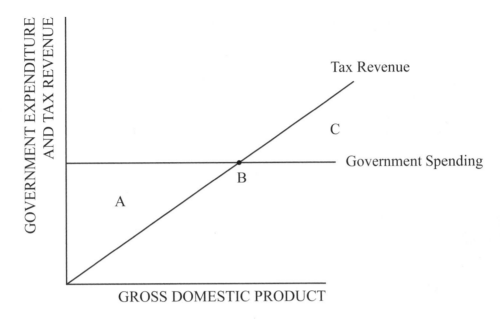

(A) surplus, in balance, deficit.
(B) in balance, deficit, surplus.
(C) deficit, in balance, surplus.
(D) deficit, surplus, in balance.
(E) surplus, deficit, in balance.

5. An advocate of supply-side policies would argue for

(A) tax cuts to spur savings and investment.
(B) tax increases to spur savings and investment.
(C) government spending increases to spur savings and investment.
(D) government spending decreases to increase interest rates.
(E) budget deficits to combat recession and budget surpluses to combat inflation.

6. An advocate of a demand-side (Keynesian) fiscal policy would argue for

(A) tax cuts to spur savings and investment.
(B) tax increases to spur savings and investment.
(C) government spending increases to spur savings and investment.
(D) government spending decreases to increase interest rates.
(E) budget deficits to combat recession and budget surpluses to combat inflation.

7. Which of the following combinations would have the greatest contractionary effect on an economy?

	Taxes	Government Spending	Transfer Payments
(A)	increase	increase	increase
(B)	increase	increase	decrease
(C)	increase	decrease	decrease
(D)	decrease	decrease	decrease
(E)	decrease	increase	increase

8. Expansionary fiscal policy is most appropriate as a response to

(A) recession.
(B) disinflation.
(C) stagflation.
(D) inflation.
(E) deflation.

9. Given an MPC of 0.75, the maximum amount by which GDP could increase with an increase in government spending of $200 is

$$\frac{1}{.25} = \frac{100}{25} = 4$$

(A) $25
(B) $75
(C) $200
(D) $400
(E) $800

10. An increase in which of the following would decrease the numerical value of the simple spending multiplier?

(A) marginal propensity to consume
(B) marginal propensity to save
(C) budget deficit
(D) budget surplus
(E) national debt

11. The simple spending multiplier is correctly expressed as

(A) 1/MPS
(B) 1/MPC
(C) 1/MPS + MPC
(D) MPS/MPC
(E) MPC/MPS

12. The numerical value of the MPS for the economy shown is

Income	Consumption
$1,000	$800
$2,000	$1,600
$3,000	$2,400

$$\frac{800}{1000} = \frac{8}{10} = .80 \rightarrow MPC$$

$$1 - .8 = .2$$

(A) .10
(B) .20
(C) .40
(D) .80
(E) 1.0

Questions 13-16 refer to the graph below:

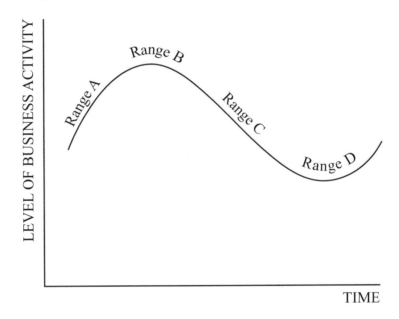

13. The correct labels for the four ranges in the graph above, starting with Range A, would be

(A) peak, contraction, trough, expansion.
(B) contraction, trough, expansion, peak.
(C) trough, expansion, peak, contraction.
(D) expansion, peak, contraction, trough.
(E) trough, contraction, peak, expansion.

14. Based on the graph, which of the following would be the most appropriate response by the federal government to an economy in Range C?

    (A) increase taxes
    (B) balance the current budget deficit
    (C) eliminate programs like unemployment compensation
    (D) reduce transfer payments
    (E) increase government spending

15. The graph depicts a

    (A) Laffer curve.
    (B) short-run Phillips curve.
    (C) business cycle.
    (D) long-run Phillips curve.
    (E) secular trend.

16. Based on the information shown in the graph, a Keynesian would argue for

    (A) expansionary fiscal policy in Range B.
    (B) expansionary fiscal policy in Range A.
    (C) expansionary fiscal policy in Range C.
    (D) contractionary fiscal policy in Range C.
    (E) contractionary fiscal policy in Range D.

---

17. A series of persistent federal budget deficits will

    (A) add to the national surplus.
    (B) decrease the national debt.
    (C) increase the national debt.
    (D) have no effect on the national debt.
    (E) have a contractionary effect on the economy.

18. Which of the following is a basic tenet of proponents of an income policy?

    (A) Inflation is perpetuated by expectations of inflation.
    (B) There should be wage-price controls.
    (C) There is a need to break the link between wage increases and price increases.
    (D) all of the above
    (E) none of the above

19. If the marginal propensity to consume is .5 and the federal government increases spending by $200 billion and increases taxes by $200 billion to pay for the spending increase, which of the following correctly describes the result?

    (A) $200 billion increase in GDP
    (B) $200 billion decrease in GDP
    (C) no change in GDP
    (D) $400 increase in GDP
    (E) $400 decrease in GDP

20. Purposeful attempts by the federal government to act in a counter-cyclical manner are called

    (A) economics.
    (B) fiscal policy.
    (C) monetary policy.
    (D) incomes policy.
    (E) destabilization policy.

21. A Keynesian economist would argue for

    (A) the active use of discretionary fiscal policy to correct for short-term business cycle fluctuations.
    (B) the active use of discretionary monetary policy to correct for short-term business cycle fluctuations.
    (C) the active use of both fiscal and monetary policy to correct for short-term business cycle fluctuations.
    (D) leaving short-term business cycle fluctuations to take care of themselves and would discourage the use of discretionary policies to correct these short-term fluctuations.
    (E) using discretionary fiscal policy and monetary policies to correct for short-term business cycle fluctuations only to combat inflation and not to combat recession.

22. An increase in which of the following is likely to have the largest and most immediate contractionary effect on an economy?

    (A) taxes
    (B) transfer payments
    (C) government spending
    (D) entitlement programs
    (E) federal government budget deficit

23. The belief that short-term business cycle fluctuations take care of themselves and the use of discretionary policies to correct these short-term fluctuations only makes things worse is the view held by

 (A) Keynesians.
 (B) supply side economists.
 (C) the federal government.
 (D) classical economists.
 (E) the Federal Reserve.

24. If government expenditures exceed government revenues, the government has

 (A) a debt.
 (B) a surplus.
 (C) a deficit.
 (D) an expansion.
 (E) a contraction.

25. If the marginal propensity to consume is .8, the marginal propensity to save is

 (A) .8
 (B) 8
 (C) 0
 (D) 2
 (E) .2

26. The national debt and a budget deficit are referred to by economists as

 (A) a stock and a flow.
 (B) a flow and a stock.
 (C) flows.
 (D) stocks.
 (E) neither a flow nor a stock.

27. Over time, economies such as the United States have shown a long-term growth trend. This trend for real GDP to grow over time is referred to as

 (A) the Laffer curve.
 (B) the Phillips curve.
 (C) the business cycle.
 (D) the cyclical trend.
 (E) the secular trend.

MACROECONOMICS: UNIT VII

FREE-RESPONSE QUESTIONS

1. Analyze the economy depicted by the following figures:

Unemployment	5%
Inflation rate	5%
Annual rate of real GDP growth	4%

(a) What is the biggest problem this economy is facing?

(b) List two fiscal policy measures that could be used to correct the problem you identified in part (a), and then explain how/why each would fix the problem.

2. Provide the requested information for an economy with a marginal propensity to consume of 75% and that is currently operating at a level of GDP that is $2,000 less than the desired level.

(a) Identify two specific fiscal policy tools that could be used to increase GDP to the desired level.

(b) Identify the appropriate dollar amount of each fiscal policy measure you listed in part (a).

3. The government of Chaseystan has decided to build a moat separating the liberal and conservative sides of Chaseystan. The moat construction is expected to cost $250 billion. Address each of the following regarding the proposed moat construction project:

   (a) If the government of Chaseystan is committed to the moat construction project, how could they complete it without having a budget deficit in the short-run?

   (b) What would be the effect of the moat project on the economy of Chaseystan? Explain your answer.

   (c) If Chaseystan had a $12 trillion national debt prior to the moat project, how would the project affect the national debt in the short-run?

MONEY, BANKING & MONETARY POLICY

The previous chapter discussed one way of encouraging a healthy economy: using fiscal policy. Monetary policy – controlling the money supply – can also treat an ailing economy, and is the focus of this chapter.

Before talking about the money supply, we need to know what is **money**, exactly? Various items have been used as "money" throughout the centuries with varying degrees of success. The most successful attempts at money follow these guidelines:

Characteristics of money:	Functions of money:
Portable	Medium of exchange
Uniform	Store of value
Durable	Standard of value
Stable in value	
Widely accepted	
Not easily counterfeited	

Money

Before money existed, society exchanged goods and services via **bartering**. Later came **commodity money**, where people used goods such as salt, animal furs or gold as money. When paper money was first introduced, it represented the value of a store of goods – a specific weight of gold or silver, for example. Currently, the money we use is **fiat money**. It derives its value simply from the fact that the government declares it to be legal tender – merchants and others must accept it as a medium of exchange. There is no commodity, be it gold or anything else, that determines its value. Rather, its value is a perception driven by what a person can obtain with it – food, clothing, a haircut, a yacht, whatever.

The Money Market

The amount of money in circulation is measured in two categories: **M1** and **M2**. M1 includes all currency, demand deposits in your local banks such as a checking account, other checkable deposits and travelers' checks. The key difference between M1 and M2 is the liquidity of the money – how easy is it for you to get your money right now? If you can pull it out of your wallet or go to the bank and easily withdraw it, then it is counted in M1. M2, in contrast, is everything else: (1) savings deposits; (2) small-denomination time deposits (time deposits in amounts of less than $100,000); (3) balances in retail money market mutual funds (minus IRA and Keogh balances); and (4) M1. These figures make up the **money supply**.

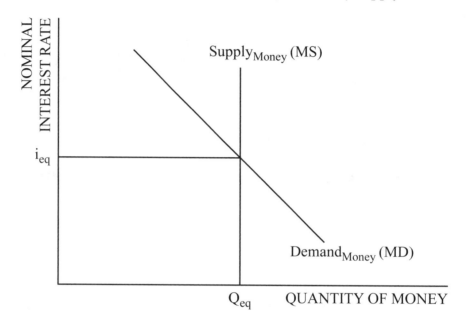

Graph A: The Money Market

Graph A shows the **money market**. The money supply is represented by a vertical line. This is because the money supply is fixed at any one point in time. The amount of money in circulation as measured by M1 and M2 is determined by the central bank (more on that in a minute).

The demand for money (or the **money demand**) is the sum of **transaction demand** and **asset demand** (sometimes called speculative demand). Transaction demand is the demand for currency necessary to purchase goods and services – money needed for the daily operation of a household or business. Asset demand is the inverse relationship between the price of money (the interest rate) and the desire to hold money as an asset (the opportunity cost of not spending it). For example, when interest rates are high, the demand for money is low, as people would rather hold assets than cash. When interest rates are low, the demand for money is high, as people would rather hold cash than invest in assets such as bonds. A third component of money demand is the **precautionary demand** for money, which is cash held aside for a rainy day – emergency funds needed on short notice.

On a graph of the money market, the intersection of the money supply and money demand curves represents the **nominal interest rate**, which is the price of money. As the money supply and money demand curves shift, the interest rate is affected accordingly. *Graph B* shows these shifts and the resulting nominal interest rate.

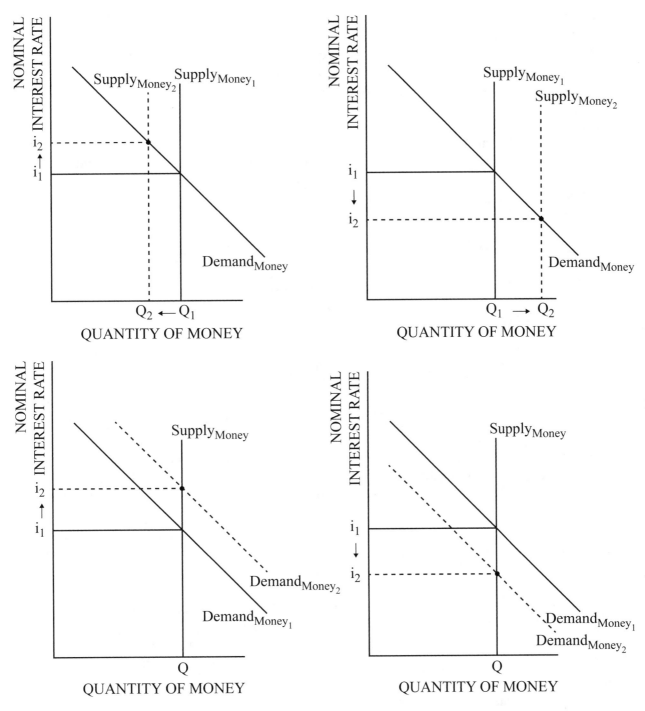

Graph B: Shifting Curves in the Money Market

The Federal Reserve

The money supply is set by the central bank. In the case of the United States, this is the **Federal Reserve Bank,** or "the Fed." The Fed's role in the economy is the following:

- Conducting the nation's monetary policy in pursuit of maximum employment, stable prices, and moderate long-term interest rates
- Supervising and regulating banking institutions
- Maintaining the stability of the financial system
- Providing financial services to depository institutions, the U.S. government, and foreign official institutions[1]

The Fed uses its 12 branches to survey their respective districts and determine the state of the economy. Interest rates, the stock market, vendor deliveries, commodities prices, productivity, factory orders and order backlogs are all examples of information the Fed gathers (these are the economic indicators referred to in Unit VII). This information is used to formulate the Fed's **monetary policy**, which adjusts the money supply as needed.

Monetary Policy

The Fed has three tools it can use to adjust the money supply.

Fed Reserve Tool:	Definition:	How it works:
Open Market Operations	This is the buying and selling of securities in order to manipulate the amount of money held by the public. This is the most commonly used tool of the Fed.	When the Fed would like to encourage public spending, it offers to buy securities from anyone holding them. This puts money into the hands of the public, resulting in a rightward-shift in the money supply curve and an expansionary/ easy monetary policy. When spending should be curtailed, the Fed sells securities, thus taking money out of circulation and enacting a contractionary/ tight monetary policy and shifting the money supply curve to the left.
Reserve Requirement	This is the amount of money from each deposit that must be set aside and not loaned out. This is a seldom-used tool of the Fed.	If the reserve requirement (RR) is high, then banks have fewer funds to loan out and the result is a contractionary or tight money policy. The money supply curve shifts to the left. If the RR is lowered, then banks may lend out a larger percentage of their deposits, putting money in the hands of the public. This is expansionary/easy monetary policy. The money supply curve shifts to the right.
Discount Rate	This is the interest rate the Fed charges member banks to cover overnight shortages in the required reserves.	If the discount rate is high, banks are discouraged from borrowing from the Fed, and thus discouraged from making loans to the public. This is a contractionary/tight policy that shifts the money supply curve to the left. If the discount rate is low, banks are more likely to loan out money and borrow from the Fed to cover reserves. This is expansionary/ easy monetary policy that shifts the money supply curve to the right.

[1] "The Federal Reserve System: Purposes and Functions," http://www.federalreserve.gov/pf/pf.htm, last updated August 24, 2011.

The Fed also uses the **federal funds rate**, which is the interest rate on loans between banks, to control the money supply. Similar to the discount rate, this rate is the price of borrowing from member banks (rather than from the Fed) as the level of reserves fluctuates. When banks and financial institutions accumulate reserves in excess of their requirements, they may lend these reserves overnight to other banks and financial institutions that have not met their reserve requirement. The Fed sets the target level for the federal funds rate, but the actual rate is determined by supply and demand. Contrasting with the discount rate is the fact that this rate changes constantly, where the discount rate does not.

To clarify the leftward (contractionary/tight) and rightward (expansionary/easy) shifts in the money supply:

Type of monetary policy:	Definition:	How it works:
Contractionary or tight money policy	When the economy is suffering from inflation greater than 2-3%, the Fed can shift the money supply curve to the left, decreasing the amount of money in circulation. This is meant to bring the price level down as the nominal interest rate falls.	Excess reserves decrease, leading to an increase in the nominal interest rate, which decreases the amount of investment (I), which causes aggregate demand to decrease and GDP to decrease as well.
Expansionary or easy money policy	When the economy is suffering from unemployment greater than 4-6%, the Fed can shift the money supply curve to the right, increasing the amount of money in circulation. This is meant to increase aggregate demand and thus GDP. The price level might increase as well.	Excess reserves increase, decreasing the nominal interest rate and increasing the amount of investment (I), which causes aggregate demand to increase and GDP to increase as well.

The effectiveness of these shifts in the money supply on the economy depends on how responsive both investment and the money demand are to the change in the nominal interest rate.

Using the Money Multiplier

When the reserve requirement changes, the amount that banks can lend out to potential borrowers changes as well. Increases in the reserve requirement are contractionary, while decreases in the reserve requirement are expansionary.

> If the reserve requirement (RR) is 25%, and a deposit of $100 is made, the bank must keep on reserve 25%, or $25. It may loan out $75.
>
> Conversely, if the RR is lowered to 10%, now only $10 of that $100 deposit is required reserves, and the bank may loan out $90.

This $90 is added to the money supply and, if spent, increases aggregate demand. But by how much does this $90 increase aggregate demand? The **money multiplier** determines that value.

Just as money spent by one person ripples through the economy via the spending multiplier from Unit VII, the ability to loan out a fraction of each deposit causes a ripple effect in the money supply. These ripples enlarge the money supply with each deposit and subsequent loan. The total effect of these expansions are calculated using the money multiplier and the following equation:

The money multiplier $= \dfrac{1}{RR}$

Excess reserves (E) = actual deposits $-$ RR

Maximum expansion of the money supply $= E \times \dfrac{1}{RR}$.

Using numbers from the previous example,

> The RR is 10% for a deposit of $100. Ten dollars must be kept on reserve, but $90 may be loaned out.
> Thus, E = $90
> Maximum expansion of the money supply $= E \times \dfrac{1}{RR} = \$90 \times \dfrac{1}{.10} = \$900$
>
> Thus, $900 is "created" using monetary policy.
> The total money supply is now $1000 ($100 original deposit + $900 created from loaning out the $90 excess reserves).
>
> If one wanted to decrease AD in the case of inflation, for example, then the RR would be raised to, say, 25%. Now, only $75 may be lent out (25% of the original $100 deposit must be kept on reserve). Excess reserves are $75.
>
> $E \times \dfrac{1}{RR} = \$75 \times \dfrac{1}{.25} = \$300$ created by expanding the money supply.
>
> The total money supply is now $400 ($100 original deposit + $300 created = $400).

Thus, a relatively small change in the reserve requirement (from 10% to 25%) led to a large decrease in the money supply (from $1000 to $400). This is contractionary/tight monetary policy at work.

Just as fiscal policy has strengths and weaknesses, monetary policy does as well.

What are the strengths of monetary policy?	Speed and flexibility: The Fed can make decisions on a daily basis via open market operations. Thus, it is extremely flexible. Isolation from political pressures: Fed Board of Governors members are appointed, not elected. Also, the tools used by the Fed are not subject to political debate.

What are the weaknesses of monetary policy?	Issues of changing asset liquidities: People can move money around from various accounts – within the U.S. or even overseas – thus offsetting the goal of the Fed by making it harder to quantify M1 and M2. Issues of Asymmetry: The Fed can make the money available to banks, but it cannot guarantee that people will borrow or that banks will make loans. In addition, those people who do borrow might use the loans to pay off outstanding debt, and thus not increase consumption or investment. Issues of Velocity: The circulation of money in the economy varies with the interest rate. For example, if interest rates are low because the Fed wants to encourage spending, people might actually hold on to money longer because of a lower asset demand. Issues of Investment: If investment demand is high, this might offset the Fed's attempts to lower the interest rate. Issues of Interest: If people view the interest rate as income, their behavior will be different from those who view it as an expense. The "target dilemma": Should the Fed target the money supply or the interest rate?

The **quantity theory of money** is the idea that changes in the money supply directly affect the price level via the equation $MV = PQ$, where

M = money supply
V = the velocity of money, or how quickly money changes hands in an economy
P = price level
Q = quantity of real output (or GDP)

If it is assumed that the velocity of money is relatively stable, then the only thing that can affect inflation and GDP is a change in the money supply. Thus the value of money is determined by the money supply, as an increase in the money supply leads to an increase in inflation. A higher inflation rate reduces the purchasing power of the dollar – it costs more to purchase the same amount of goods. However, often the velocity is not stable. It slows down in times of economic contraction, and speeds up when the economy expands. Thus, the Fed needs to consider velocity when adjusting the money supply in order for monetary policy to be most effective.

One way to visualize the information presented in the macroeconomic units thus far is as follows:

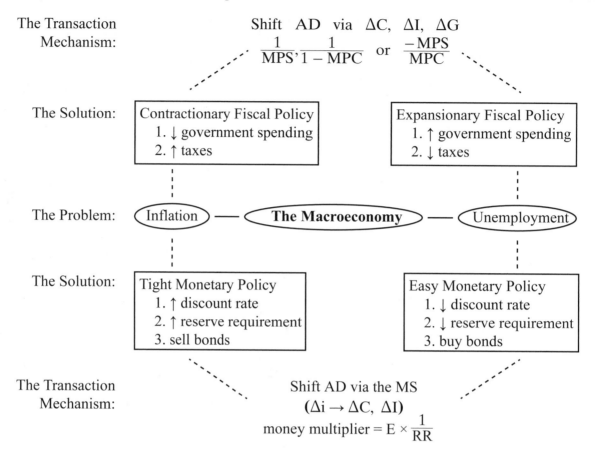

The Transaction Mechanism:

$$\text{Shift AD via } \Delta C, \Delta I, \Delta G$$
$$\frac{1}{MPS}, \frac{1}{1-MPC} \quad \text{or} \quad \frac{-MPS}{MPC}$$

The Solution:

Contractionary Fiscal Policy
1. ↓ government spending
2. ↑ taxes

Expansionary Fiscal Policy
1. ↑ government spending
2. ↓ taxes

The Problem: Inflation — **The Macroeconomy** — Unemployment

The Solution:

Tight Monetary Policy
1. ↑ discount rate
2. ↑ reserve requirement
3. sell bonds

Easy Monetary Policy
1. ↓ discount rate
2. ↓ reserve requirement
3. buy bonds

The Transaction Mechanism:

$$\text{Shift AD via the MS}$$
$$(\Delta i \rightarrow \Delta C, \Delta I)$$
$$\text{money multiplier} = E \times \frac{1}{RR}$$

The Bond Market

In order to encourage the Federal Funds Rate to stay near the Fed's target rate, the Fed buys and sells government securities on the open market. These movements change the nominal interest rate, which in turn affects the price of securities in the bond market.

Type of security:	Maturity date from issuance:
Treasury bill	Less than one year
Treasury note	2, 3, 5, or 10 years
Treasury bond	10 years or more

An example:

You own a 5-year Treasury note that sells for $10,000 at a 5% coupon rate ("the interest") paid every six months.

However, nominal interest rates increase to 6% because of an increase in the money demand in the money market.

You have two options:

Keep your note until maturity OR sell it on the open market (but why would someone want it if it only pays 5%, considering that the interest rate available on other assets is 6%?)

If you sell it, the note is now only worth $8,333 instead of $10,000. This is because the annual payment of $500 earned when the $10,000 note earned 5% interest now needs to adjust to the reality of a 6% interest rate.

$$\$8,333 \times 6\% = \$500$$

Thus, in order to sell the note, bill or bond on the open market, the price of the security would have to fall when the interest rate rises. If the interest rate were falling, security prices would have to increase to make up the difference.

The key is the inflation rate: higher inflation means that the Fed will decrease the money supply (contractionary/tight monetary policy), which increases nominal interest rates. When the Fed announces it will raise interest rates:

- the dollar appreciates because foreigners find the dollar more attractive (so they invest in dollar-denominated investments); and
- mortgage rates usually increase as well (mortgage rates are tied to bond rates – as bond prices decrease and the nominal interest rate increases, banks add a premium to the bond rate in order to make a profit).

Of course the opposite is true as well.

Important Terms in this chapter:

- Money
- Barter
- Commodity money
- M1 and M2
- Fiat money
- Money Supply
- Money Demand
- Transaction demand
- Asset demand
- Precautionary demand
- Nominal interest rate
- Federal Reserve Bank
- Monetary policy
- Open market operations
- Reserve requirement
- Discount rate
- Federal funds rate
- Contractionary/tight policy
- Expansionary/easy policy
- Quantity theory of money
- Money multiplier
- Bond market

MULTIPLE-CHOICE QUESTIONS

1. A type of money that has no intrinsic value in and of itself, like currency in the United States, is referred to as

   (A) full bodies money.
   (B) silver certificates.
   (C) fiat money.
   (D) commodity money.
   (E) Gresham's money.

2. The effect of contractionary monetary policy on the money supply and nominal interest rate is

   (A) increase; increase.
   (B) increase; decrease.
   (C) decrease; decrease.
   (D) decrease; constant.
   (E) decrease; increase.

3. The "quantity theory of money" is best expressed by which of the following?

   (A) marginal propensity to consume = marginal propensity to save
   (B) gross domestic product = consumption + investment + government spending + net exports
   (C) 1/reserve requirement
   (D) money supply × velocity of money = price level × output
   (E) interest = principal × rate × time

4. In the graphs below, the transactions demand and the asset demand for money would be shown as:

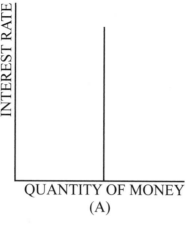

QUANTITY OF MONEY
(A)

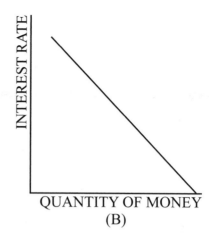

QUANTITY OF MONEY
(B)

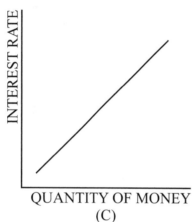

QUANTITY OF MONEY
(C)

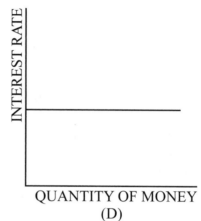

QUANTITY OF MONEY
(D)

(A) A, B
(B) A, C
(C) A, D
(D) B, A
(E) B, D

5. A fractional reserve system with a reserve requirement of 20% into which a new deposit of $5,000 is made could experience a maximum change in the money supply of

(A) an increase of $5,000.
(B) an increase of $20,000.
(C) an increase of $25,000.
(D) a decrease of $25,000.
(E) a decrease of $5,000.

6. The effect of expansionary monetary policy on nominal interest rates and GDP is

   (A) increase; increase.
   (B) increase; decrease.
   (C) decrease; decrease.
   (D) decrease; constant.
   (E) decrease; increase.

7. The money supply in the United States is controlled by

   (A) Congress.
   (B) the President.
   (C) the U. S. Treasury.
   (D) the Federal Reserve.
   (E) the market.

8. Which of the following combinations represents the monetary policy that would increase real GDP the most?

	Open Market Operations	Reserve Requirement	Discount Rate
(A)	sell	decrease	decrease
(B)	buy	decrease	decrease
(C)	sell	increase	increase
(D)	buy	increase	decrease
(E)	sell	decrease	increase

Questions 9-11 refer to the graphs below:

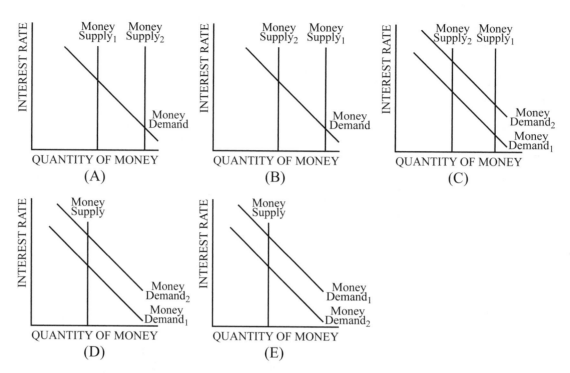

9. Which of the graphs demonstrates the appropriate monetary policy to achieve decreased consumer spending on durable goods?

(A) A
(B) B
(C) C
(D) D
(E) E

10. Which of the graphs demonstrates the appropriate response by the Federal Reserve to a severe and prolonged recession?

(A) A
(B) B
(C) C
(D) D
(E) E

11. Which of the graphs demonstrates the effect of an expanding economy with no action by the Federal Reserve?

   (A) A
   (B) B
   (C) C
   (D) D
   (E) E

12. Contractionary monetary policy would be most effective to combat

   (A) a recession.
   (B) inflation.
   (C) stagflation.
   (D) a contraction.
   (E) a trough.

13. Which of the following correctly depicts the Keynesian monetary policy transmission mechanism after a decrease in the money supply?

   (A) A decrease in interest rates, followed by an increase in investment demand, followed by an increase in aggregate demand, followed by an increase in GDP.
   (B) An increase in interest rates, followed by an increase in investment demand, followed by an increase in aggregate demand, followed by an increase in GDP.
   (C) An increase in interest rates, followed by a decrease in investment demand, followed by an increase in aggregate demand, followed by an increase in GDP.
   (D) An increase in interest rates, followed by a decrease in investment demand, followed by a decrease in aggregate demand, followed by an increase in GDP.
   (E) An increase in interest rates, followed by a decrease in investment demand, followed by a decrease in aggregate demand, followed by a decrease in GDP.

14. The simple money multiplier is correctly expressed as

   (A) 1/MPC
   (B) 1/MPS
   (C) 1/reserve requirement
   (D) 1/tax rate
   (E) reserve requirement × tax rate

15. Which of the following combinations would be the most expansionary?

	Open Market Operations	Reserve Requirement	Fed Funds Rate
(A)	sell	increase	increase
(B)	buy	increase	increase
(C)	sell	decrease	decrease
(D)	buy	decrease	decrease
(E)	sell	decrease	increase

16. The most widely-cited factor that would render ineffective the discretionary use of monetary policy as a tool of stabilization policy is

   (A) the inability of the Federal Reserve to act quickly.
   (B) the inability of the Federal Reserve to reach consensus.
   (C) the inability of the Federal Reserve and Congress to agree on the appropriate policy to implement.
   (D) the uncertainty as to the time lags involved between the implementation of policy and the resulting effect on the economy.
   (E) the uncertainty as to which tool of policy to actually use.

17. If interest rates rise,

   (A) bond prices rise.
   (B) money demand rises.
   (C) money supply rises.
   (D) money demand falls.
   (E) bond prices fall.

18. Money definitions would include all of the following components EXCEPT:

   I. medium of exchange
   II. store of value
   III. unit of account
   IV. backed by gold

   (A) I.
   (B) II.
   (C) III.
   (D) IV.
   (E) All of the above are components of the definition of money.

19. Which of the following accurately shows the result of a person signing a 60-month fixed-rate loan contract with an interest rate of 10% in an economy with an inflationary expectation of 4%?

	The Real Interest Rate	The Nominal Interest Rate
(A)	2%	4%
(B)	4%	10%
(C)	6%	10%
(D)	10%	6%
(E)	14%	6%

20. Beginning at equilibrium E in the graph below, if there is a sudden increase in the supply of money, which of the following is the chain of events that will result?

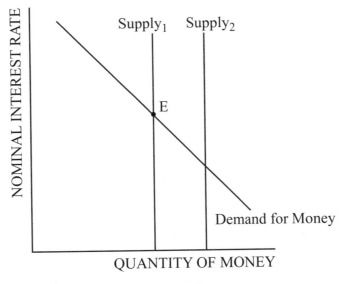

Money Market

(A) a temporary shortage of money followed by an increase in interest rates
(B) a temporary shortage of money followed by a decrease in interest rates
(C) a temporary surplus of money followed by an increase in interest rates
(D) a temporary surplus of money followed by a decrease in interest rates
(E) a permanent shortage of money with no adjustment in interest rates

21. When the Fed engages in the contractionary use of open market operations it is

(A) selling government bonds.
(B) buying government bonds.
(C) increasing the reserve requirement.
(D) decreasing the reserve requirement.
(E) decreasing taxes.

22. Expansionary fiscal and monetary policies will have what effect on interest rates, respectively?

    (A) increase; increase
    (B) increase; constant
    (C) increase; decrease
    (D) decrease; increase
    (E) decrease; decrease

23. The relationship that exists between the purchasing power of the dollar and the Consumer Price Index is

    (A) direct.
    (B) inverse.
    (C) as likely to be either direct or inverse.
    (D) non-existant.
    (E) one to one.

24. Which of the following correctly describes the relationship between real and nominal interest rates?

    (A) real + expected inflation = nominal
    (B) real – expected inflation = nominal
    (C) nominal + expected inflation = real
    (D) nominal and real are always equal
    (E) nominal + real = expected inflation

25. Which of the following would be included in the M_1 definition of the money supply?

    I. $100 in the vault of, and owned by, the Chicago Federal Reserve Bank
    II. $100 in the vault of, and owned by, the First National Bank of Chicago
    III. $100 in your wallet
    IV. $100 in your checking account at the Last National Bank of Chicago

    (A) I only
    (B) I and II
    (C) I, III, and IV
    (D) II, III, and IV
    (E) I, II, III, and IV

Questions 26-28 refer to the balance sheet shown below.

Last National Bank of Econville

Assets		Liabilities	
Required reserves	$10,000	Demand deposits	$100,000
Excess reserves	$0	Stockholders equity	$40,000
Land and buildings	$100,000		
Government bonds	$20,000		
Loans	$10,000		

26. Based on the balance sheet above, the reserve requirement for the Last National Bank of Econville is

(A) 10%
(B) 20%
(C) 30%
(D) 40%
(E) 50%

27. Based on the balance sheet above, if the Federal Reserve purchases $10,000 in government bonds from the Last National Bank of Econville, what will be the change in excess reserves immediately after the purchase?

(A) They will increase by $1,000.
(B) They will increase by $9,000.
(C) They will increase by $10,000.
(D) They will decrease by $10,000.
(E) They will decrease by $9,000.

28. Based on the balance sheet above, if the Federal Reserve purchases $10,000 in government bonds from the Last National Bank of Econville, what will be the change in demand deposits immediately after the purchase?

(A) They will not change.
(B) They will increase by $10,000.
(C) They will increase by $9,000.
(D) They will decrease by $9,000.
(E) They will decrease by $10,000.

29. Beginning with a discount rate of 3%, if the Federal Reserve increases the discount rate by 25 basis points, the new discount rate will be

(A) .5%
(B) 2.75%
(C) 3.25%
(D) 5.5%
(E) 28%

30. The rate of interest banks charge each other for short-term loans to cover reserve accounts is the

(A) reserve rate.
(B) discount rate.
(C) bond rate.
(D) treasury rate.
(E) fed funds rate.

FREE-RESPONSE QUESTIONS

1. Analyze the economy described by the following figures:

Unemployment	8%	4-5%
Inflation rate	2%	2-3%
Annual rate of real GDP growth	2%	3-3.5%

(a) What is the biggest problem this economy is facing?

(b) List two fiscal policy measures that could be used to correct the problem you identified in part (a), and then explain why they would correct the problem.

(c) List two monetary policy measures that could be used to correct the problem you identified in part (a), and then explain why they would correct the problem.

a) Unemployment rate is too high — recession

b) Increase gov. spending or decrease income taxes,
   Increase in aggregate demand results in a higher output, reducing
   unemployment

c) Buy bonds, lower the reserve requirement,
   Increase money supply, decreasing ir, increasing investment
   and consumption, increasing AD & GDP

2. Assume the reserve requirement for a banking system is 10%. Under the typical assumptions corresponding with the money multiplier, if the Fed buys government bonds in the amount of $20,000 from a member bank how will it affect each of the following:

(a) the initial required reserves of the individual bank from whom the Fed bought the bonds
(b) the initial excess reserves of the individual bank from whom the Fed bought the bonds
(c) the total deposits in the entire banking system after all of the repercussions of the Fed purchase
(d) What factors might limit the actual amount of money created by all of the banks in the system to less than the maximum possible in theory?

a) Won't change, Fed purchases don't affect reserve

b) $20,000

c) $200,000

d) People save money, banks can choose to keep excess reserves

3. Draw and correctly label a graph of the money market.

    (a) On your graph, identify the equilibrium interest rate.

    (b) Explain if the rate you identified in part (a) is a nominal or a real rate.

    (c) Draw a new money market graph and demonstrate the effect of the Federal Reserve engaging in expansionary monetary policy. Identify the effect this expansionary monetary policy would have on the interest rate on your graph.

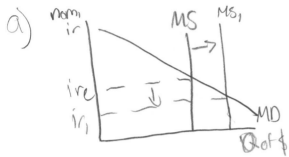

a) nom ir, ire, ir₁, MS, MS₁, MD, Q of $

b) Nominal because the money market

c)

AGGREGATE SUPPLY
AGGREGATE DEMAND

In the previous chapters, we discussed GDP and its determinants, the effects of unemployment and inflation on GDP, as well as how the economy is affected when GDP increases or decreases. What we haven't done yet is graph the aggregate economy, and because it is difficult to separate economists from their graphs, this chapter focuses on just that.

Similar to the supply/demand graph in microeconomics, the axes for the main macroeconomic graph – called the **Aggregate Supply/Aggregate Demand** graph, or AS/AD – reference price and quantity. However, because the AS/AD graph represents <u>all</u> goods and services produced in the entire economy (hence the name "aggregate" which means "total") rather than one particular market (as in micro), the labels for the axes are a bit different.

Micro Vocabulary	**Macro Vocabulary**
Price or P	Price Level or PL
Quantity or Q	Real GDP (or National Output or National Income). Remember the circular flow diagram. These measurements should be equal to each other.
Supply or S	Aggregate Supply or AS
Demand or D	Aggregate Demand or AD

The graph looks similar to a micro supply/demand graph, with upward-sloping supply and downward-sloping demand curves, as shown on the following page. The reasons for the slopes of the curves are different however. (The causes for the downward slope of the micro demand curve were explained in Unit III).

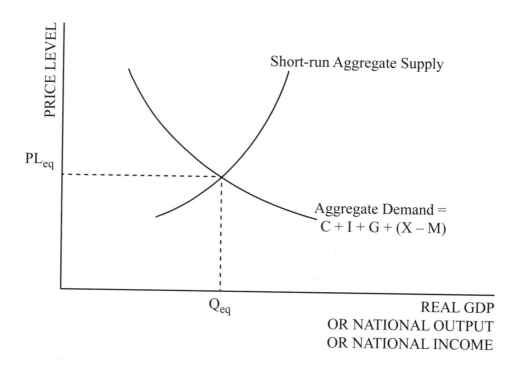

The key point for both micro and macro demand curves is the same: there is an inverse relationship between the vertical axis and the horizontal axis. When prices or overall price levels are low, the quantities consumed increase and vice versa. For both macro and micro supply curves, quantity produced increases as the opportunity for increased revenues grows. Thus, both micro and macro supply curves have a direct relationship between P (or PL) and Q (or output). The chart below summarizes this.

	Micro	Macro
Upward Slope of Supply Curve	Law of Supply: Low prices represent low marginal costs and low opportunity costs; high prices represent high opportunity and marginal costs.	Higher prices for goods and services make output more profitable, enabling businesses to expand their production; lower prices discourage production.
Downward Slope of Demand Curve	Law of Demand: Income effect rate Substitution effect Diminishing marginal utility	Interest rate effect Wealth effect Foreign purchases effect

The Downward-sloping Macro Demand Curve

The **wealth effect** (or **"real balances" effect**) is assumed to occur when people feel as if they have more money. For example, "Every $1 increase in stock prices raises consumer spending by 3 cents to 5 cents," according to calculations by Joseph Gagnon, a former Federal Reserve official. So if the market value of the Standard & Poor's 500 Stock Index is currently $13.9 trillion, and it increased 10 percent, consumer spending would rise $40 billion to $70 billion.[1] Rising housing prices can have the same effect.

---

[1] As quoted in "Fed Aims For 'Wealth Effect' To Revive The Economy" by the Associated Press, National Public Radio, September 14, 2012.

The **interest rate effect** says that when interest rates change due to a change in the price level, the cost of borrowing money to purchase capital (the investment component of AD) is affected, as are interest-rate sensitive consumption purchases such as cars and appliances. Thus, when interest rates rise, consumption and investment fall, and vice versa.

The **foreign purchases effect** states that our economy is sensitive to price changes worldwide. When the price level in the United States rises relative to the price level in other countries (that is, when the same goods are more expensive in the U.S. than they are overseas), Americans will substitute cheaper foreign goods for more expensive American goods. Likewise, foreigners will import fewer of our goods. Net exports fall, and quantity of overall goods purchased decreases.

Determinants of AS and AD

The determinants that cause the curves to shift are unique to macro. Remember that aggregate demand is the sum of consumption spending, investment spending, government spending and net foreign purchases (or, $AD = C + I + G + [X - M]$). Anything that affects one of those components will shift the curve.

Determinants of Aggregate Demand	How do they work?
Changes in Consumer Spending (C)	
Consumer wealth	When consumers have more money, they tend to purchase more goods and services (and vice versa).
Consumer expectations	When consumers expect that the economy will grow in the future, they tend to purchase more goods and services (and vice versa).
Consumer indebtedness	When consumers own less debt (owe less money), they tend to purchase more goods and services (and vice versa).
Taxes	When consumers pay less of their income in taxes (their disposable income increases), they tend to purchase more goods and services (and vice versa).
Changes in Investment (I)	
Interest rates (i)	When interest rates are low, the cost of borrowing is low. Businesses tend to purchase more capital, and investment increases (and vice versa).
Profit expectations	When businesses expect that profits will be positive, they tend to purchase more capital, and investment increases (and vice versa).

Business taxes	When business taxes are low, businesses have more money to re-invest in their companies. Businesses tend to purchase more capital, and investment increases (and vice versa).
Technology	Technology helps increase productivity, which increases profit opportunities for businesses. Businesses tend to purchase more capital, and investment increases (and vice versa).
Amount of excess capacity	When aggregate demand is straining a country's current production capabilities (production lines are running around the clock, for example), businesses expand in order to keep up with demand. Businesses tend to purchase more capital, and investment increases (and vice versa).
Changes in Government Spending (G)	If government spending increases, the amount of goods and services purchased in an economy increases (and vice versa).
Changes in Foreign Trade (X – M)	
National income abroad	When the income of consumers overseas increases, they tend to import more goods and services produced in the U.S. Thus our exports rise (and vice versa).
Exchange rates	When the dollar depreciates relative to other currencies, consumers overseas tend to import more of our goods and services produced in the U.S. Thus our exports rise (and vice versa).

Aggregate supply reflects the output of all the producers in an economy. Their production is affected by a number of determinants.

Determinants of Aggregate Supply	How do they work?
Changes in Input Prices	
Domestic resource availability	Falling domestic input prices often lead to increases in AS as businesses have the confidence to increase production (and vice versa).
Prices of imported resources	Falling foreign input prices often lead to increases in AS as businesses have the confidence to increase production (and vice versa).
Market power	The ability to avoid the costs of competition often leads to increases in AS as businesses have the confidence to increase production (and vice versa).
Changes in productivity	An increase in the productivity of workers (say, through increased training or added technology) often leads to increases in AS as businesses increase production (and vice versa).
Changes in the legal environment	Legislation that favors property rights, for example, often leads to increases in AS as businesses have the confidence to increase production (and vice versa).
Government regulations	Fewer government regulations mean lower production costs, which often leads to increases in AS as businesses have the confidence to increase production (and vice versa).
Business taxes/subsidies	When business taxes are low and/or subsidies rise, AS increases because businesses have the confidence to increase production (and vice versa).

Demand and Supply Shocks

Occasionally events occur that are not predicted by the regular movement of AS and AD as outlined by the determinants listed above. A war or a recession overseas, a natural disaster, or a collapse of a housing price bubble all have unexpected impacts on the macroeconomy. Examples of these shocks and their effects are listed in the following chart.

Demand shock:	How it affects AD:
Capital investment boom (or bust)	Increases (or decreases) investment (I)
Rise (or fall) of the interest rate	Decreases (or increases) investment (I) or consumption (C)
Consumer boom (or bust) in the country of one of our major trading partners	Increases (or decreases) net exports (X –M)
Rise (or fall) in the exchange rate	Decreases (or increases) net exports (X – M)

Supply shock:	How it affects AS:
An unexpected rise (or fall) in the price of essential inputs	Oil is used in the production process of almost everything, and so an increase in the price of oil has large repercussions throughout the economy, thus shifting AS to the left. A decrease in the price of oil would shift AS to the right.
The invention of a new technology (or sudden absence of technology)	The invention of the Internet vastly increased the productivity of workers, shifting AS to the right. Likewise, a natural disaster that cuts off electricity and access to servers decreases productivity, shifting AS to the left.

Shifting the Curves

The effects of these determinants and shocks are shown on the following graphs. *Graphs A* and *B* show an increase in AD and a decrease in AD, respectively. *Graphs C* and *D* show an increase in AS and a decrease in AS, respectively. Note the new equilibrium created by each shift, and the resulting changes in price level and output reflected on each graph.

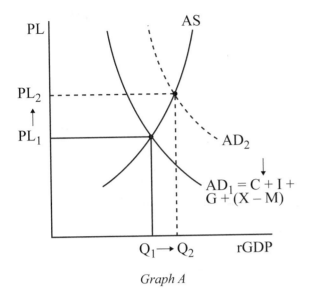

Graph A

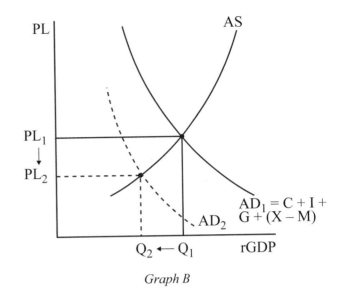

Graph B

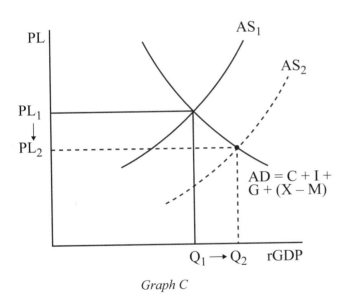

Graph C

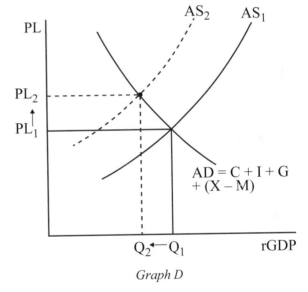

Graph D

Sometimes the AS curve is shown as a curve with three distinct sections; this is simply a more specific version of the AS curve, and it makes the status of the economy more clear. These specific sections are labeled in *Graph E* below:

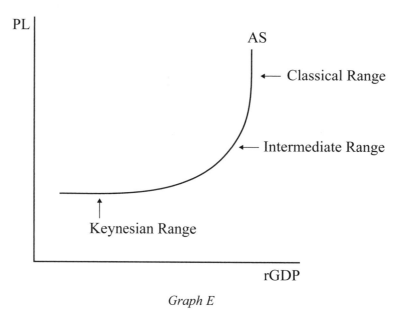

Graph E

When the equilibrium is in the **Keynesian** section, the economy is in a recession, or worse, a depression. This is synonymous with saying that the economy is operating inside its production possibility curve, or close to the trough of the business cycle. Factories are operating at less than capacity, a significant percentage of office space is vacant, and unemployment is higher than desired. Notice in *Graph F* below that aggregate demand can increase, which increases GDP, but the price level does not change when the economy is operating in this part of the AS.

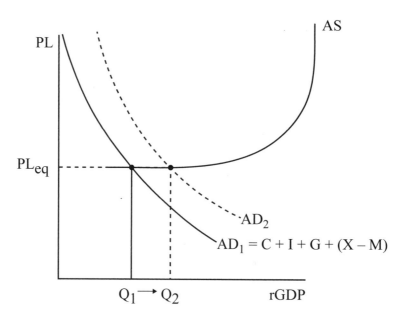

Graph F: The Keynesian Range

An equilibrium in the **intermediate** section reflects a more healthy economy where increases in GDP correspond with acceptable increases in the price level, as shown in *Graph G*.

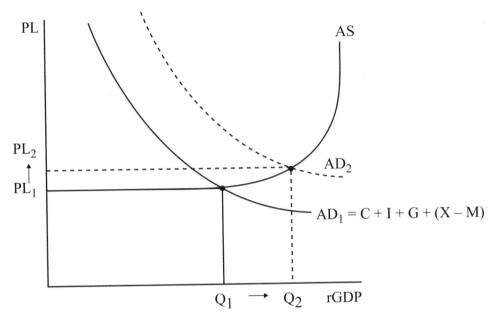

Graph G: The Intermediate Range

Equilibrium in the **classical** part of the AS curve reflects the situation where the economy is at full production and any further increases in AD will only drive up the price level – it is not possible to produce any more goods or services because the economy is already operating at full throttle. This is shown in *Graph H*.

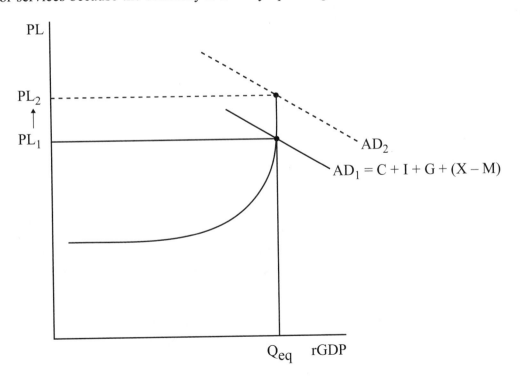

Graph H: The Classical Range

The classical and Keynesian parts of the AS curve represent the two views about macroeconomics in general: classical and Keynesian economics. The goal of both policies is the same: increased production at the natural rate of unemployment and a stable price level. How they reach this goal is different, however. The **classical viewpoint** states that markets should be able to operate free from any intervention – no fiscal or monetary policy. Prices are free to fluctuate as needed to return any imbalance in the economy to equilibrium. Changes in productivity, and thus policies that increase AS in the long-run, will improve society when needed. **Keynesianism**, named after John Maynard Keynes, is the theory that the means to an appropriate equilibrium is via changes to AD in the short-run and that the government should engage in monetary and/or fiscal policy when the need arises. Thus, the government should encourage or influence changes to C, I and/or G in order to shift AD in the correct direction. While classicalists think that prices and wages are flexible, Keynesians believe prices do not adjust downward easily – rather, they are "sticky". Keynesian economists believe this makes it difficult for the economy to self-correct and thus government needs to step in temporarily.

Long-Run Aggregate Supply vs. Short-Run Aggregate Supply

Up to this point, the AS we've discussed is a short-run concept: a snapshot of where the economy is currently. In order to understand where an economy's current equilibrium is relative to its potential, it is necessary to include a long-run aggregate supply curve in our AS/AD graph.

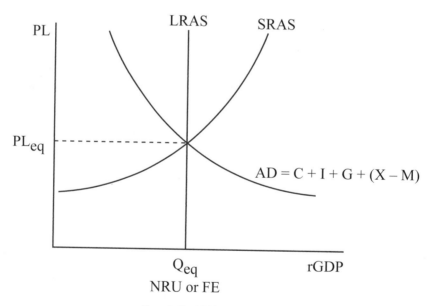

Graph I: AS/AD with LRAS

This **long-run aggregate supply** (or LRAS) shown in *Graph I* is a measure of potential output, synonymous with the idea of the production possibilities frontier from Unit I. It is drawn as a vertical line because it is independent of price level – regardless of changes in the price level, LRAS is fixed at a certain level of output. This output level is determined by:

1) the quality and quantity of human and physical capital available;
2) the productivity of the factors of production (land, labor and capital); and
3) the availability of technology.

Notice these are the same determinants that shift the production possibilities curve. In addition, the assumption is that at this level of output the economy will be at the natural rate of unemployment, meaning that everyone who wants a job has one. Only frictional unemployment will exist. As a result, often AS/AD graphs include notation where the LRAS intercepts the x-axis that that point represents full employment. This can be abbreviated as FE (for full employment) or NRU (for natural rate of unemployment) or any other way that communicates the idea.

Recessionary and Inflationary Gaps

If equilibrium at the LRAS is viewed as the goal of macroeconomic policy, what happens when the equilibrium is either short of or beyond LRAS?

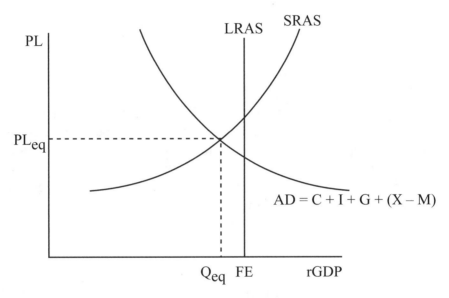

Graph J: Recessionary Gap

In the case of the former, this is called a **recessionary gap** and is shown in *Graph J*. The "gap" is the difference between Q_{eq} and FE. In order to return to full capacity, either AD, AS or both need to shift to the right. For example, suppose real GDP is less than potential real GDP as shown by the location of the LRAS; this also means that employment is low (the unemployment rate is greater than the natural rate of unemployment or $Q_{eg} <$ FE). As people are looking for jobs, they tend to settle for a lower wage. This decrease in input prices will shift the AS curve to the right, causing the price level to decrease. Lower price levels will increase consumption, thus shifting AD to the right. This process will continue until the economy readjusts to its LRAS.

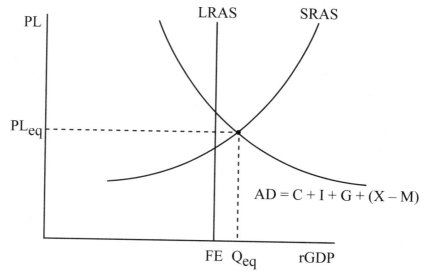

Graph K: Inflationary Gap

With an **inflationary gap**, shown in *Graph K*, real GDP is greater than potential real GDP (or $Q_{eq} > FE$). While this sounds as if it should not be a problem (what is wrong with producing more than expected?), it can lead to inflation beyond the acceptable 2-3% range. With an inflationary gap, employment is high and there are not enough bodies to fill the available job openings (this is another way of saying the unemployment rate is less than the natural rate of unemployment). Employers are forced to raise wages to attract new workers. High wages increase input costs, which shift AS to the left. The price level rises, lowering consumption and shifting AD to the left. Eventually, the economy will realign itself with its long-run equilibrium.

The Phillips Curve

Another way to show the relationship between unemployment and inflation is to use the **Phillips Curve**. The short-run version (or, SRPC) looks like *Graph L*:

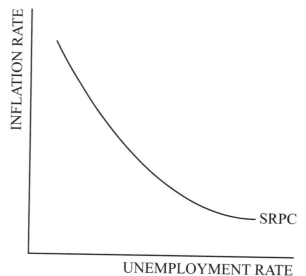

Graph L: Short-Run Phillips Curve

Notice that as inflation increases, unemployment decreases and vice versa. When AD shifts left or right, the changes in price level and unemployment are reflected by movement along the SRPC. When AS shifts, the changes in price level and unemployment cause the SRPC to shift in the opposite direction. These relationships are shown in *Graphs M* and *N* respectively. One trick to understanding how the change in unemployment as shown by the SRPC relates to changes in rGDP and the AS/AD graph is to remember that as rGDP increases, more resources, including labor, are employed. Thus, as the employment rate increases, unemployment must necessarily decrease (and vice versa).

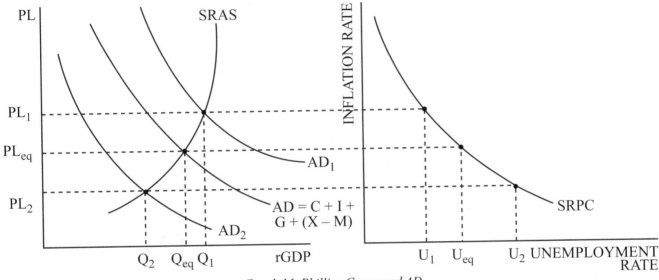

Graph M: Phillips Curve and AD

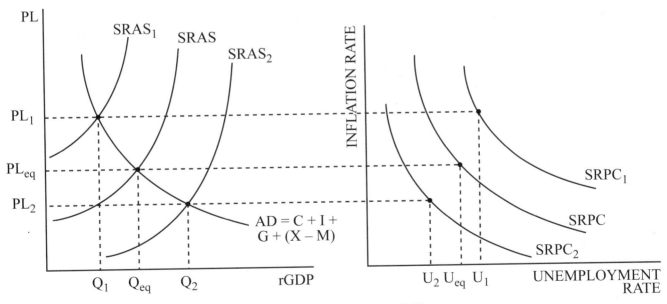

Graph N: Phillips Curve and AS

This theory about the short-run tradeoff between inflation and unemployment shown in the short-run Phillips Curve was widely accepted until the 1970s. At that time, the U.S. economy experienced stagflation

– high unemployment and high inflation at the same time (see Unit VI) – a situation unexplainable by the SRPC. Economists have come to agree that while the SRPC has its limitations, the idea behind the **long-run Phillips Curve** (LRPC) holds true: inflation has no effect on unemployment in the long-run. Thus, the LRPC is a vertical line at the natural rate of unemployment. See *Graph O* for this depiction.

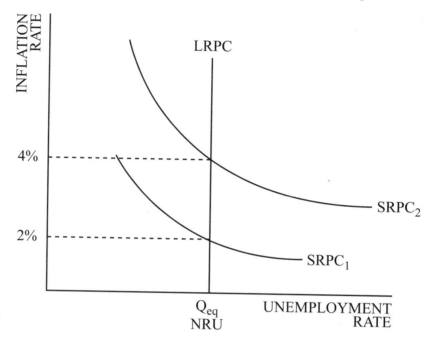

Graph O: The Phillips Curve

Changes in the inflation rate only cause movements along the LRPC, not a movement of the LRPC itself. For example, suppose AD has increased, temporarily increasing output, employment and the price level. Eventually, this will cause nominal wages to rise (as workers feel more confident in asking for a raise), which leads to a decrease in AS. Profits fall, workers are laid off, and the economy is back to its orignal employment level (that is, its natural rate of unemployment). Thus, only the price level has changed; the level of employment has remained constant in the long run. The opposite is true, of course, as well.

Loanable Funds Market

Just as there is a market for oranges or oil (or any other good or service), there is a market for borrowing money from lending institutions. This is the **loanable funds market**, and it is where funds for capital purchases are obtained. The loanable funds market is represented on *Graph P*.

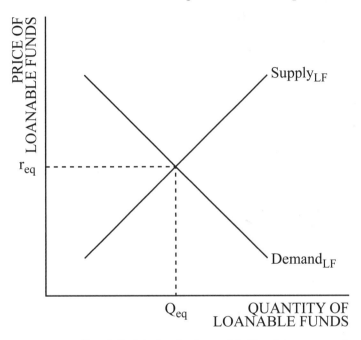

Graph P: Market for Loanable Funds

The price of loanable funds is the "**real interest rate**, shown here as "r". This is the price of borrowing money, adjusted for inflation. It assumes that borrowers (in this case, the individuals, business and government entities who would like to take out a loan) and the lenders (the savers – those who make deposits in banks and other lending institutions) take into account the inflation rate when making decisions. Thus the real interest rate is used in the loanable funds market (rather than the nominal interest rate which is used in the money market).

This market works like any other supply/demand market: when the demand for loans increases, the quantity of loanable funds exchanged in the market and the price of such funds – the real interest rate – increases. When people increase savings, the supply of loanable funds increases, and thus real interest rates fall and the equilibrium quantity increases. The opposite is true for decreases in demand and supply. These changes are shown in *Graph Q* on the following page.

One thing to keep in mind: when we discuss real interest rates from a domestic perspective, interest is the cost of borrowing money. High interest rates discourage borrowing as shown in *Graph Q*. However, from an international perspective, interest is an income opportunity. High interest rates attract investment from abroad, and countries will purchase financial assets in those countries where interest rates are highest in order to take advantage of the opportunity to earn interest.

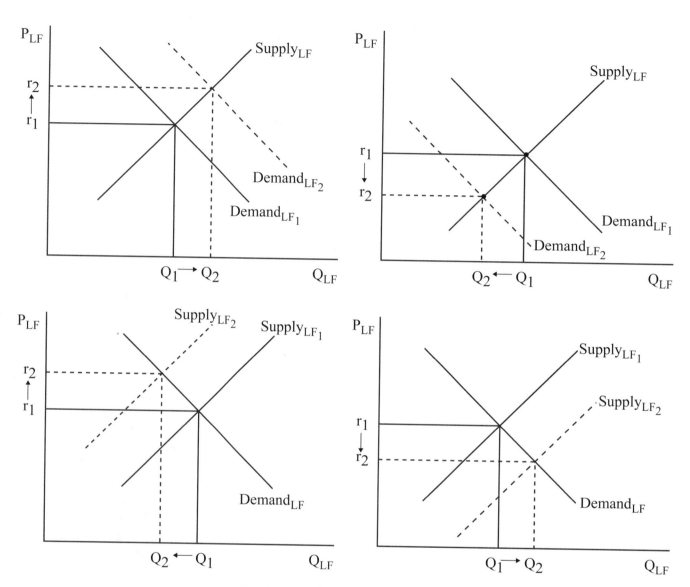

Graph Q: Market for Loanable Funds

Crowding Out and Crowding In

The loanable funds graph illustrates the concept of "**crowding out**" that was mentioned in Unit VII. The theory is that as real interest rates rise – either from an increase in the demand for loanable funds (say, the government needs to use deficit spending in order to finance a new project) or a decrease in the supply (private savers are discouraged from making deposits in lending institutions) – private borrowers will be "crowded out" of the market because they will not be willing or able to borrow at the current higher rates. The opposite can be true as well – as real interest rates fall, "**crowding in**" happens as borrowers rush to take advantage of new low rates.

As with many macroeconomic theories, there is debate as to how much crowding out occurs as a result of government borrowing. If the deficit spending occurs as part of expansionary fiscal policy in order to address a recession, then there probably is not much private borrowing taking place anyway. However, if the government is borrowing during times when private investment is occurring, there is a greater risk of crowding out those private investors. At that point, one must ask if public investment is as effective in encouraging economic growth as is private investment. The answer determines how large a worry the idea of "crowding out" really is.

Time Value of Money

Another topic of relevance is the **time value of money**. As interest rates rise, savers earn more interest on their deposits. For example, if $1000 is deposited into a savings account at 10% interest, one year from now it will be worth $1100. This incentive leads the supply of loanable funds to shift to the right. Borrowers of loanable funds, though, will have to pay more for the privilege of borrowing. For example:

To calculate the time value of money, use the following equation:

Future value = present value $(1 + \text{interest rate})^n$, n being the time period in question.

A firm borrows $1000 for one year at an annual interest rate of 10%. At the end of the year, the firm will have to pay the lender $1100 – the original amount owed plus the $100 in interest. This is the future value. The firm must realize, though, that the value of this money now is really $910 ($1000 divided by 1.10). This is the present value.

If the interest rate were only 4%, then the present value of $1000 spent or earned one year from now would be about $960 ($1000/1.04).

When interest rates are low, the higher the present value of money, and the more likely borrowers will use these funds to increase investment. When interest rates are high, borrowers are less likely to use the loanable funds market, and investment may decrease.

To Sum It Up

Putting the macroeconomic graphs together gives economists a vibrant picture of the economy. Suppose there is a recession and the central bank increases the supply of money with easy monetary policy. This lowers nominal interest rates, which increases the quantity of investment demanded. Borrowers go to the loanable funds market and borrow money, which leads to increases in investment and some big-ticket consumption items. Increases in investment and consumption lead to an increase in AD, which increases GDP and the price level rises to an acceptable 2-3%. The opposite is also true. *Graph R* shows this chain of events.

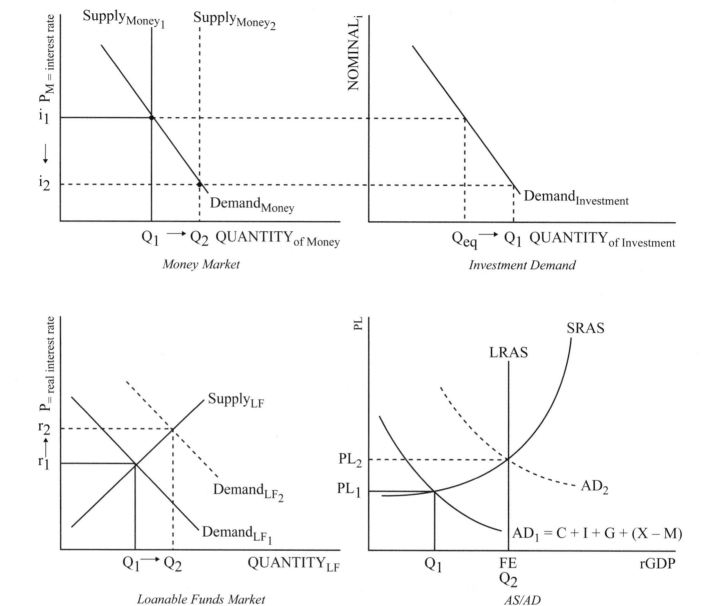

Graph R: The Macroeconomy

Thus, the easy monetary policy shown in the money market graph has led to an increase in AD and cured the recessionary gap by the end of the transmission process. Problem solved!

Important terms:

- Aggregate supply
- Aggregate demand
- Wealth effect
- Interest rate effect
- Foreign purchases effect
- Demand shock
- Supply shock
- Keynesian vs. classical economic theory

- Long-run aggregate supply
- Recessionary gap
- Inflationary gap
- Phillips curve
- Loanable funds market
- Crowding out/crowding in
- Time value of money

MACROECONOMICS: UNIT IX

MULTIPLE-CHOICE QUESTIONS

1. If the federal government engages in a spending plan that results in a deficit, what will be the effect on each of the following?

	Loanable Funds Market	Real Interest Rate
(A)	increase in demand	increase
(B)	decrease in demand	decrease
(C)	increase in demand	decrease
(D)	decrease in supply	decrease
(E)	increase in supply	increase

2. Which of the following is the most likely outcome of simultaneous contractionary fiscal policy and contractionary monetary policy?

	Interest Rate	Price Level	Real Output
(A)	increase	increase	increase
(B)	increase	decrease	decrease
(C)	decrease	decrease	decrease
(D)	indeterminate	decrease	decrease
(E)	indeterminate	increase	increase

Questions 3-5 refer to the graph below:

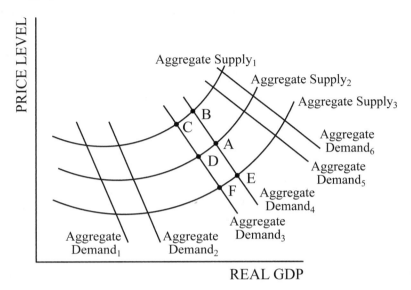

3. If this economy is nearing full employment levels of output and consumers suddenly take a pessimistic view toward the future and businesses experience a decrease in expectations of profitability, the most likely shift to describe this series of events is:

   (A) aggregate demand$_6$ to aggregate demand$_5$
   (B) aggregate demand$_3$ to aggregate demand$_4$
   (C) aggregate demand$_2$ to aggregate demand$_1$
   (D) aggregate supply$_1$ to aggregate supply$_2$
   (E) aggregate supply$_2$ to aggregate supply$_1$

4. Beginning at equilibrium point A, in the graph, contractionary monetary policy could be demonstrated by a single curve shift that would result in a new equilibrium at point:

   (A) B
   (B) C
   (C) D
   (D) E
   (E) F

5. Beginning at equilibrium point A, in the graph, a series of natural disasters such as floods, hurricanes, and tornadoes could be demonstrated by a single curve shift that would result in a new equilibrium at point:

(A) B
(B) C
(C) D
(D) E
(E) F

_____

6. Which of the following explains the downward slope of an aggregate demand curve?

(A) increasing price level effect
(B) foreign purchases effect
(C) interest rate effect
(D) diminishing marginal utility effect
(E) production possibility effect

7. Which of the following will decrease short-run aggregate supply?

(A) a decrease in consumer optimism
(B) an increase in business optimism
(C) a decrease in price level
(D) an increase in business taxes
(E) an increase in government spending

8. If you believe there is a short-run tradeoff between inflation and unemployment, which of the following economic concepts would be the basis of your belief?

(A) Okun's law
(B) Phillips curve
(C) Gresham's law
(D) Monetary rule
(E) Keynesian economics

9. In the graph below

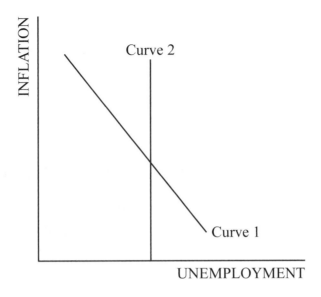

(A) curve 1 is a short-run Phillips curve.
(B) curve 1 is a long-run Phillips curve.
(C) curve 2 is a short-run Phillips curve.
(D) curve 1 is a long-run aggregate supply curve.
(E) curve 2 is a long-run aggregate supply curve.

10. Limitations of expansionary fiscal policy would include all of the following EXCEPT:

(A) crowding out
(B) net export effect
(C) demand-pull inflation
(D) offsetting savings (Ricardian equivalence)
(E) uncertain time lags

11. If an increase in deficit spending by the federal government results in an increase in the real interest rate, the resulting effect on the economy will be

(A) an increase in consumer spending only.
(B) an increase in investment spending only.
(C) a decrease in consumer spending and a decrease in investment spending.
(D) a decrease in consumer spending and an increase in investment spending.
(E) a decrease in investment spending only.

Questions 12-14 refer to the graph below:

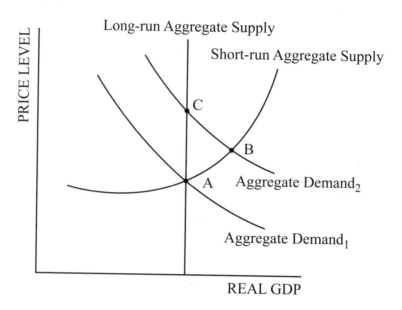

12. In the graph above, expansionary fiscal policy would be demonstrated by a movement from

   (A) point B to point C.
   (B) point C to point B.
   (C) point C to point A.
   (D) point B to point A.
   (E) point A to point B.

13. In the graph above, contractionary monetary policy would be demonstrated by a movement from

   (A) point B to point A.
   (B) point A to point B.
   (C) point C to point A.
   (D) point C to point B.
   (E) point B to point C.

14. In the graph above, if the economy is presently operating at point B, in the absence of any fiscal or monetary policy action, we could conclude that

   (A) point B is the short-run equilibrium and long-run equilibrium will be established at point B.
   (B) point B is the short-run equilibrium and long-run equilibrium will be established at point A.
   (C) point B is the short-run equilibrium and long-run equilibrium will be established at point C.
   (D) point C is the short-run equilibrium and long-run equilibrium will be established at point C.
   (E) point A is the short-run equilibrium and long-run equilibrium will be established at point B.

15. Which of the following will decrease aggregate demand?

(A) an increase in government spending
(B) an increase in business optimism
(C) an increase in the price level
(D) an increase in taxes
(E) a decrease in taxes

16. In the country of Econostan, an island nation previously closed to contact with the rest of the world, the citizens tend to spend 80 percent of any increase in income. Based on this information, if a traveler from outside were to visit and spend $10,000 on a newly produced product, the GDP of Econostan could increase by a maximum of

(A) $5,000
(B) $9,000
(C) $10,000
(D) $45,000
(E) $50,000

17. A simultaneous and equally sized tax decrease and spending decrease by the federal government would have which of the following effects?

(A) increase the price level and increase real output
(B) increase the price level and decrease real output
(C) decrease the price level and decrease real output
(D) decrease the price level and increase real output
(E) have no effect on the price level or real output

18. An outward shift (to the right) on a production possibility curve would be most closely synonymous with a (an)

(A) increase in long-run aggregate supply.
(B) decrease in long-run aggregate supply.
(C) increase in aggregate demand.
(D) decrease in aggregate demand.
(E) decrease in the capacity utilization rate.

19. A series of natural disasters like fires, floods, and earthquakes in the short-run could cause

   (A) demand shocks and inflation.
   (B) supply shocks and inflation.
   (C) demand shocks and deflation.
   (D) supply shocks and deflation.
   (E) demand shocks and stagflation.

20. A commonly cited shortcoming of the effectiveness of fiscal policy is that

   (A) the interest rate effect and the foreign purchases effect tend to support the policy action.
   (B) the interest rate effect and the foreign purchases effect tend to run counter to the policy action.
   (C) the interest rate effect runs counter to the policy and the foreign purchases effect tends to support the policy action.
   (D) the interest rate effect supports the policy and the foreign purchases effect runs counter to the policy action.
   (E) time lags that exist between implementation and effect are uncertain and varied.

21. Based on the findings of the Council of Economic Advisors, the complex multiplier is

   (A) greater than the simple spending multiplier.
   (B) less than the simple spending multiplier.
   (C) equal to the simple spending multiplier.
   (D) equal to the reserve requirement.
   (E) equal to the simple money multiplier.

22. Cost-push inflation is caused by

   (A) an increase in aggregate demand and an increase in aggregate supply.
   (B) a decrease in aggregate demand only.
   (C) an increase in aggregate supply only.
   (D) a decrease in aggregate supply only.
   (E) a decrease in aggregate demand and an increase in aggregate supply.

23. In the graph below, the intersection of which of the aggregate demand curves with the existing aggregate supply curve demonstrates an economy in the most severe recession?

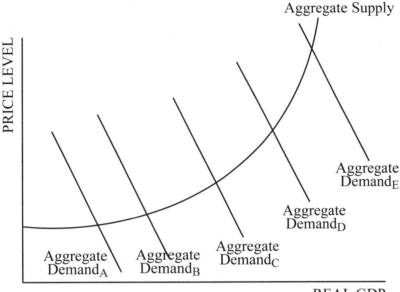

(A) A
(B) B
(C) C
(D) D
(E) E

24. Which of the following represents a valid potential limitation of the effectiveness of fiscal policy and monetary policy respectively?

(A) crowding out; a weak link between interest rate changes and investment changes
(B) a weak link between interest rate changes and investment changes; crowding out
(C) the inability of Congress to decide on the correct fiscal policy to use; the inability of the Federal Reserve to decide on the correct monetary policy to use
(D) crowding out; crowding in
(E) crowding in; crowding out

25. In the graph below, crowding out is demonstrated by which of the following shifts?

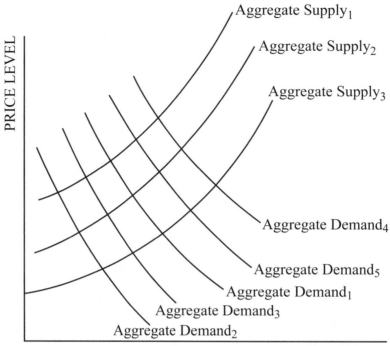

(A) Aggregate Demand$_1$ to Aggregate Demand$_4$ to Aggregate Demand$_5$
(B) Aggregate Demand$_1$ to Aggregate Demand$_5$ to Aggregate Demand$_4$
(C) Aggregate Demand$_1$ to Aggregate Demand$_2$ to Aggregate Demand$_3$
(D) Aggregate Demand$_1$ to Aggregate Demand$_3$ to Aggregate Demand$_2$
(E) Aggregate Supply$_1$ to Aggregate Supply$_2$ to Aggregate Supply$_3$

26. The effect of a simultaneous decrease in government spending and a decrease in the money supply would be correctly shown in which of the graphs below?

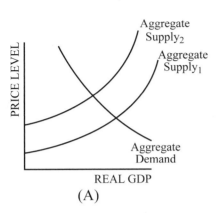

(A)

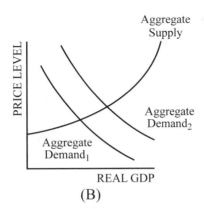

(B)

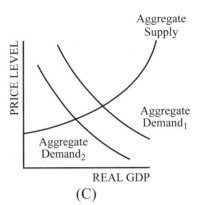

(C)

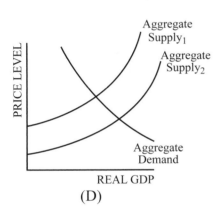

(D)

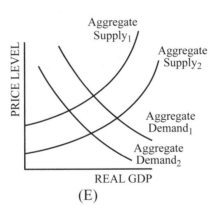

(E)

(A) A
(B) B
(C) C
(D) D
(E) E

27. The long-run aggregate supply curve is most similar to the

(A) Phillips curve.
(B) Laffer curve.
(C) aggregate demand curve.
(D) production possibilities curve.
(E) investment demand curve.

28. Which of the following correctly sums up the difference between the classical and Keynesian views of macroeconomic stability?

   (A) The classical view is that the economy is inherently unstable and needs active counter-cyclical policies to provide stability, while the Keynesian view is that the best course of action is to allow market forces (through flexible wages and prices) to correct for any short-term economic fluctuations.

   (B) The Keynesian view is that the economy is inherently unstable and needs active counter-cyclical policies to provide stability, while the classical view is that the best course of action is to allow market forces (through flexible wages and prices) to correct for any short-term economic fluctuations.

   (C) The Keynesian view favors the active use of fiscal policy to correct for short-term economic fluctuations in the economy, while the classical view favors the active use of monetary policy to correct for short-term economic fluctuations in the economy.

   (D) Both the Keynesian and classical views support the idea that the economy is inherently unstable and needs active counter-cyclical policies to provide economic stability.

   (E) Both the Keynesian and classical views support the idea that the best course of action is to allow market forces (through flexible wages and prices) to correct for any short-term economic fluctuations.

29. Which of the graphs below demonstrates an economy experiencing long-run economic growth?

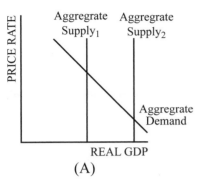
(A)

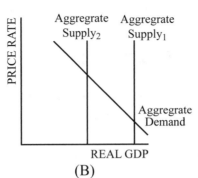
(B)

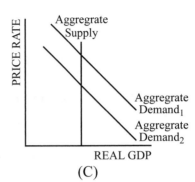
(C)

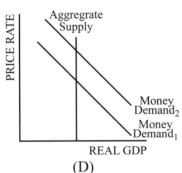
(D)

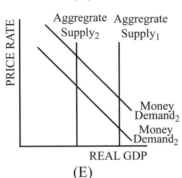
(E)

(A) A
(B) B
(C) C
(D) D
(E) E

30. The concept of crowding out (or crowding in) is generally regarded as a limitation of the effectiveness of

(A) fiscal policy only.
(B) monetary policy only.
(C) both fiscal and monetary policy.
(D) incomes policy.
(E) open-market operations.

MACROECONOMICS: UNIT IX

FREE-RESPONSE QUESTIONS

1. Assume the following figures represent the existing condition in the U.S. economy:

Unemployment rate	6% 4-5%
Inflation rate	6% 2-3%
Annual rate of real GDP growth	3% 2-3.5%

(a) Is the economy facing any economic problems as described by the data above? Explain.

(b) Draw an aggregate supply and aggregate demand diagram to demonstrate the effect of the federal government instituting a massive new tax increase on consumers and businesses in the economy described above.

(c) Describe the effect of the Federal Reserve decreasing the money supply on each of the following:
   (i) interest rate
   (ii) the level of output
   (iii) the level of unemployment
   (iv) the price level

a) High inflation, healthy inflation is about 2-3%

b)

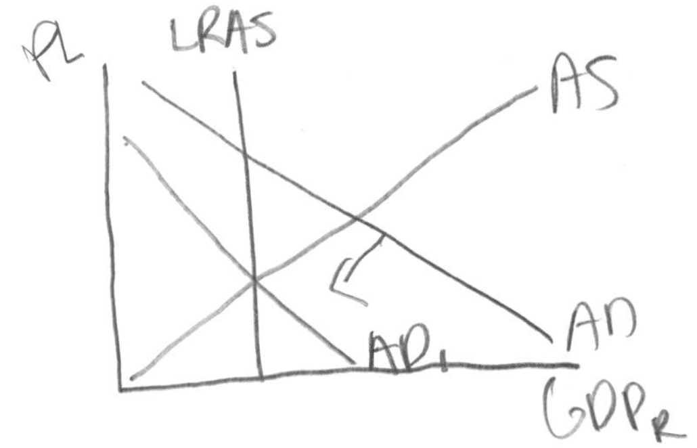

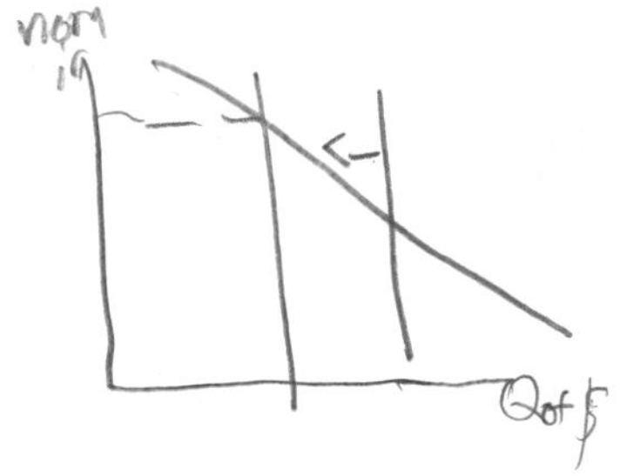

c) i) ↑
   ii) ↓
   iii) ↑
   iv) ↓

2. Draw a correctly labeled short-run Phillips curve and then redraw the curve to demonstrate the effect of each of the following:

(a) a leftward shift of the aggregate demand curve
(b) a rightward shift of the aggregate supply curve

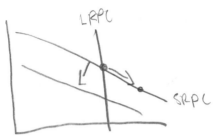

3. Draw a correctly labeled loanable funds graph and then redraw the curve to demonstrate each of the following:

   (a) an increase in deficit spending by the federal government
   (b) an increased desire on the part of consumers to save for their retirement

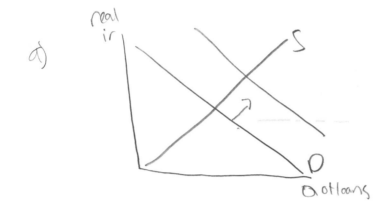

MACROECONOMICS: UNIT X

INTERNATIONAL ECONOMICS

In the previous units, much of the discussion was about GDP and its components. Left out of those discussions were net exports – the $(X - M)$ of the equation $C + I + G + (X - M) = GDP$. This unit attempts to explain how the rest of the world impacts our economy, as well as how our economy interacts with the rest of the world.

Remember that in order for economic growth to take place, goods and services need to be produced. However, production isn't enough – if there isn't sufficient demand, these goods and services will pile up as inventories. While our domestic demand (the $C + I + G$ in GDP) is vital to ensuring this does not happen, our foreign market plays an increasingly important role in maintaining the health of the economy.

American trade with China receives a lot of attention in the media. Total trade (imports and exports) with the European Union and Canada, though, are larger in terms of dollars spent, ranking first and second respectively[1]. And, while we want China and the countries of the European Union to buy our products, what good would a pile of Chinese currency (the renminbi) or the currency of the European Union (the euro) do us? Not much. Thus, other countries must convert their currencies to the American dollar in order to purchase American goods, and we must convert our currency to theirs in order to import foreign goods. This exchanging of currencies takes place in the **foreign exchange market**.

The foreign exchange market (or FOREX market) exists in cities around the world, New York, London and Hong Kong being the most important. It is in these markets that countries, companies and individuals exchange one currency based on its value relative to another currency (for example, the value of euros to dollars, or dollars to yen). Like the other markets we have discussed, the FX market has its own supply and demand graphs:

---

[1] Mexico and Japan round out the top five trading partners of the United States.

301

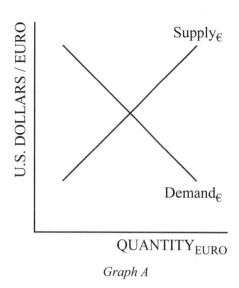

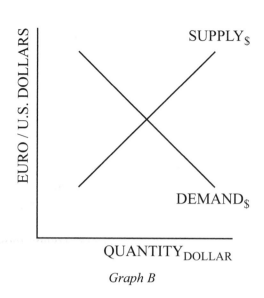

Graph A   *Graph B*

Notice that there are two graphs here, as the value of one currency affects the value of the other. The price axis for the first graph (*Graph A*) is labeled USD/EUR; this reflects the value of euros in terms of dollars. The second graph (*Graph B*), the market for dollars, reflects the price of the dollar in terms of euros (EUR/USD).

Determinants for Shifting Curves

Like other supply/demand graphs, there are specific **determinants** that cause the curves to shift:

A country's relative income	As people grow wealthier overseas, they tend to want to import more. In order to buy American goods, they exchange their foreign currency for U.S. dollars in the FX market. This means that the demand for the U.S. dollar would rise relative to the overseas currency, and the dollar's value would appreciate. At the same time, the supply of the foreign currency in the FX market increases (because foreigners are getting rid of their currency), depreciating the value of the foreign currency. As incomes fall overseas, the opposite occurs: imports fall, and demand for the foreign currency falls as well.
A country's relative prices	If inflation is occurring here, it might be cheaper to import foreign goods as substitutes. Thus, American demand for foreign currency rises (and its value appreciates), and the supply of U.S. dollars made available in the FX market increases (the value of the U.S. dollar depreciates). The opposite is true as well.
A country's relative interest rates	Overseas investment will flow to the country where it receives the highest rate of return (where interest rates are highest). If interest rates are higher in Europe relative to the U.S., the demand for the euro will increase (causing the value of the euro to appreciate) as Americans buy European financial assets. The supply of U.S. dollars will increase, as Americans want to trade their dollars for euros (and the value of the dollar will depreciate). If interest rates are higher here than in Europe, the opposite will occur.

Changes in tastes	If it becomes trendier to wear imported shoes, for example, then the demand for foreign goods will increase, and the demand for foreign currency will increase as well. The value of the foreign currency will appreciate. The domestic currency will depreciate in value, as the supply made available for trade on the FX market will increase. If domestically-made goods are desired, the opposite will occur in the FX market.
Speculation	In the 1970's, about 80% of FX transactions were for the purchase of goods and services. The remainder was speculative, meaning that FX traders were looking to profit based on the trade of the currencies themselves as they appreciated and depreciated in the FX market. Today, those percentages have flipped – 80% of FX trade is speculation. Following the maxim of "buy low, sell high," speculators attempt to purchase currencies when their relative values have depreciated and sell them when they have appreciated.

Assume that Americans want to purchase more iPhones. Even though iPhones are produced by an American company, the components are built primarily in China. Apple has to pay its Chinese partners for the assembly of the iPhone, and it must pay in Chinese currency. So, as American demand for iPhones rises, so does the demand for the renminbi needed to purchase the components. Thus, the demand curve for renminbi in the FX market shifts to the right (*Graph C*). At the same time, Americans are trading U.S. dollars to purchase renminbi. The supply of U.S. dollars made available in the FX market increases, shifting the supply curve to the right (*Graph D*). Thus, the FX graphs with the appropriate shifts look like this:

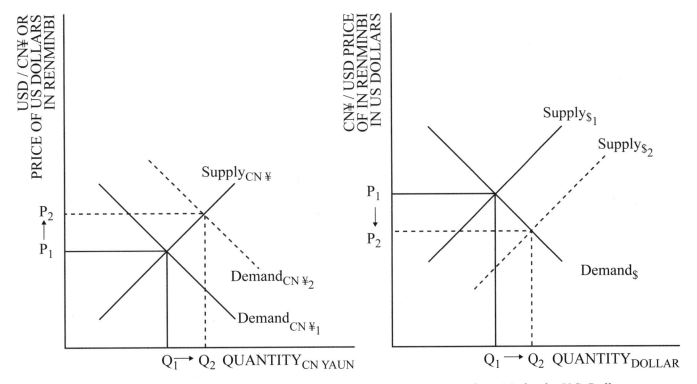

Graph C: Market for Renminbi   *Graph D: Market for U.S. Dollar*

Keep in mind that the FX market is a relative one – there needs to be two graphs in order to compare the movement of one currency to another.

Tariffs, Quotas and Embargoes

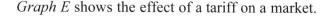

As foreign companies compete with domestic ones, the global price for a good can be less than what domestic producers want to charge. The political response to this difference might be the enactment of a tariff, a quota, or an embargo.

A **tariff** is a tax on an imported good. Early tariffs in U.S. history were instituted solely with the intention of raising revenue for the new government; later, tariffs were legislated with the intention of protecting domestic markets. As the foreign good becomes more expensive relative to its domestic version, the hope is that the higher price will cause domestic consumers to look for domestic substitutes.

Graph E shows the effect of a tariff on a market.

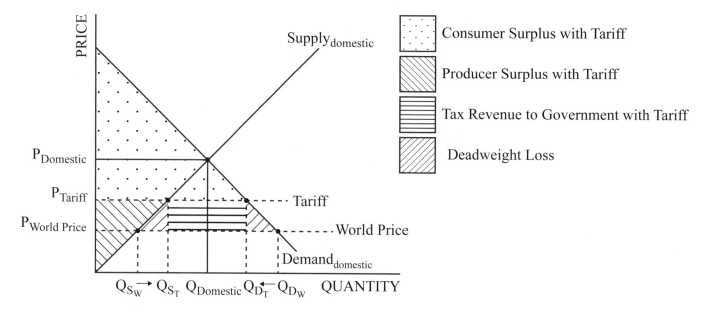

Q_{S_W} = Quantity supplied at the world price

Q_{S_T} = Quantity supplied at the tariff price

$Q_{Domestic}$ = Equilibrium with no foreign trade

Q_{D_T} = Quantity demanded at tariff price

Q_{D_W} = Quantity demanded at the world price

Graph E: Market with Tariff

Notice that there is a perfectly elastic international supply curve that is established by the world price. This world price is below the domestic equilibrium price, which is why consumers benefit from open trade but producers are unhappy as they lose market share to overseas producers. The tariff price is placed between the domestic equilibrium price and the world price. Because the tariff price is higher than the world price, quantity demanded decreases and quantity supplied increases, making domestic suppliers happy (although not as happy as they would be if all international trade were halted). The government receives the revenue from the tariff, making the government happy. However, consumers are hurt by the tariff, as higher prices and deadweight loss are the result.

A **quota** is a limit on the number of goods that can be imported into a country. The hope is that consumers will purchase more domestically-made goods because there is a limited supply of the foreign-made ones. Notice on *Graph F* that the supply of imported goods is restricted with a quota.

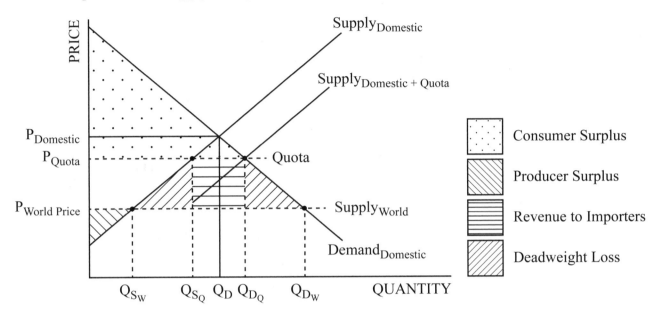

Q_{S_W} = Quantity supplied at the world price

Q_{S_Q} = Quantity supplied at the quota price

Q_D = Equilibrium with no foreign trade

Q_{D_Q} = Quantity demanded at quota price

Q_{D_W} = Quantity demanded at the world price

Graph F: Market with Quota

Instead of the government collecting revenue as it did from the tariff, here the higher revenue brought in by the quota goes to those importers lucky enough to distribute the good in question.

An **embargo** is a restriction on trade with a foreign country. For example, to protest the government of Fidel Castro in Cuba, the U.S. government began an economic embargo of Cuba in 1962. The graph for an embargo (*Graph G*) shows a leftward shift of the supply curve as fewer goods are available for purchase in the domestic market.

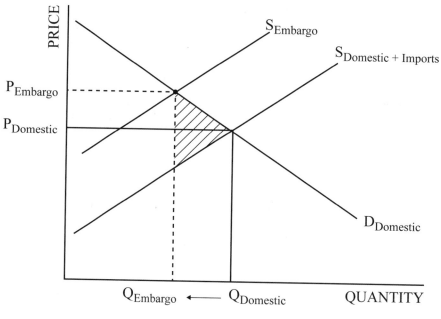

Graph G: Embargo

Why might a government want to use these protections? There are a number of arguments made for and against protectionism:

Argument:	Pro:	Con:
Infant Industries	A certain industry might be new to a country and have difficulty competing with more established industries abroad that benefit from economies of scale.	It is hard to identify when and how much help a new industry might need, and it is unpopular to end support once the industry is up and running.
National Security	A country would not want to be at risk of lacking necessary technology in the case of war; those industries need to be encouraged, and thus protected, at home.	Given comparative advantage and economies of scale, very few technologies are solely produced in one place; the likelihood of being completely cut-off in a time of war is usually overblown.
Jobs	As labor costs decrease in other countries, domestic industries might move overseas, taking those jobs with them to other countries. Thus, those industries should receive certain protections in order to keep local jobs.	If one industry is protected, and the price of its output is now higher, the potential exists to hurt other domestic industries that depend on its production. For example, if the domestic steel industry is protected and its price is higher than the world price, local industries that buy steel will now have to pay a higher price for their inputs, potentially costing jobs. Whose job is more important? Hard to say…

Dumping	Countries whose production costs are lower can flood overseas markets with cheap goods, wiping out those local overseas industries.	It is difficult to prove which countries are maliciously "dumping" their goods and which ones simply benefit from economies of scale.
Cultural Issues	It is necessary to protect the heritage of a country when threatened due to competition. For example, strict rules exist regarding the production of chocolate in European countries in order to ensure the consumer is receiving authentic "Belgian" or "Swiss" chocolate.	Care must be taken to make sure the prized domestic industry is not simply inefficient.
Environmental or Health Reasons	Imports from certain countries might be banned if they contain high-fructose corn syrup or are genetically-modified products. Likewise, products from countries with less-strict (or unenforced) environmental standards are discouraged.	Care must be taken to make sure the prized domestic industry is not simply inefficient.

You can see that the decision to enact some form of protection is a complicated one, one that often falls along political lines rather than economical ones.

Comparative and Absolute Advantage

Absolute advantage and **comparative advantage** were discussed in Unit I. These concepts can be used to determine how work should be divided, or which country should produce what goods. Thus, comparative and absolute advantage apply to both microeconomics and macroeconomics.

The following examples show two ways to determine comparative advantage. The first example calculates comparative advantages for individuals; in a later example, we'll calculate comparative advantage for countries. Either method of determining comparative advantage is acceptable – what matters most is that you are able to determine which option has the least opportunity cost, as that determines comparative advantage.

Sam and Bob live in an apartment on campus. Bob is a little bit lazy, and takes his time doing chores around the apartment. Sam, on the other hand, likes to "get things done" – no messing around, no wasting time…

For example, it takes Bob 20 minutes to wash a load of dishes and 75 minutes to cook a chicken dinner. Sam can do the same tasks in 18 minutes and 60 minutes, respectively.

Sam wants to split up the work, but Bob says, "Hey, you're so good at both of them. Why don't you just clean the kitchen and whip up some food while I sit here and watch TV?"

Sam realizes he is the best at both jobs, but he doesn't like having a slouch for a roommate. So, he tells Bob, "Pick one of the jobs to do, and do it, or move out." (It is Sam's apartment, so he can do this). Bob thinks for a minute about this one, and quickly realizes that the opportunity cost of finding a new apartment would definitely be a bigger hassle than sharing jobs. But which job should he do, and which one should Sam do? How does he figure out the answer?

	Washing 1 load of dishes takes this long:	Cooking one chicken dinner takes this long:	
Bob	20 minutes	75 minutes	
Sam	18 minutes	60 minutes	<= Sam has an "absolute advantage" – he does both jobs the fastest. But we want to know who has a "comparative advantage" – who has the least to lose by picking one of these jobs? Whose opportunity cost is the lowest?

Table I

Some simple math will help us figure this out:

	Task	Time				Opportunity Cost
Bob:	cooking 1 chicken dinner	$\times \dfrac{75 \text{ minutes}}{1 \text{ cooking one chicken}}$	$\times \dfrac{1 \text{ load of dishes}}{20 \text{ minutes}}$	$= \dfrac{75}{20}$	$= 3.75$	Bob gives up doing 3.75 loads of dishes to cook 1 chicken dinner

Complete the same equation for Sam:

	Task	Time				Opportunity Cost
Sam:	cooking 1 chicken dinner	$\times \dfrac{60 \text{ minutes}}{1 \text{ cooking one chicken}}$	$\times \dfrac{1 \text{ load of dishes}}{18 \text{ minutes}}$	$= \dfrac{60}{18}$	$= 3.53$	Sam gives up doing 3.53 loads of dishes to cook 1 chicken dinner

As you can see, Sam has the lowest opportunity cost, so Sam should cook the chicken. This means he gives up less than does Bob by cooking the chicken.

Now, do the equations for washing dishes:

	Task	Time		Opportunity Cost
Bob:	washing 1 load of dishes	$\times \dfrac{20 \text{ minutes}}{1 \text{ load of dishes}} \times \dfrac{1 \text{ chicken dinner}}{75 \text{ minutes}} = \dfrac{20}{75}$	$= .26$	Bob gives up cooking .26 chicken dinners to wash 1 load of dishes.

	Task	Time		Opportunity Cost
Sam:	washing 1 load of dishes	$\times \dfrac{18 \text{ minutes}}{1 \text{ load of dishes}} \times \dfrac{1 \text{ chicken dinner}}{60 \text{ minutes}} = \dfrac{18}{36}$	$= .30$	Sam gives up cooking .30 chicken dinners to wash 1 load of dishes.

Thus, Bob should wash dishes because he has the lowest opportunity cost.

The result of sharing jobs? Bob keeps a roof over his head and Sam gets 18 minutes of time he didn't have when he was doing both dishes and chicken – therefore, both benefit.

What if we switched the comparison by talking about goods/services produced (output) rather than the time it took to complete a task (input)?

Some new, hypothetical numbers:

	# of loads of dishes that can be completed in one hour:	# of chicken dinners that can be cooked in one hour:
Bob	3	1
Sam	2.5	.75

Here Bob has the "absolute advantage" – he can produce the most in a given time period. But we want to know who has a "comparative advantage" – who has the least to lose by picking one of these jobs? Whose opportunity cost is the lowest?

	Task	Time		Opportunity Cost
Bob:	cooking 1 chicken dinner	$\times \dfrac{1 \text{ hour}}{1 \text{ chicken dinner}} \times \dfrac{3 \text{ loads of dishes}}{1 \text{ hour}} = \dfrac{3}{1}$	$= 3$	Bob gives up 3 loads of dishes in the time he can cook 1 chicken dinner.

	Task	Time			Opportunity Cost
Sam:	cooking 1 chicken dinner	$\times \dfrac{1 \text{ hour}}{.75 \text{ chicken dinner}} \times \dfrac{2.5 \text{ loads of dishes}}{1 \text{ hour}}$	$= \dfrac{2.75}{.75}$	$= 3.5$	Sam gives up 3.5 loads of dishes in the time he can cook one chicken dinner.

Bob gives up less if he cooks the chicken than does Sam; therefore, Bob should cook dinner.

Another way to calculate comparative advantage is to make a chart, which is basically the same as above but without the equations. In this example, we'll calculate which country has the comparative advantage in trade.

Two countries, Chaseyland and Waldronia, both produce golf clubs and t-shirts. Chaseyland is better at producing both. It can produce more t-shirts and golf clubs than Waldronia can in the same amount of time; therefore, it has the absolute advantage in such production. A more important question, though, is which country has the lowest opportunity cost when producing golf clubs or t-shirts? Determining this piece of information will help determine which country should specialize in the production of one good and trade for the other.

	Golf clubs (per hour)	T-shirts (per hour)
Chaseyland	10	8
Waldronia	4	4

In order to calculate lowest opportunity cost, we set up ratios – similar to what we did in the Sam and Bob problems:

	T-shirts/Golf Clubs	Golf Clubs/T-shirts
Chaseyland	8/10	10/8
Waldronia	4/4	4/4

Chaseyland has a lower opportunity cost of producing golf clubs (as seen by the ratio 8/10 vs. 4/4) while Waldronia has a lower opportunity cost of producing t-shirts (shown by the ratio 10/8 vs. 4/4). This means Chaseyland should produce golf clubs and trade the surplus golf club production for t-shirts; Waldronia should produce t-shirts and trade its remaining quantity for golf clubs. Both countries will end up producing more total goods because they will specialize, and both can trade for goods needed but produced elsewhere.

The above discussion of trade between Chaseyland and Waldronia concerns output – how much can be produced within a given time frame. What if the discussion was focused on inputs – how many resources does each country use in the production of two goods or services? How would that problem be solved?

	Number of hours to wire a house for electricity	Number of hours to write a multiple-choice test
Chaseyland	16	5
Waldronia	7	2

Notice that Waldronia is more efficient – it takes less time to perform both tasks. Waldronia has the absolute advantage. How would one solve for comparative advantage, though? Which country has the least opportunity cost in its use of inputs/resources? When setting up an output problem, as with the t-shirts and golf clubs, we created ratios by putting one number over the other. With input problems, however, putting one number under the other sets up the proper ratios.

	Number of hours to wire a house for electricity/number of hours to write a multiple choice test	Number of hours to write a multiple choice test/number of hours to wire a house for electricity
Chaseyland	16/5	5/16
Waldronia	7/2	2/7

In this case, Chaseyland has the comparative advantage in wiring a house (16/5 vs. Waldronia's 7/2) but Waldronia has the comparative advantage in writing tests (2/7 vs. Chaseyland's 5/16). Thus, Chaseyland's workers should stick to wiring houses and Waldronia's workers should write tests. Again, the gains in productivity attained by specializing means that more overall output will be produced and services can be traded. Thus, both Sam and Bob and Chaseyland and Waldronia are more productive when they consider the opportunity costs involved.

Balance of Payments

One aspect of international trade that is often confusing is the **balance of payments**. The balance of payments is a record of all international transactions for a country. A "credit" or a plus in the balance of payments is money flowing into the country. A "debit" or a minus is money flowing out of the country.

There are three categories of international transactions:

	Current Account	**Capital Account**	**Financial Account**
Type of transaction:	Short term	Long term	Long term
What is included:	- Raw materials - Manufactured goods - Services - Income from stocks ("dividends") and bonds ("interest") - Transfers of money from abroad - Direct foreign aid	- Rights to natural resources - Patents/copyrights/ trademarks - Franchises/leases - Migrants' transfers - Transfers of title or funds from the sale of fixed assets	The purchase of assets: - Businesses - Bonds - Stocks - Real estate - U.S.-owned assets abroad - Foreign-owned assets here
Also think of it as:	Imports, exports and factor payments	Anything else that isn't produced ("Current Account") or financial ("Financial Account")	Money to businesses, government and infrastructure

Capital and financial accounts were only recently described as such. Before, both categories were listed simply as "capital" (so don't get confused when you see only two categories, not three).

Current Account = Capital Account + Financial Account
Σ = 0 always!

As we buy many goods and services from abroad (a "negative current account," or a "current account deficit"), we must exchange our dollars for foreign currency. These dollars come back to the U.S. as foreigners invest in infrastructure (plants and buildings), finance our businesses (buy stock) and/or make loans to our government (buy bonds) – a "capital account surplus." They do this because they need to get rid of the U.S. dollars accumulated in the foreign exchange market. Thus, the sum must equal 0.

****

When studying microeconomics and macroeconomics, it is easy to forget that the goal is really the same for both – how to determine the most efficient allocation of scarce resources. Here is one way to connect many of the ideas discussed (and their graphs) to this fundamental goal:

Microeconomics:

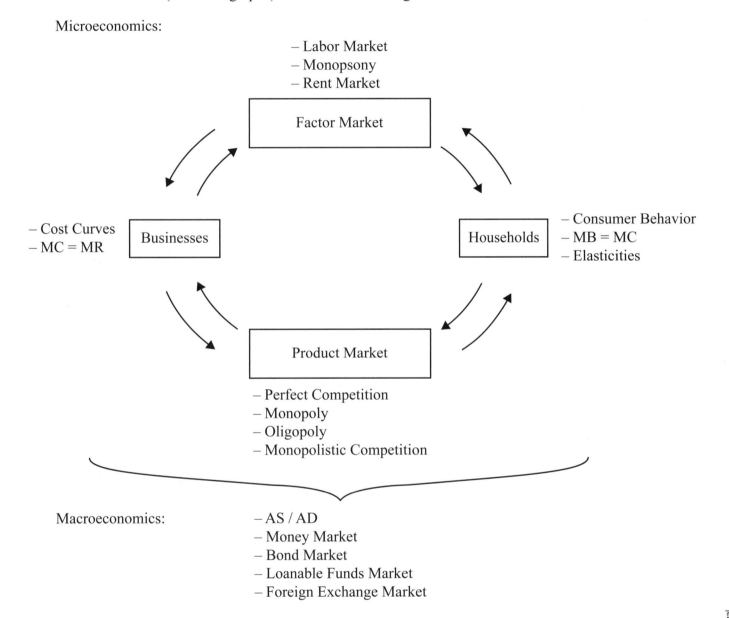

Important Terms:

- Foreign exchange market
- Tariff
- Quota
- Embargo
- Absolute advantage

- Comparative advantage
- Current account
- Capital account
- Financial account
- Balance of payments

MULTIPLE-CHOICE QUESTIONS

1. If a nation experiences a decrease in real interest rates while those of other countries remain constant, we could expect

   (A) the value of that nation's currency to decrease.
   (B) the value of that nation's currency to be unaffected.
   (C) the long-run aggregate supply curve of that nation to decrease.
   (D) the amount of that nation's imports to increase.
   (E) the amount of that nation's exports to decrease.

2. Which of the following would contribute to a nation having a current account deficit?

   (A) an increase in imports
   (B) an increase in exports
   (C) an active fiscal policy
   (D) an active monetary policy
   (E) a domestic recession

3. If foreigners suddenly find products made in the United States increasingly unpopular, which of the following will most likely occur?

   (A) an increase in the demand for the dollar and an increase in its price in foreign exchange markets
   (B) an increase in the demand for the dollar and a decrease in its price in foreign exchange markets
   (C) a decrease in the demand for the dollar and an increase in its price in foreign exchange markets
   (D) a decrease in the demand for the dollar and a decrease in its price in foreign exchange markets
   (E) no change in the demand for the dollar or its price in foreign exchange markets

4. An exchange rate is best defined as

   (A) the rate at which goods and services are exchanged for money.
   (B) the rate at which a nation's currency exchanges for gold.
   (C) the price of one nation's currency from one year to the next.
   (D) the price of one nation's currency expressed in terms of another nation's currency.
   (E) the ratio between a nation's currency and its price level.

Questions 5-6 refer to the graph below:

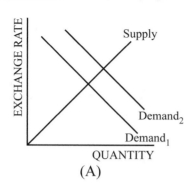
(A)

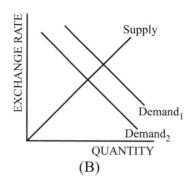
(B)

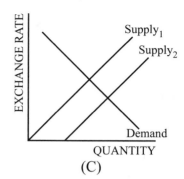
(C)

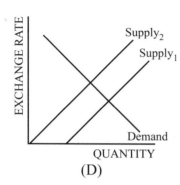
(D)

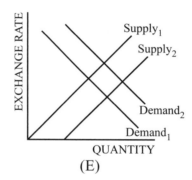
(E)

5. If interest rates in a country increased, which of the graphs shows the effect this would have on that nation's currency in the foreign exchange market?

(A) A
(B) B
(C) C
(D) D
(E) E

6. A decrease in the popularity of American made products around the world would impact the value of the United States dollar in foreign exchange markets as shown in which graph?

(A) A
(B) B
(C) C
(D) D
(E) E

7. The stance of most economists on international trade issues is

    (A) pro-free trade, as it results in a more efficient allocation of resources.
    (B) anti-free trade, as it results in a less efficient allocation of resources.
    (C) pro-protectionism, as it results in a more efficient allocation of resources.
    (D) as likely to be free trade as protectionist.
    (E) noncommittal – few economists embrace one view or the other.

8. Which of the following would lead to decreases in real GDP over time?

    (A) decreases in taxes
    (B) decreases in government spending
    (C) decreases in the size of the capital stock
    (D) decreases in interest rates
    (E) increases in government spending

9. If a nation found its central bank willing to finance increases in government spending by printing money, the most likely chain of events that would result is a(an)

    (A) depreciation of its currency, and a decrease in exports.
    (B) depreciation of its currency, and an increase in exports.
    (C) appreciation of its currency, and a decrease in exports.
    (D) appreciation of its currency, and an increase in exports.
    (E) appreciation of its currency, and no change in exports.

10. A sudden decrease in the worldwide popularity of American made products would have what effect on the demand for, the supply of, and the international value of the dollar?

	Demand	Supply	International Value
(A)	no change	decrease	decrease
(B)	no change	decrease	increase
(C)	decrease	no change	decrease
(D)	increase	no change	increase
(E)	decrease	increase	decrease

11. Expansionary monetary policy has which of the following effects on income, imports, and exchange rates?

	Income	Imports	Exchange Rate
(A)	increase	increase	increase
(B)	increase	decrease	increase
(C)	decrease	decrease	decrease
(D)	decrease	increase	increase
(E)	increase	increase	decrease

12. Contractionary fiscal policy has which of the following effects on income, interest rates, and imports?

	Income	Interest Rates	Imports
(A)	increase	increase	increase
(B)	increase	decrease	increase
(C)	decrease	decrease	decrease
(D)	decrease	decrease	increase
(E)	decrease	increase	decrease

13. Which of the following is NOT regarded as a barrier to international trade?

(A) tariffs
(B) quotas
(C) embargos
(D) General Agreement on Tariffs and Trade (GATT)
(E) voluntary export restrictions

Questions 14-16 refer to the graph below.

Waldronstan and Chaseland produce only two goods, computers and cattle. The figure below shows each nation's production possibility curve for these two goods. The graphs reflect the amount of each good that can produced using all available resources.

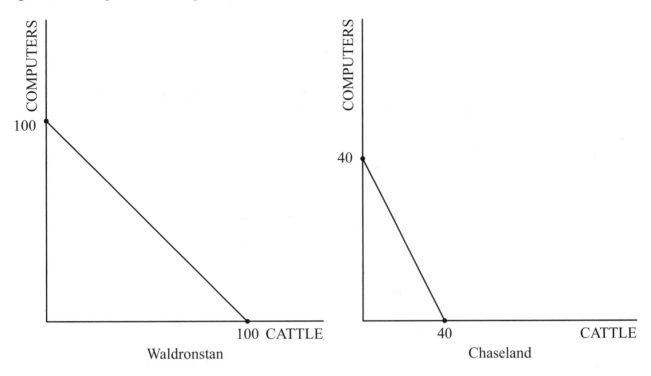

14. Waldronstan has an absolute advantage in

(A) computers only.
(B) cattle only.
(C) both computers and cattle.
(D) neither computers nor cattle.
(E) a combination of computers and cattle.

15. Chaseland has a comparative advantage in

(A) computers only.
(B) cattle only.
(C) both computers and cattle.
(D) neither computers nor cattle.
(E) a combination of computers and cattle.

16. Based on the graphs, the opportunity cost of producing one unit of cattle for Chaseland is

(A) 1/2 unit of computers.
(B) 1 unit of computers.
(C) 2 units of computers.
(D) 4 units of computers.
(E) 8 units of computers.

17. If the federal government suddenly engages in a dramatic contractionary fiscal policy move which results in the sale of government bonds, each of the following will be affected in what way?

	Loanable Funds Market	Value of Currency	Imports
(A)	demand decrease	decrease	decrease
(B)	demand increase	increase	increase
(C)	demand decrease	increase	increase
(D)	demand increase	increase	decrease
(E)	demand increase	decrease	increase

18. Economic growth would be best characterized by

(A) a rightward shift of the production possibilities curve and a rightward shift in the long-run aggregate supply curve.
(B) a leftward shift of the production possibilities curve and a rightward shift in the long-run aggregate supply curve.
(C) a rightward shift of the production possibilities curve and a leftward shift in the long-run aggregate supply curve.
(D) a leftward shift of the production possibilities curve and a leftward shift in the long-run aggregate supply curve.
(E) a leftward shift of the production possibilities curve but no shift in the long-run aggregate supply curve.

19. An economist would point out that a nation which purposely pursues a policy of protectionism does so

(A) at a cost to society in general, but a possible benefit to some domestic producers.
(B) at a cost to some domestic producers, but a benefit to society in general.
(C) at a cost to society in general, and a cost to all domestic producers.
(D) with a benefit to all domestic producers and consumers.
(E) only during periods of rapid economic growth.

20. Tariffs, quotas, and embargos are all forms of

(A) incomes policy.
(B) fiscal policy.
(C) monetary policy.
(D) free trade.
(E) protectionism.

21. If the nation of Econstan suddenly becomes a worldwide popular vacation spot for tourists, what can we expect to happen in the market for the Econstan unit of money, the moohlah?

(A) The demand for the moohlah will increase.
(B) The demand for the moohlah will decrease.
(C) The supply of the moohlah will increase.
(D) The supply of the moohlah will decrease.
(E) The demand for the moohlah will increase and the supply of the moohlah will decrease.

Questions 22-24 refer to the table below:

	Day 1	Day 2
U.S.	$1	$1
W.E.	1 peso	2 pesos

22. Based on the information in the table, we can conclude that from Day 1 to Day 2

(A) the U.S. dollar appreciated.
(B) the U.S. dollar depreciated.
(C) the U.S. dollar floated.
(D) the U.S. dollar sunk.
(E) the U.S. dollar devalued.

23. Based on the information in the table, we can conclude that on Day 2, (relative to Day 1)

(A) the U.S. will export more to W.E.
(B) the U.S. will import more from W.E.
(C) the U.S. will import less from W.E.
(D) W.E. will import more from the U.S.
(E) W.E. will export less to the U.S.

24. Based on the information in the table, we can conclude that

   (A) the U.S. will certainly experience a recession.
   (B) W.E. will certainly experience a recession.
   (C) capital flows will enter the U.S. at a faster rate.
   (D) capital flows will exit the U.S. at a faster rate.
   (E) capital flows will not be affected.

25. Which of the following combinations of circumstances would limit the ability of an economy to experience a rapid rate of economic growth?

	Interest Rate	Savings Rate	Capacity Utilization Rate
(A)	high	high	high
(B)	high	low	low
(C)	low	low	low
(D)	low	low	high
(E)	low	high	high

FREE-RESPONSE QUESTIONS

1. Draw and correctly label an aggregate supply and aggregate demand diagram in short-run equilibrium at a level of output below the full-employment level, and include each of the following on your diagram: recession

   (a) short-run aggregate supply curve
   (b) aggregate demand curve
   (c) long-run aggregate supply curve
   (d) demonstrate the effect of an increase in exports
   (e) explain how long-run economic growth would be demonstrated

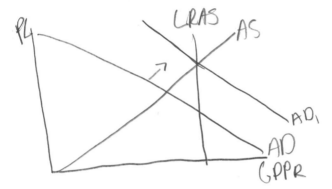

2. A country experiences an inflationary episode.

    (a) List one fiscal policy and one monetary policy action that can be used to lower the rate of inflation.
    (b) Explain how the fiscal policy action you described would affect the exchange rate.
    (c) Explain how the monetary policy action you described would affect the exchange rate.

a) Reduce gov't. spending, sell bonds

b) decrease GDP, demand for dollars increase, er↑

c) decrease ir, demand of dollars decrease, er↓

3. Based on the information in the table below, answer the questions that follow.

Exchange Rates			
	U.S. Dollar	W.E. Peso	E.C.O.N. Euro
Year 1	1	4	2
Year 2	1	3	3

(a) What happened to the value of the U.S. dollar relative to the W.E. Peso from year 1 to year 2?

(b) What happened to the value of the E.C.O.N. Euro relative to the W.E. Peso from year 1 to year 2?

(c) What will happen to tourism in the U.S. from year 1 to year 2? Why?

NO TESTING MATERIAL ON THIS PAGE

MACROECONOMICS

SAMPLE EXAMINATION I

1. An increase in the amount people save for retirement will result in which of the following?

	Supply of Loanable Funds	Real Interest Rate
(A)	increase	increase
(B)	increase	decrease
(C)	decrease	decrease
(D)	decrease	increase
(E)	no change	no change

Questions 2-4 refer to the graph below:

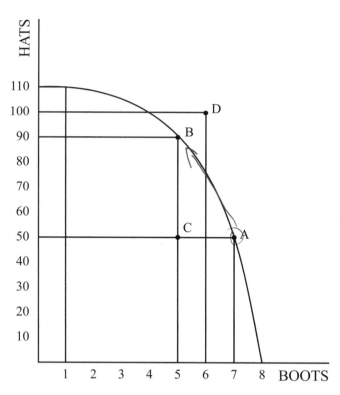

2. Which of the following could cause the movement from point A to point B in the production possibility curve shown above?

   (A) an increase in consumer confidence
   (B) an increase in consumer preference for hats
   (C) an increase in production costs
   (D) a decrease in production costs
   (E) an improvement in the technology used to make hats and boots

3. An economy that is in recession would be shown by which point in the production possibility curve shown above?

   (A) A
   (B) B
   (C) C
   (D) D
   (E) E

4. Based on the graph, which of the following is correct?

   (A) The opportunity cost of moving from point A to point C is two boots.
   (B) The opportunity cost of moving from point A to point B is two boots.
   (C) The opportunity cost of moving from point A to point B is two hats.
   (D) The opportunity cost of moving from point A to point B is forty hats.
   (E) The opportunity cost of moving from point A to point D is two boots.

5. To correct for a severe recession, what fiscal policy measure would be appropriate?

   (A) decrease the reserve requirement
   (B) decrease the discount rate
   (C) increase government spending
   (D) increase taxes
   (E) increase interest rates

6. If real GDP grew by 5% during a period when anticipated inflation was 4%, then

   (A) nominal GDP fell by 9%.
   (B) nominal GDP grew by 1%.
   (C) nominal GDP grew by 4%.
   (D) nominal GDP grew by 5%.
   (E) nominal GDP grew by 9%.

   real = nominal - inflation
   5 = x - 4

7. Of the following people who is least likely to be affected by cyclical unemployment?

   (A) a real estate agent
   (B) a new car salesperson
   (C) a local firefighter
   (D) a travel agent
   (E) an airline pilot

8. Which of the following combinations of events would result in the most contractionary effect on an economy?

	Taxes	Government Spending	Net Exports	Reserve Requirement
(A)	decrease	increase	increase	decrease
(B)	increase	increase	increase	decrease
(C)	decrease	increase	decrease	decrease
(D)	decrease	decrease	decrease	decrease
(E)	increase	decrease	decrease	increase

9. If the consumer price index (CPI) is 400 at the end of 2013, and 460 at the end of 2014, then inflation during 2014 was

$$\frac{460-400}{400} = \frac{60}{400} = \frac{15}{100}$$

(A) 6 percent.
(B) 15 percent.
(C) 20 percent.
(D) 25 percent.
(E) 60 percent.

10. If actual inflation is less than anticipated inflation, then real wages

(A) rise.
(B) fall.
(C) remain unchanged.
(D) rise or fall depending on the actual wage rate.
(E) are indeterminate.

11. The "full-employment unemployment rate" is defined as the unemployment rate when

(A) cyclical unemployment is zero.
(B) structural unemployment is zero.
(C) frictional unemployment is zero.
(D) seasonal unemployment is zero.
(E) the total unemployment rate is zero.

Questions 12-13 refer to the table below:

Population	400 million
Number in labor force	320 million
Number employed	296 million
Number unemployed	24 million

12. Based on the data above, what is the labor force participation rate?

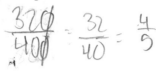

(A) 100 percent
(B) 90 percent
(C) 80 percent
(D) 60 percent
(E) 20 percent

13. Based on the data above, what is the unemployment rate of this economy?

(A) 24 percent
(B) 8.1 percent
(C) 7.5 percent
(D) 6 percent
(E) 2.4 percent

14. If the demand for financial assets of the United States increases, the most likely short-run effect will be:

(A) an increase in the value of the U.S. dollar.
(B) a decrease in the value of the U.S. dollar.
(C) a decrease in interest rates in the U.S.
(D) a decrease in inflation in the U.S.
(E) an increase in unemployment in the U.S.

15. The Fed Funds Rate is the rate of interest

(A) the federal government pays on bonds.
(B) the Federal Reserve charges member banks to borrow money.
(C) the Federal Reserve charges the federal government to borrow money.
(D) that banks charge each other for overnight loans to cover reserve accounts.
(E) that large businesses are charged to borrow for investment purposes.

16. Economic growth would be encouraged the most by which of the following combinations of events?

	Investment	Interest Rate	Savings Rate
(A)	high	high	low
(B)	low	low	low
(C)	low	high	low
(D)	low	low	high
(E)	high	low	high

17. Which of the following would increase the size of GDP?

    I. purchasing a used textbook from the bookstore for an economics class at the local college
    II. purchasing a download from an online music seller
    III. renting an apartment
    IV. purchasing a memory upgrade package for an old computer

(A) II only
(B) II and III only
(C) III and IV only
(D) II, III, and IV only
(E) I, II, III, and IV

18. Which of the following would be the correct Keynesian fiscal policy response to a contractionary episode for an economy?

(A) Increase taxes and increase federal government spending.
(B) Increase taxes and decrease federal government spending.
(C) Decrease taxes and decrease federal government spending.
(D) Decrease taxes and increase federal government spending.
(E) Increase taxes and decrease the federal deficit.

Questions 19-20 refer to the graph below:

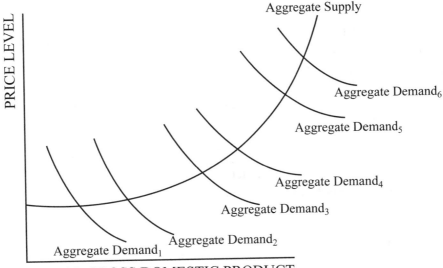

19. Based on the graph, the largest increase in real output with the smallest change in the price level would be shown by a movement from

   (A) Aggregate Demand$_1$ to Aggregate Demand$_2$
   (B) Aggregate Demand$_2$ to Aggregate Demand$_3$
   (C) Aggregate Demand$_3$ to Aggregate Demand$_4$
   (D) Aggregate Demand$_4$ to Aggregate Demand$_5$
   (E) Aggregate Demand$_5$ to Aggregate Demand$_6$

20. Based on the graph, the result of an increase in government spending as the economy approaches full employment would be shown by a movement from

   (A) Aggregate Demand$_1$ to Aggregate Demand$_2$
   (B) Aggregate Demand$_2$ to Aggregate Demand$_3$
   (C) Aggregate Demand$_3$ to Aggregate Demand$_4$
   (D) Aggregate Demand$_4$ to Aggregate Demand$_5$
   (E) Aggregate Demand$_5$ to Aggregate Demand$_6$

21. If a nation experiences a series of natural disasters and a significant decline in worker productivity, the likely result of these combined factors is:

	GDP	Price Level
(A)	increase	increase
(B)	decrease	decrease
(C)	increase	decrease
(D)	decrease	increase
(E)	decrease	no change

Questions 22-24 refer to the graph below:

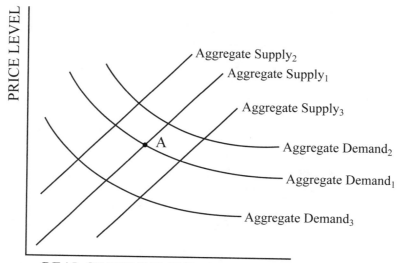

22. Beginning at the equilibrium position shown by point A in the graph above, which single movement could cause demand-pull inflation?

(A) Aggregate Supply$_1$ to Aggregate Supply$_2$
(B) Aggregate Supply$_1$ to Aggregate Supply$_3$
(C) Aggregate Demand$_1$ to Aggregate Demand$_2$
(D) Aggregate Demand$_1$ to Aggregate Demand$_3$
(E) None of the above would cause demand-pull inflation.

23. Beginning at the equilibrium position shown by point A in the graph, which single movement could cause cost-push inflation?

(A) Aggregate Supply₁ to Aggregate Supply₂
(B) Aggregate Supply₁ to Aggregate Supply₃
(C) Aggregate Demand₁ to Aggregate Demand₂
(D) Aggregate Demand₁ to Aggregate Demand₃
(E) None of the above would cause cost-push inflation.

24. Economic stagnation combined with inflation (stagflation) could be caused by which single shift in the graph?

(A) Aggregate Supply₁ to Aggregate Supply₂
(B) Aggregate Supply₁ to Aggregate Supply₃
(C) Aggregate Demand₁ to Aggregate Demand₂
(D) Aggregate Demand₁ to Aggregate Demand₃
(E) Any of these has an equal chance of creating stagflation.

25. Which of the following is most likely to be reduced by countercyclical fiscal and monetary policies?

(A) seasonal unemployment
(B) cyclical unemployment
(C) frictional unemployment
(D) structural unemployment
(E) classical unemployment

26. Which of the following would be the appropriate monetary policy to reduce inflation?

(A) increase taxes
(B) decrease taxes
(C) sell bonds
(D) buy bonds
(E) lower the reserve requirement

27. The combined effect of expansionary fiscal policy and expansionary monetary policy would be which of the following?

	GDP	Interest Rates	International Value of the Dollar
(A)	increase	increase	increase
(B)	increase	decrease	increase
(C)	increase	indeterminate	indeterminate
(D)	decrease	indeterminate	increase
(E)	decrease	indeterminate	indeterminate

Questions 28-29 refer to the graph below:

28. The graph above is a

(A) short-run Keynesian aggregate demand curve.
(B) long-run Laffer curve.
(C) short-run Laffer curve.
(D) long-run Phillips curve.
(E) short-run Phillips curve.

29. A movement from point 1 to point 2 on the graph could be caused by which of the following?

 (A) a leftward shift in aggregate demand
 (B) a rightward shift in aggregate demand
 (C) a leftward shift in aggregate supply
 (D) a rightward shift in aggregate supply
 (E) a rightward shift in the production possibilities curve

30. If an economy finds that real GDP increases by $10,000 as a result of a $2000 government spending program, then for that economy the marginal propensity to save must be:

 (A) .05
 (B) .10
 (C) .20
 (D) .25
 (E) .50

Spending mult: 5

31. Which of the following correctly describes the national debt of the U.S.?

 (A) It is equal to the deficit.
 (B) It is equal to the sum of all the previous deficits minus the sum of all the previous surpluses.
 (C) It is smaller than the deficit.
 (D) It is mostly held by the federal government.
 (E) It rises when GDP rises and falls when GDP falls.

32. If labor costs fall in the personal computer industry, which of the following correctly describes the effect this will have on the quantity and price of personal computers?

	Quantity Sold	Price
(A)	increase	increase
(B)	increase	decrease
(C)	no change	increase
(D)	decrease	decrease
(E)	decrease	increase

33. Aggregate demand is comprised of which of the following?

    (A) Consumption expenditures + Investment expenditures + Government expenditures + Export spending – Import spending
    (B) Consumption expenditures + Investment expenditures + Government expenditures + Savings + Export spending – Import spending
    (C) Consumption expenditures + Investment expenditures + Government expenditures - Export spending – Import spending
    (D) Consumption expenditures + Investment expenditures + Government expenditures + Business spending + Savings + Export spending + Import spending
    (E) Consumption expenditures + Investment expenditures + Government expenditures + Business spending + Export spending + Import spending

34. Rising interest rates have a tendency to hinder economic growth because

    (A) the capital stock will decrease.
    (B) the capital stock will increase.
    (C) consumers will spend more.
    (D) aggregate demand will increase.
    (E) money will be worth more.

35. A recessionary gap could be eliminated by

    (A) an increase in the federal government's budget deficit.
    (B) an increase in the federal government's budget surplus.
    (C) an increase in the reserve requirement.
    (D) an increase in the Fed Funds rate.
    (E) a decrease in government spending.

36. The way that monetary policy is transmitted through the economy is correctly described in which of the following?

Money Supply	Interest Rates	Investment	GDP
(A) increase	increase	increase	increase
(B) increase	increase	increase	decrease
(C) increase	decrease	increase	increase
(D) increase	decrease	decrease	decrease
(E) decrease	decrease	decrease	decrease

37. If an economy was operating at an equilibrium level of output of $500 billion and full-employment equilibrium was $700 billion, with a marginal propensity to save of .10, a Keynesian economist would recommend

(A) increasing government spending by $20 billion.
(B) increasing government spending by $200 billion.
(C) decreasing taxes by $200 billion.
(D) decreasing taxes by $500 billion.
(E) decreasing taxes by $20 billion.

recession
expansionary
$\frac{1}{.10} = 10$

38. If a banking system has a reserve requirement of 20% and experiences an autonomous deposit of $5,000, which of the following is the maximum amount of money that the banks in that system could create?

$\frac{100,000}{100} = 1000$

$\frac{1}{.2} = 5$

(A) $2,000
(B) $5,000
(C) $7,000
(D) $20,000
(E) $50,000

39. If the government and the Federal Reserve both attempt to expand the economy, which of the following describes the most likely result of these actions? (FP=fiscal policy, MP=monetary policy)

	Interest Rate		Price level		Output	
	FP	MP	FP	MP	FP	MP
(A)	increase	increase	increase	increase	increase	increase
(B)	decrease	decrease	decrease	decrease	decrease	decrease
(C)	increase	decrease	increase	increase	increase	increase
(D)	decrease	increase	decrease	decrease	decrease	decrease
(E)	decrease	increase	decrease	increase	decrease	increase

40. Which of the following is most likely to occur during a period of rapidly falling GDP?

    (A) increasing employment rates
    (B) increasing federal budget surpluses
    (C) decreasing inflationary pressure in the economy
    (D) increasing inflationary pressure in the economy
    (E) a shift in the long-run Phillips curve

    real ≠ nominal - inflation

41. The relationship between real interest rates and nominal interest rates is correctly described by which of the following?

    (A) real interest rate = nominal interest rate + anticipated inflation
    (B) nominal interest rate = real interest rate + anticipated inflation
    (C) real interest rate = nominal interest rate + actual inflation
    (D) nominal interest rate = real interest rate + actual inflation
    (E) nominal interest rate = real interest rate – actual inflation

42. Based on the graph, if country X and country Y are both currently producing 50 units of guns and 50 units of butter, the opportunity cost of increasing the amount of gun production is

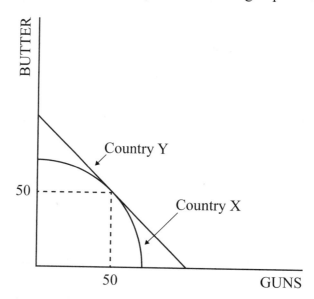

    (A) the same in both countries.
    (B) greater in country X.
    (C) greater in country Y.
    (D) positive in country X and negative in country Y.
    (E) positive in country Y and negative in country X.

43. Based on the Keynesian model, which of the following would increase aggregate demand?

(A) an increase in exports
(B) an increase in imports
(C) an increase in business taxes
(D) an increase in the price level
(E) a decrease in the price level

44. Which of the graphs below correctly shows a long-run Phillips curve?

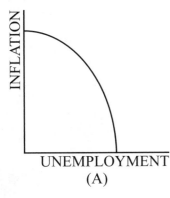

UNEMPLOYMENT
(A)

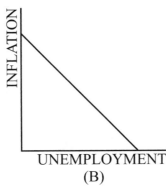

UNEMPLOYMENT
(B)

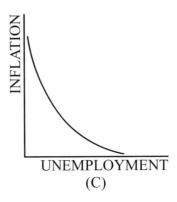

UNEMPLOYMENT
(C)

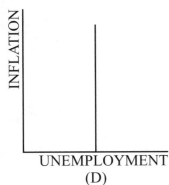

UNEMPLOYMENT
(D)

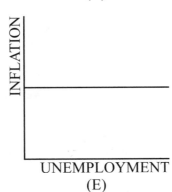

UNEMPLOYMENT
(E)

(A) A
(B) B
(C) C
(D) D
(E) E

45. Which of the following would be included in the U.S. financial or capital account?

(A) an American company builds a factory in Germany
(B) an American receives dividends on Japanese stock she owns
(C) a Chinese citizen tours the United States
(D) a Canadian citizen buys an American made car
(E) an American buys a British made coat

46. If an effective price ceiling is established on a good, which of the following correctly describes the effect the price ceiling has on quantity and price?

	Quantity	Price
(A)	increase	increase
(B)	increase	no change
(C)	increase	decrease
(D)	decrease	decrease
(E)	decrease	increase

Questions 47-48 refer to the graph below:

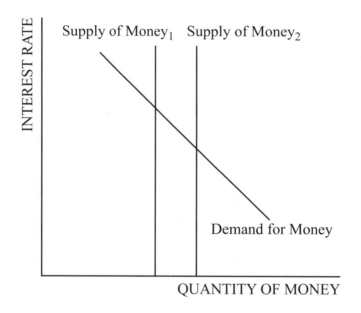

47. What is the most likely cause of the shift in the graph?

(A) expansionary fiscal policy
(B) contractionary fiscal policy
(C) expansionary monetary policy
(D) contractionary monetary policy
(E) wage and price controls

48. What is the most likely consequence of the shift in the graph?

(A) an increase in business investment spending
(B) a decrease in business investment spending
(C) a decrease in new home construction
(D) a decrease in inflation
(E) an increase in unemployment

49. Which of the following has the potential to improve conditions the most in an economy with an 8% annual rate of inflation and an 8% unemployment rate?

    (A) an increase in aggregate demand
    (B) a decrease in aggregate demand
    (C) an increase in aggregate supply
    (D) a decrease in aggregate supply
    (E) a decrease in aggregate supply and an increase in aggregate demand

50. The national debt of a country would decrease with which of the following actions?

    (A) expansionary fiscal policy
    (B) a budget surplus for the current year
    (C) a budget deficit for the current year
    (D) a balanced budget for the current year
    (E) contractionary monetary policy

51. If the simple spending multiplier is 4, then the

    (A) tax multiplier is also 4.
    (B) marginal propensity to consume is 75%.
    (C) marginal propensity to consume is 25%.
    (D) savings rate is 25%.
    (E) reserve requirement is 75%.

    $1 - MPC = MPS$

    $\frac{1}{MPS} = $ spending mult

52. Which of the following transactions would contribute to a current account surplus for the United States?

    (A) an American company expanding operations by building a factory in Mexico
    (B) an American touring Australia
    (C) a Canadian firm paying dividends to a retired American citizen
    (D) a California based firm paying dividends to a resident of Illinois
    (E) an American buying a television made in Japan

53. If a country experienced a rightward shift of its long-run aggregate supply curve, one likely result would be

    (A) a rightward shift of its short-run Phillips curve.
    (B) a rightward shift of its production possibility curve.
    (C) a rightward shift of its aggregate demand curve.
    (D) a leftward shift of its aggregate demand curve.
    (E) a leftward shift of its money supply curve.

Questions 54-55 refer to the graph below.

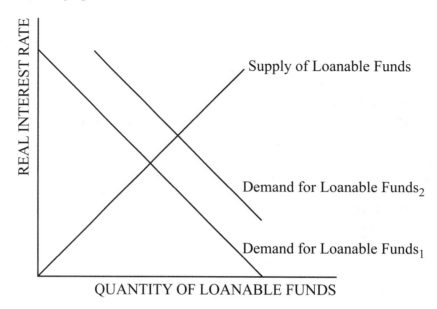

U.S. Loanable Funds Market

54. Which of the following would cause the change in the loanable funds market shown in the graph above?

(A) an increase in the money supply
(B) a decrease in the money supply
(C) an increase in federal income tax revenue
(D) an increase in federal borrowing
(E) an increase in the tax rate

55. The likely result of the change shown in the graph above is

(A) an increase in the demand for U.S. financial assets.
(B) an increase in tourism in the U.S. by foreigners.
(C) a decrease in the value of the U.S. dollar.
(D) a decrease in the demand for the U.S. dollar.
(E) a current account surplus for the U.S.

56. An aggregate demand curve slopes down and to the right because of all of the following EXCEPT:

(A) the wealth (real balances) effect.
(B) the interest rate effect.
(C) the international effect.
(D) the price level effect.
(E) none of the above are reasons for the downward and to the right slope of the aggregate demand curve.

57. If real interest rates in an economy fall, what will happen to each of the following?

International Value of Currency	Exports	GDP	Capital Flow
(A) increase	increase	expand	inflow
(B) decrease	decrease	contract	outflow
(C) increase	decrease	expand	outflow
(D) increase	decrease	contract	inflow
(E) decrease	increase	expand	outflow

58. Based on the information in the exchange rate table below, which of the following is a logical conclusion?

May	1 U.S. dollar = 2 Fergi francs
June	1 U.S. dollar = 3 Fergi francs

(A) The U.S. dollar has become stronger and exports to Fergi will rise.
(B) The U.S. dollar has become stronger and exports to Fergi will fall.
(C) The U.S. dollar has become weaker and exports to Fergi will rise.
(D) The U.S. dollar has become weaker and exports to Fergi will fall.
(E) The U.S. dollar has become weaker and imports from Fergi will fall.

59. If the federal government and the Federal Reserve cooperate in implementing higher real interest rates, which of the following will occur?

(A) an increase in the capital stock and a capital inflow
(B) an increase in the capital stock and a capital outflow
(C) a decrease in the capital stock and a capital inflow
(D) a decrease in the capital stock and a capital outflow
(E) a decrease in the capital stock and a balance in capital flows

60. If the Federal Reserve buys bonds, which of the following will result?

   (A) increased demand for money and lower interest rates
   (B) decreased demand for money and higher interest rates
   (C) decreased supply of money and higher interest rates
   (D) increased supply of money and lower interest rates
   (E) increased supply of money and higher interest rates

1.

(a). Draw a correctly labeled aggregate supply and aggregate demand graph for an economy in long-run equilibrium at full employment. On your graph include each of the following:
i. a short-run aggregate supply curve
ii. a long-run aggregate supply curve
iii. an aggregate demand curve

(b) Assume that the government decides to engage in a plan to reduce the national debt. List two actions the government could use to reduce the debt.

(c) Explain what will happen to each of the following as a result of the debt reduction plan in part (b) on the graph you drew in part (a):
i. aggregate demand
ii. output and the price level
iii. unemployment

(d) Draw a correctly labeled loanable funds market graph to demonstrate the effect of the debt reduction plan. Explain what will happen to interest rates.

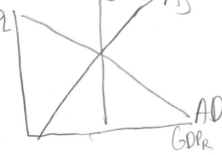

a) PL LRAS AS AD GDPᵣ

d) Real ir Sloans 0 Loans Qof loans

⇓ less people can invest

b) reduce govt. spending
   increase income taxes

c) i) ↓
   ii) ↓↓
   iii) ↑

2. Use the information in the exchange rate table below to answer the questions that follow. The U.S. currency is the dollar ($). The currency for W.E. is the "P":

	U.S. ($)		W.E. (P)
Day 1	1	trades for	3
Day 2	1	trades for	2

(a) What has happened to the value of the U.S. ($) from Day 1 to Day 2?
(b) What has happened to the value of the W.E. (P) from Day 1 to Day 2?
(c) What will happen to exports from the U.S. to W.E. on Day 2 relative to Day 1?
(d) What will happen to imports into the U.S. from W.E. on Day 2 relative to Day 1?

a) depreciate

b) appreciate

c) increase

d) decrease

3. The United States economy enters a recession and the federal government and the Federal Reserve both decide to act in a countercyclical manner.

   (a) List two actions the federal government could take to correct for the recession.
   (b) List two actions the Federal Reserve could take to correct for the recession.
   (c) Explain the effect of the federal government's actions on interest rates.
   (d) Explain the effect of the Federal Reserve's actions on interest rates.

a) increase gov't,
   reduce income tax
b) buy bonds
   decrease RR
c) ↑
d) ↓

SAMPLE EXAMINATION II

1. If real interest rates in an economy rise, what will happen to each of the following?

	International Value of Currency	Exports	GDP
(A)	increase	increase	expand
(B)	decrease	decrease	contract
(C)	increase	decrease	expand
(D)	increase	decrease	contract
(E)	decrease	increase	expand

Questions 2-4 refer to the graph below:

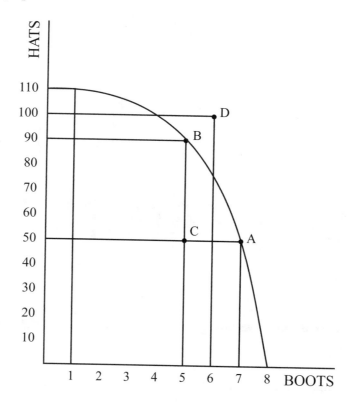

2. Which of the following statements about point D in the graph is correct?

(A) Point D represents a production level of boots that exceeds the production capability of the economy.

(B) Point D represents a production level of hats that exceeds the production capability of the economy.

(C) Point D represents a production level at which consumer demand is too low to purchase all of the boots and hats produced.

(D) Point D represents a level of production of hats and boots that exceeds the production capability of the economy.

(E) Point D represents a level of production at which some resources would be idle.

3. The opportunity cost for this economy to move production from point C to point B

(A) is the loss of 40 boots.

(B) is the loss of 5 hats.

(C) is zero.

(D) is increased unemployment.

(E) is infinite and therefore not possible.

4. Based on the graph, which of the following is correct?

(A) The opportunity cost of moving from point A to point C is two boots.
(B) The opportunity cost of moving from point B to point A is two boots.
(C) The opportunity cost of moving from point C to point B is two hats.
(D) The opportunity cost of moving from point B to point A is forty hats.
(E) The opportunity cost of moving from point A to point D is two boots.

5. If labor costs rise in the United States auto industry at the same time that the demand for United States-made autos increases, which of the following correctly describes the effect this will have on the quantity and the price of autos sold?

	Quantity Sold	Price
(A)	increase	indeterminate
(B)	increase	decrease
(C)	decrease	increase
(D)	decrease	decrease
(E)	indeterminate	increase

6. Of the following, who is the most likely to be affected by cyclical unemployment?

(A) a law enforcement officer
(B) a member of the military
(C) a local firefighter
(D) a real estate agent
(E) a school teacher

7. Which of the following combinations of events would have the most expansionary effect on an economy?

	Interest Rates	Exports	Imports
(A)	increase	increase	increase
(B)	decrease	decrease	decrease
(C)	increase	decrease	decrease
(D)	decrease	increase	decrease
(E)	increase	increase	decrease

8. If inflation is expected to be 3% and the nominal interest rate is 8%, the real interest rate must be

   (A) −5 percent.
   (B) 3 percent.
   (C) 5 percent.
   (D) 8 percent.
   (E) 11 percent.

Questions 9-10 refer to the graph below:

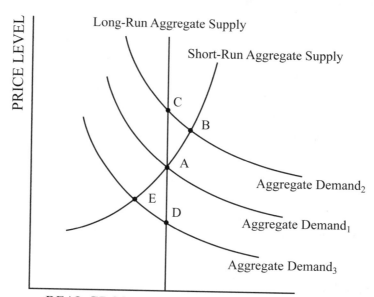

9. Assume that the United States economy has achieved long-run equilibrium at full employment. Suddenly, American products become less attractive in world markets. If no fiscal or monetary actions are taken, which equilibrium point on the graph above represents the new long-run equilibrium that will result?

   (A) A
   (B) B
   (C) C
   (D) D
   (E) E

10. If an economy finds itself in short-run equilibrium at a point like B on the graph, the appropriate counter-cyclical policy would be to

(A) increase government spending.
(B) sell bonds.
(C) decrease taxes.
(D) decrease the reserve requirement.
(E) drive down the Fed Funds rate.

---

11. If the consumer price index (CPI) is 400 at the end of 2013, and 440 at the end of 2014, then inflation during 2014 was

(A) 4 percent.
(B) 9 percent.
(C) 10 percent.
(D) 20 percent.
(E) 40 percent.

12. If a nation experiences a period of positive supply shocks, the likely result is:

	GDP	Price Level
(A)	increase	increase
(B)	decrease	decrease
(C)	increase	decrease
(D)	decrease	increase
(E)	decrease	no change

13. Which of the following combinations of events would have the most expansionary effect on an economy?

	Taxes	Government Spending	Exports	Imports
(A)	decrease	increase	increase	decrease
(B)	increase	increase	increase	decrease
(C)	decrease	increase	decrease	decrease
(D)	decrease	decrease	decrease	decrease
(E)	increase	decrease	decrease	increase

Questions 14-15 refer to the graph below:

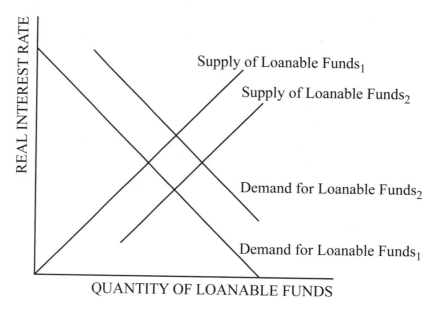

U.S. Loanable Funds Market

14. Which of the following combinations of events would account for the change in the loanable funds market shown in the graph above?

   (A) an increase in the federal deficit and an increased amount of personal savings for retirement
   (B) a decrease in the federal deficit and a decreased amount of personal savings for retirement
   (C) an increase in the federal deficit and a decreased amount of personal savings for retirement
   (D) a decrease in the federal deficit and an increased amount of personal savings for retirement
   (E) a balanced federal budget and equilibrium in the money market

15. The result of the change in the loanable funds market shown in the graph is

   (A) an increase in the equilibrium interest rate and an indeterminate effect on the equilibrium quantity of loanable funds.
   (B) an increase in the equilibrium interest rate and a decrease in the equilibrium quantity of loanable funds.
   (C) a decrease in the equilibrium interest rate and an increase in the equilibrium quantity of loanable funds.
   (D) a decrease in the equilibrium interest rate and a decrease in the equilibrium quantity of loanable funds.
   (E) an indeterminate effect on the equilibrium interest rate and an increase in the equilibrium quantity of loanable funds.

16. If actual inflation is greater than anticipated inflation over a period for which wages were adjusted purely to account for expected inflation, then real wages will

(A) rise.
(B) fall.
(C) remain unchanged.
(D) rise or fall depending on the actual wage rate.
(E) be indeterminate.

17. The natural rate of unemployment is defined as the unemployment rate when

(A) cyclical unemployment is zero.
(B) structural unemployment is zero.
(C) frictional unemployment is zero.
(D) seasonal unemployment is zero.
(E) the total unemployment rate is zero.

Questions 18-19 refer to the table below:

Population	500 million
Number in labor force	400 million
Number employed	360 million
Number unemployed	40 million

18. Based on the data above, what is the labor force participation rate?

(A) 100 percent
(B) 90 percent
(C) 80 percent
(D) 60 percent
(E) 20 percent

19. Based on the data above, what is the unemployment rate of this economy?

(A) 8 percent
(B) 10 percent
(C) 40 percent
(D) 60 percent
(E) 90 percent

20. If fiscal and monetary policies both result in lower real interest rates, which of the following will occur?

   (A) an increase in the capital stock and a capital inflow
   (B) an increase in the capital stock and a capital outflow
   (C) a decrease in the capital stock and a capital inflow
   (D) a decrease in the capital stock and a capital outflow
   (E) a decrease in the capital stock and no change in capital flows

21. An increase in the money supply will result in

   (A) a decrease in GDP.
   (B) a decrease in the Fed Funds rate.
   (C) a decrease in the inflation rate.
   (D) an increase in the unemployment rate.
   (E) a decrease in the price of existing bonds.

22. Economic growth would be encouraged the most by which of the following combinations of events?

	Investment	Interest Rates	Savings Rate
(A)	high	high	low
(B)	low	low	low
(C)	low	high	low
(D)	low	low	high
(E)	high	low	high

23. Which of the following would be the most appropriate fiscal policy to reduce inflation?

   (A) increase the money supply
   (B) decrease the money supply
   (C) increase government spending
   (D) increase taxes
   (E) increase deficit spending

24. The combined effect of contractionary fiscal policy and contractionary monetary policy would be which of the following?

GDP	Interest Rates	International Value of the Dollar
(A) decrease	increase	increase
(B) increase	decrease	increase
(C) increase	indeterminate	decrease
(D) increase	indeterminate	increase
(E) decrease	indeterminate	indeterminate

Questions 25-27 refer to the graph below:

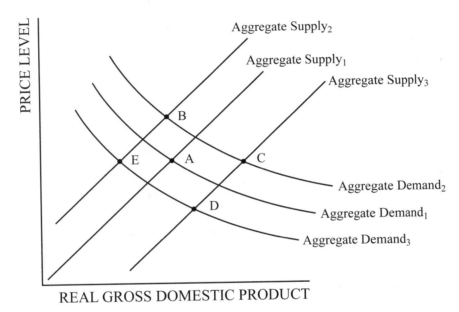

25. Beginning at the equilibrium position shown by point A in the graph above, which single movement could cause cost-push inflation?

(A) Aggregate Supply$_1$ to Aggregate Supply$_2$
(B) Aggregate Supply$_1$ to Aggregate Supply$_3$
(C) Aggregate Demand$_1$ to Aggregate Demand$_2$
(D) Aggregate Demand$_1$ to Aggregate Demand$_3$
(E) None of the above could cause cost-push inflation

26. Beginning at the equilibrium position shown by point A in the graph, which of the following could cause a movement to point C?

(A) increased input costs and increased consumer confidence
(B) decreased input costs and decreased consumer confidence
(C) increased input costs and increased taxes
(D) decreased input costs and decreased taxes
(E) increased input costs and decreased government spending

27. An increase in inflation with no change in real GDP can be demonstrated by a movement from

(A) point A to point B.
(B) point A to point C.
(C) point A to point D.
(D) point D to point C.
(E) point B to point E.

28. Which of the following would contribute to a surplus in the U.S. current account?

(A) an American citizen touring Spain
(B) an American receiving dividends on Japanese stock she owns
(C) an American citizen buying only American made products
(D) a Canadian company building a factory in California
(E) an American company paying stock dividends to a British citizen

29. The national debt of a country would increase with which of the following actions?

(A) contractionary fiscal policy
(B) a budget surplus for the current year
(C) a budget deficit for the current year
(D) balanced budget for the current year
(E) expansionary monetary policy

30. If the simple spending multiplier is 5, then the

(A) tax multiplier is also 5.
(B) marginal propensity to consume is 5 percent.
(C) marginal propensity to consume is 50 percent.
(D) marginal propensity to consume is 80 percent.
(E) savings rate is 20 percent.

31. If a banking system has a reserve requirement of 10% and experiences an autonomous deposit of $7,000, which of the following is the maximum amount by which the money supply could expand if every bank in the system loaned out all of its excess reserves?

(A) $3,000
(B) $6,000
(C) $7,000
(D) $63,000
(E) $70,000

32. Which of the following would be the correct Keynesian fiscal policy response to an inflationary episode?

(A) increase taxes and increase government spending
(B) increase taxes and decrease government spending
(C) decrease taxes and decrease government spending
(D) decrease taxes and increase government spending
(E) decrease taxes and increase the federal budget deficit

Questions 33-34 refer to the graph below:

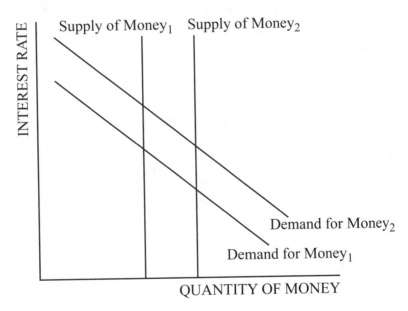

33. Which shift in the graph would cause monetary policy to be contractionary?

(A) Supply of Money$_1$ to Supply of Money$_2$
(B) Demand for Money$_1$ to Demand for Money$_2$
(C) Supply of Money$_1$ to Demand for Money$_1$
(D) Demand for Money$_2$ to Demand for Money$_1$
(E) Supply of Money$_2$ to Supply of Money$_1$

34. A shift of Money Supply$_1$ to Money Supply$_2$ and a shift of Money Demand$_1$ to Money Demand$_2$ in the graph would be the result of which of the following?

   (A) expansionary monetary policy and an expanding GDP
   (B) expansionary monetary policy and a contracting GDP
   (C) contractionary monetary policy and an expanding GDP
   (D) contractionary monetary policy and a contracting GDP
   (E) contractionary monetary policy and contractionary fiscal policy

35. If the Federal Reserve sells bonds, which of the following will result?

   (A) increased demand for money and lower interest rates
   (B) increased demand for money and higher interest rates
   (C) decreased supply of money and lower interest rates
   (D) decreased supply of money and higher interest rates
   (E) increased supply of money and lower interest rates

36. Which of the following will increase real GDP?

   (A) an increase in the price level
   (B) a social security recipient receiving his monthly check in the mail
   (C) an American buying a foreign made product
   (D) a local police department building a new police station
   (E) an antique collector buying a vintage car

37. Economic growth would be hindered the most by which of the following combinations of events?

	Investment	Interest Rates	Literacy Rate
(A)	high	high	low
(B)	low	low	low
(C)	low	high	low
(D)	high	low	high
(E)	high	high	high

38. Based on the information in the exchange rate table below, which of the following is a logical conclusion?

May	1 U.S. dollar = 1 W.E. franc
June	2 U.S. dollar = 1 W.E. franc

(A) The U.S. dollar has become stronger and exports to W.E. will rise.
(B) The U.S. dollar has become stronger and exports to W.E. will fall.
(C) The U.S. dollar has become weaker and exports to W.E. will rise.
(D) The U.S. dollar has become weaker and exports to W.E. will fall.
(E) The U.S. dollar has become weaker and imports from W.E. rise.

Questions 39-40 refer to the table below:

Output Per Unit of Labor Input

	U.S.	T.H.E.M.
Cars	3	2
Computers	30	4

39. Based on the information in the table, we can conclude the

(A) U.S. has a comparative advantage in the production of cars and computers.
(B) T.H.E.M. has a comparative advantage in the production of cars and computers.
(C) U.S. has an absolute advantage in the production of cars and computers.
(D) T.H.E.M. has an absolute advantage in the production of cars and computers.
(E) U.S. has a comparative advantage in cars and the T.H.E.M. has a comparative advantage in computers.

40. Based on the information in the table, we can conclude

(A) the U.S. will export both cars and computers to T.H.E.M.
(B) T.H.E.M. will import cars from the U.S.
(C) the U.S. will export cars to T.H.E.M.
(D) T.H.E.M. will import computers from the U.S.
(E) there is no basis for mutually advantageous trade between U.S. and T.H.E.M.

41. When the Federal Reserve engages in expansionary open market operations, it

    (A) raises the Fed Funds rate.
    (B) sells bonds.
    (C) lowers the discount rate.
    (D) buys bonds.
    (E) lowers the reserve requirement.

42. If an economy suddenly experiences a significant decrease in interest rates, which of the following is most likely to increase?

    (A) the money supply
    (B) investment
    (C) government spending
    (D) unemployment
    (E) imports

43. An inflationary gap could be eliminated by

    (A) a decrease in federal government spending.
    (B) a decrease in federal taxes.
    (C) a decrease in the reserve requirement.
    (D) a decrease in the Fed Funds rate.
    (E) a decrease in interest rates.

44. Falling interest rates have a tendency to help economic growth because

    (A) the capital stock will decrease.
    (B) the capital stock will increase.
    (C) consumers will spend less.
    (D) aggregate demand will decrease.
    (E) money will be worth less.

45. Movement from point 2 to point 1 on the graph below could be caused by which of the following?

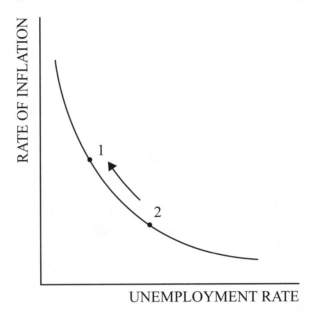

(A) a leftward shift in aggregate demand
(B) a rightward shift in aggregate demand
(C) a leftward shift in aggregate supply
(D) a rightward shift in aggregate supply
(E) a rightward shift in the production possibilities curve

46. If an economy finds that real GDP increases by $400 as a result of a $100 tax cut, then for that economy the marginal propensity to save must be

(A) 0.10.
(B) 0.20.
(C) 0.25.
(D) 0.30.
(E) 0.50.

47. Which of the following is most likely to occur during a prolonged period of rapidly rising GDP?

(A) a decrease in employment rates
(B) a decrease in the federal budget deficit
(C) a decrease in interest rates
(D) decreasing inflationary pressure
(E) a shift of the long-run Phillips curve

48. The way that fiscal policy is transmitted through the economy is correctly described in which of the following?

	Taxes	Disposable Income	Consumption	GDP
(A)	increase	increase	increase	increase
(B)	increase	increase	increase	decrease
(C)	increase	decrease	increase	increase
(D)	increase	decrease	decrease	decrease
(E)	decrease	decrease	decrease	decrease

49. If a nation experiences a series of technological innovations which result in a significant increase in worker productivity, the likely result of these combined factors is:

	GDP	Price Level
(A)	increase	increase
(B)	decrease	decrease
(C)	increase	decrease
(D)	decrease	increase
(E)	decrease	no change

50. Which of the following groups would be hurt the most if actual inflation is greater than anticipated inflation?

(A) banks that loaned out money with a fixed interest rate
(B) banks that loaned out money with a variable interest rate
(C) consumers who purchased homes with a fixed rate mortgage
(D) consumers who purchased homes with a variable interest rate mortgage
(E) banks and consumers would both be hurt equally

51. If an effective price floor is established on a good, which of the following correctly describes the effect the price floor has on quantity and price?

	Quantity	Price
(A)	increase	increase
(B)	increase	no change
(C)	increase	decrease
(D)	decrease	decrease
(E)	decrease	increase

52. Which of the following would be the appropriate monetary policy to reduce unemployment?

   (A) increase taxes
   (B) decrease taxes
   (C) sell bonds
   (D) buy bonds
   (E) raise the Fed Funds rate

53. If the federal government engages in contractionary fiscal policy, which of the following is most likely to occur?

   (A) an increase in the demand for loanable funds and an increase in interest rates
   (B) an increase in the demand for loanable funds and a decrease in interest rates
   (C) a decrease in the demand for loanable funds and a decrease in interest rates
   (D) an increase in the demand for money and a decrease in interest rates
   (E) a decrease in the demand for money and a decrease in interest rates

54. If real interest rates in an economy are 7% and nominal interest rates in the same country are 6%, then the anticipated rate of inflation in that economy must be

   (A) –13 percent.
   (B) –1 percent.
   (C) 1 percent.
   (D) 7 percent.
   (E) 13 percent.

55. Which of the following would increase the size of GDP?

   I. purchasing a textbook from an online seller of new books
   II. renting an apartment in the town where you attend college
   III. a business increasing the amount of inventory in stock
   IV. purchasing a computer at a garage sale

   (A) I and III only
   (B) II and III only
   (C) III and IV only
   (D) I, II, and III only
   (E) I, II, III, and IV

56. A long-run aggregate supply curve can be shifted to the right by which of the following?

    (A) an increase in aggregate demand
    (B) an increase in short-run aggregate supply
    (C) a decrease in exports
    (D) a decrease in imports
    (E) a decrease in interest rates

57. Which of the following is most likely to have a positive influence on long-run economic growth?

    (A) a decrease in interest rates
    (B) a decrease in exports
    (C) an increase in government spending
    (D) an increase in taxes
    (E) an increase in unemployment

58. If real interest rates in an economy rise, what will happen to each of the following?

International Value of Currency	Exports	GDP	Capital Flow
(A) increase	increase	expand	inflow
(B) decrease	decrease	contract	outflow
(C) increase	decrease	expand	outflow
(D) increase	decrease	contract	inflow
(E) decrease	increase	expand	outflow

59. When a country follows a protectionist policy

    (A) it does so at a possible gain to domestic consumers and at a possible expense to domestic producers.
    (B) it does so at a possible gain to domestic producers and at a possible expense to domestic consumers.
    (C) both domestic consumers and domestic producers will benefit.
    (D) both domestic consumers and domestic producers will be hurt.
    (E) it maximizes the benefits of specialization and comparative advantage.

60. Based on the Keynesian model, which of the following would increase aggregate demand?

    (A) an increase in aggregate supply
    (B) an increase in the price level
    (C) an increase in exports
    (D) an increase in imports
    (E) an increase in business taxes

FREE-RESPONSE QUESTIONS

1.
   (a) Draw a correctly labeled aggregate supply and aggregate demand graph for the United States economy operating at a short-run equilibrium beyond full employment. On your graph include each of the following:
      i. a short-run aggregate supply curve
      ii. a long-run aggregate supply curve
      iii. an aggregate demand curve

   (b) Assume that the government decides to engage in fiscal policy to correct the situation you described in part (a). List one fiscal policy action the government could take.
   (c) Assume that instead the Federal Reserve decides to engage in monetary policy to correct the situation in part (a). List two monetary policy actions the Federal Reserve could take.
   (d) Create a correctly labeled graph to demonstrate the effect the fiscal policy action in part (b) would have on interest rates.
   (e) Create a correctly labeled graph to demonstrate the effect the monetary policy action in part (c) would have on interest rates.

369

2. Answer the following questions based on the balance sheet for the Last National Bank of Frankfort shown below:

Last National Bank of Frankfort

Assets		Liabilities	
Required reserves	$100,000	Demand deposits	$500,000
Excess reserves	$50,000		
Loans	$350,000		

(a) What is the reserve requirement for this bank?
(b) How much additional money does the Last National Bank have available to loan?
(c) A new customer comes into the bank and deposits $100,000 into her checking account. Redraw the balance sheet of the Last National Bank to reflect the new transaction.
(d) What is the maximum amount by which the money supply can increase as a result of the new $100,000 deposit?

3. Economic indicators are frequently used to measure the performance of an economy like the United States.

(a) The unemployment rate is one of the economic indicators used in the United States. Explain why the full-employment rate of unemployment is not 0%.

(b) Inflation is another economic indicator used in the United States. Define:
   i. Inflation
   ii. Disinflation
   iii. Deflation
   iv. Stagflation

(c) GDP is another economic indicator used in the United States. Explain the difference between nominal GDP and real GDP.